About the author

Chris Kyriacou is Professor of Educational Psychology at the University of York,
Department of Education. His writings have
focused on various aspects of teaching,
learning, and pastoral care in schools. These
include well over 100 papers in academic
journals and four books: *Effective Teaching
in Schools; Essential Teaching Skills; Stress-
Busting for Teachers*; and *Helping Troubled
Pupils*.

He graduated in Psychology at the University of Reading, going on to
complete a postgraduate teacher-training course at Goldsmiths' College,
before teaching Mathematics at a secondary school in London. He went on
to complete a PhD at the University of Cambridge on the topic of teacher
stress, before joining the University of York as a member of academic staff.

His driving passion has been to promote the quality of teaching in schools,
to help and support *all* pupils to thrive. The key theme underpinning his
work has been enhancing the welfare and well-being of pupils and teachers.
To this end, he has sought to improve our knowledge and understanding of
teaching, learning, and pastoral care in schools, by writing in an accessible
style and by highlighting the implications of policy on teaching practice in
schools. He has also regularly given talks and run workshops for teachers
in schools and at local and national conferences, aimed at improving policy
and practice.

Contents

Preface

In this book, I outline the teaching skills that are involved in effective teaching. The book is designed to meet the needs of student teachers and experienced teachers wishing to explore and develop their own practice. It will also be of use to those involved in helping others to develop teaching skills or with an interest in this topic generally.

I have been very gratified by the immense popularity of this book since it first appeared. This new (fifth) edition has been revised to take account of important developments in education policy, teaching skills, classroom practice, evidence-based teaching, and different routes into the teaching profession.

This revised text incorporates developments in classroom dialogue, assessment practices, pastoral care, using social media and e-learning, behaviour management, special educational needs and disabilities, inclusive teaching, school data systems, reflection, mentoring, and professional development.

Chapter 1

Teaching skills

Teaching in schools is a challenging profession (DfE, 2018). If you are a new teacher, developing your teaching skills may at times feel daunting. However, as a newly qualified teacher you bring to the profession many wonderful qualities with you – enthusiasm, energy, commitment, and new ideas. You also have areas of knowledge and skills in abundance that many experienced teachers do not have – not least in the use of social media, recent study of relevant subject matter, and in most cases, recent experience of what it is like to be a pupil. All of this will stand you in good stead as a beginning teacher, and you will be welcomed into the profession with open arms.

In order to start thinking about your teaching skills, you need, first of all, to think about the nature of being an effective teacher. The essence of being an effective teacher lies in you knowing what to do to foster pupils' learning and being able to do it. Effective teaching is primarily concerned with setting up a learning activity for each pupil that is successful in bringing about the type of learning that you intend.

The difference between knowing what to do and being able to do it can be well illustrated by making an analogy with playing tennis. You may know that in a particular situation a lob over the opponent's head is required, but whether that shot can be played successfully may be an entirely different matter! Your tennis skills involve three elements: first, your knowledge about possible types of shots; second, your decision-making involved in deciding that a lob is in fact the most appropriate shot required; third, your ability to action that shot successfully.

The nature of teaching skills

Successful teaching skills thus crucially involve knowledge, decision-making and action. This distinction between these three elements underpinning skills is extremely important, because skilful teaching is as much a thinking activity as it is observable actions. Developing your skills as a teacher therefore is as much about developing and extending your knowledge, and the decision you take in a particular situation, as it is about the successful execution of the observable action.

Figure 1.1: You must develop your action skills

Almost all teachers during their initial training will spend some time observing experienced teachers, and experienced teachers in many countries spend time observing colleagues as part of their own or their colleagues' programme of professional development. Such observation can be immensely valuable: seeing how another teacher performs can stimulate your own ideas about your teaching. It may do this simply by acting as a model, either good or bad (seeing a colleague use an exceptionally well-prepared worksheet or one containing some obvious shortcomings may stimulate your thinking about your own use of worksheets). Equally well, and more frequently, observation is stimulating because of the creative tension caused by trying to match your own decision-making about teaching with the decisions you infer your colleague has made. For example, in a science lesson you may normally go over some key points regarding how a particular design for an experiment might be suspect, with the class as a whole, only to see a colleague using small group discussion instead. As a result, you may be stimulated to think about the reasons for this. Indeed, the benefits of classroom observation are greatly enhanced by having some time available before and after the lesson for discussion about the teaching.

The features of teaching skills

Over the years much has been written about classroom teaching skills. The impetus for this has come from a number of sources, including those concerned with the initial training and the in-service training of teachers, those concerned with monitoring the standard and quality of teaching performance, those involved in schemes of teacher appraisal, and those concerned with understanding, as a research endeavour, what constitutes successful teaching. As such, there is now a massive body of literature available for study. Overall, it appears that teaching skills can usefully be considered in terms of three key features:

- they involve purposeful and goal-directed behaviour

- their level of expertise is evidenced by the display of precision, smoothness, and sensitivity to context

- they can be improved by training and practice.

Studies of teaching skills

Studies of teaching skills have typically focused on how such skills are developed and displayed by teachers, from beginning (novice) teachers to experienced (expert) teachers. A study by Jenkins and Ueno (2017) analysed international data on teaching and learning in schools, and concluded that the most important factor accounting for differences between countries in pupil attainment appeared to be the level of classroom teaching skills displayed by the teachers. This study indicates that the degree to which novice teachers can develop their skills and continue to remain in the profession as expert teachers is a crucial factor in enhancing pupil progress.

Focusing on particular skills in isolation can sometimes be unhelpful because they can become less meaningful out of context. Wragg (2005) believes that it is better to analyse particular skills in relation to broad areas of activity, such as class management, questioning and explaining.

Teachers' thinking

As well as studies focusing on developing skills among student teachers, a number of writers have focused on studying what teachers think about being a teacher and the skills they use in teaching (Day and Gu, 2010; Pollard et al., 2014). Such studies have viewed teaching as a complex cognitive skill, based on knowledge about how to construct and conduct a lesson, and knowledge about the content to be taught. This skill enables the teacher to construct lesson plans and make rapid decisions in the light of changing circumstances. The difference between novice teachers and expert teachers is that the latter have developed sets of well-organised actions that they can apply flexibly and adapt with little mental effort to suit the situation.

A useful analogy here is that of going to a restaurant. Once you have been to several types of restaurant, you develop knowledge about the procedure that generally operates: whether you find a table or are shown to one; how to order from a menu; and when and how you pay. Such experience enables you to go to a new restaurant and cope with getting what you want reasonably skilfully. For someone who has never been to a restaurant, few sets of organised actions have been built up. For all the person may know, you may have to go to the kitchen, select some meat, and cook it yourself! Similarly, experienced teachers have built up a repertoire of many sets of behaviours from which to select the behaviour most appropriate to the immediate demands of the situation, whether it is dealing with a pupil who is unable to answer a question, or noticing a pupil looking out of a window. Indeed, the reason why teaching is so demanding in the early years is because new teachers have to build up their expertise of knowing what to do and being able to do it.

A number of writers have pointed out that a particular feature of teaching skills is their interactive nature. A teacher's actions during a lesson continuously need to take account of changing circumstances, many of which may be unexpected. Indeed, a teacher's effectiveness in the classroom is very dependent on how well they can modify and adapt their actions in the light of how well the lesson is going. In this sense, teaching is more like driving through a series of busy roundabouts than it is like driving along a quiet motorway. With experience, much of this interactive decision-making gradually becomes routine so that the teacher is hardly aware at a conscious level of the many decisions that they are making during a lesson. In contrast, for a novice teacher, each new demand seems to require careful attention and thought.

Teachers' knowledge about teaching

Another important feature of teaching skills is that they clearly draw upon the teacher's knowledge about effective teaching (Campbell et al., 2004; Cooper, 2014; Muijs and Reynolds, 2017). Shulman (1987) famously argued that this knowledge base includes knowledge about:

- content
- broad principles and strategies of classroom management and organisation
- curriculum materials and programmes
- the teaching of particular content topics
- pupils

- educational contexts, ranging from the classroom group to aspects of the community

- educational aims and values.

For Shulman, teaching skills are bound up with teachers' thinking, which draws upon their knowledge base as a basis for judgement and action. This notion that as much emphasis in considering teaching skills must be given to the knowledge base as to the decision-making process may seem odd, since clearly all decision-making must draw on teachers' knowledge about teaching. The basic point here is that such knowledge is largely implicit and taken for granted. However, if one is concerned with how teachers develop their teaching skills, this knowledge base needs to be made more explicit. A very effective way of doing this is to show teachers a video of their teaching and probe their thinking about what they did and why through this 'stimulated recall' method. This approach essentially tries to re-create the teacher's thinking in progress while they were actually teaching (often referred to as 'reflection-in-action').

A number of researchers have argued that in order to explore the teacher's knowledge base it is important to use a range of methods, such as in-depth interview, classroom observation, stimulated recall, and task analysis, in order to probe as clearly as possible the teacher's thinking that underpins their classroom decision-making.

Mentoring

Writings and studies looking at school mentors and their role in the professional development of student teachers and newly qualified teachers have also highlighted the key skills that must be developed in the early years of teaching (Jarvis and White, 2012; Robins, 2006). Indeed, the increasingly important role played by mentors in schools during initial teacher training has indicated that turning effective teachers into effective trainers of new teachers is more complex than it may seem. A teacher may know how to teach well, but that may not translate easily into the role of how best to guide and help student teachers develop their own expertise. Writings and studies looking at effective mentoring have thus attempted to highlight the key skills involved in teaching and to explore how mentors can best foster such skills among beginning teachers. Moreover, the role of mentor is becoming broader and more complex, combining elements of coaching and counselling (Beere and Broughton, 2013; Tolhurst, 2010).

As your career progresses you will move from being mentored to someone who mentors others. However, it is important to remember that all teachers never stop being mentored. All teachers need to share ideas and advice, and those teachers who have developed particular expertise will often need to mentor those colleagues who are trying to upgrade their own teaching skills in this area.

In addition, you also need to develop skills in mentoring pupils. We have moved a long way from seeing classroom practice as essentially about high-quality whole-class teaching, and towards recognising the increasing importance that the quality of your one-to-one mentoring of pupils can play in enhancing their learning.

Defining and identifying essential teaching skills

Teaching skills can be defined as discrete and coherent activities by teachers that foster pupil learning. In the light of our consideration of teaching skills so far in this chapter, three important elements of skills are discernible:

- *Knowledge*, comprising the teacher's knowledge about the subject, pupils, curriculum, teaching methods, the influence on teaching and learning of other factors, and knowledge about one's own teaching skills.

- *Decision-making*, comprising the thinking and decision-making that occurs before, during and after a lesson, concerning how best to achieve the educational outcomes intended.

- *Action*, comprising the overt behaviour by teachers undertaken to foster pupil learning.

An overriding feature of teaching skills is that they are purposeful and goal-directed activities which are essentially problem-solving. At its broadest, the problem is how best to deliver effectively the educational outcomes required in terms of pupil learning. More specifically, teaching skills are concerned with all the short term and immediate problems faced before, during and after the lesson, such as 'How can I lay out the key points of this topic in a slideshow presentation?', 'How can I signal to a pupil to stop talking without interrupting what I am explaining to the whole class?', 'What can I write when assessing a piece of pupils' work to highlight a flaw in the pupil's argument?'

Teaching skills are also concerned with the long term problems of effective teaching, such as 'Which textbook series best meets the needs of my pupils?',

'How best can I update my subject knowledge?', 'How do I best prepare pupils for the work they will be doing in future years?'

Identifying essential teaching skills

One of the major problems in trying to identify a list of essential teaching skills is that teaching skills vary from very broad and general skills, such as the planning of lessons, to very specific skills, such as the appropriate length of time to wait for a pupil to answer a question in a particular type of situation. Overall, in considering teaching skills, it seems to be most useful to focus on fairly broad and general skills that are meaningful to teachers and relate to how they think about their teaching. More specific skills can then be discussed as and when they help illustrate and illuminate how these general skills operate. Nevertheless, given the nature of teaching, it is clear that whatever set of general skills is chosen to focus on, the overlap and interplay between them will be marked, and a good case can always be made by others for focusing on a different set.

Over the years there has been a wealth of writing about and use of lists of teaching skills, both by those involved in teacher education and by educational researchers (Cooper, 2014). At the most general level of categorisation, a useful distinction has been made between three fairly distinct dimensions of teaching quality (e.g. Fauth et al., 2014):

- *Cognitive activation:* developing pupils' knowledge and understanding of subject matter through the use of challenging learning activities and high-quality classroom dialogue that foster pupils' cognitive engagement.

- *Supportive climate:* developing a positive relationship with pupils, giving positive and constructive feedback, and displaying caring behaviour.

- *Classroom management:* establishing clear, sound and consistent classroom rules and procedures, and avoiding and coping effectively with disruptions.

Working within a general framework of dimensions of teacher quality, such as the example above, we can then identify the underlying teaching skills that contribute to teaching quality. While there is no definitive categorisation of teaching quality or agreed list of the teaching skills involved, a consideration of the various writings indicates that a fairly typical list of teaching skills can be identified. Such lists of teaching skills have proved to be very useful in helping both beginning and experienced teachers to think about and develop their classroom practice.

The effective teacher

Writings on the notion of the effective teacher have also yielded a mass of material concerning the skills displayed by teachers considered to be effective (Buckler and Castle, 2014; Kerry and Wilding, 2004; Koutrouba, 2012; Kyriacou, 2009). Teachers who are judged to be effective typically display the skills in their teaching in the following areas:

- establishing an orderly and attractive learning environment

- concentrating on teaching and learning by maximising learning time and maintaining an academic emphasis

- purposeful teaching through the use of well-organised and well-structured lessons coupled with clarity of purpose

- conveying high expectations and providing intellectual challenge

- monitoring progress and providing quick corrective feedback

- establishing clear and fair discipline.

Teacher appraisal and performance review

Another important source of information about teaching skills can be found in the wealth of material dealing with the appraisal and performance review of established teachers (Jones et al., 2006; Middlewood and Abbott, 2017). These include a whole host of lesson observation schedules and rating scales used to identify and comment on the extent to which teaching skills are displayed in the lessons observed. Such writings and schedules typically focus on areas such as:

- *preparation and planning* (e.g. selects short term objectives related to the school's curriculum guidelines, and is aware of and uses, as and when appropriate, a variety of equipment and resources)

- *classroom organisation and management* (e.g. uses time and space to maximum advantage and ensures smooth transitions from one activity to another)

- *communication skills* (e.g. uses questioning and explaining effectively)

- *the setting of work for pupils* (e.g. work is appropriate for age and ability, is of sound quality, and displays fitness for purpose)

- *assessment of pupils' work and record-keeping* (e.g. provides feedback to pupils that helps them improve their work in future)

- *knowledge of relevant subject matter* (e.g. uses knowledge of the topic to develop and guide pupils towards a secure base of understanding)

- *relationships with pupils* (e.g. shows a genuine interest in, and respect for, children's words and thoughts and focuses on children's behaviour rather than personality).

Skills identified by government agencies

In most countries there are official policy and practice documents produced by government agencies that identify the skills that need to be displayed by teachers. These documents may be drawn up by the relevant ministry, or by one of the agencies dealing with a specific aspect of education, such as the school curriculum and its assessment, the school inspection and advisory service, and the professional training and development of teachers. In some countries, these will be agencies operating with a national remit, while in other countries each regional authority may have its own set of agencies. For example, the United Kingdom has separate arrangements for England, Scotland, Wales and Northern Ireland.

Documents produced by government agencies, which draw attention to the teaching skills underpinning good classroom practice in both primary and secondary schools, are an attempt to provide some degree of consistency concerning the nature of effective teaching, and to develop and promote the government's view of what counts as good practice. As such, the list of skills identified by the government will feature heavily in the training and support materials developed for teachers, and will also be reflected in the frameworks developed by agencies dealing with school inspection and teacher education. These typically cover five areas:

- planning lessons
- teaching methods
- assessment
- creating effective learners
- creating the conditions needed for learning.

Packs dealing with teaching skills such as these have been developed by government agencies in many countries, and can often be downloaded free of charge from their websites. A number of writers have also produced useful guides to support you in understanding how best to display the standards for teaching set by government agencies in your classroom practice (e.g. Blatchford, 2017; Carroll and Alexander, 2016).

Skills looked for during school inspections

For many years in England, the Office for Standards in Education, Children's Services and Skills (Ofsted) has published reports dealing with the quality of teaching observed during their inspections of schools. This includes an annual report on standards in education, the publication of handbooks and other support materials used by inspectors in their inspection of schools, and also the findings of reports focusing on specific subjects, levels and topics, and on specific aspects of teaching, such as the quality of teaching displayed by newly qualified teachers and the quality of teaching experienced by particular groups of pupils (Ofsted, 2018). From these reports one is able to build up a clear picture of the types of skills school inspectors expect to see displayed when good teaching is taking place. These can be inferred from the following descriptions commonly used by Ofsted:

- lessons are purposeful, with high expectations conveyed
- pupils are given some opportunities to organise their own work
- lessons elicit and sustain pupils' interest and are perceived as relevant and challenging
- the work is well-matched to pupils' abilities and learning needs
- pupils' language is developed and extended through dialogue and questioning
- a variety of learning activities is employed
- teachers systematically check pupils' understanding throughout lessons
- teachers ensure pupils are engaged in learning
- pupils' learning benefits from high-quality marking and constructive feedback
- consistent behaviour management creates a positive climate for pupils' learning.

The teaching skills looked for by Ofsted are modified from time to time to take account of changes in government policies on education. This results in the criteria for a lesson to be graded as outstanding being revised, so that the characteristics which have to be displayed in the lesson are aligned with the government's description of the teaching skills that underpin good classroom practice. It is worth bearing in mind that Ofsted does not operate a simple checklist system when arriving at the overall grade for a particular lesson. As such, a good or even an outstanding lesson need not contain every feature in their list of the important qualities that school inspectors look for.

Skills to be developed during initial training and beyond

A further source of information comes from writings and materials concerned with the teaching skills that student teachers are expected to develop during their initial teacher training. These include a variety of profiling documents developed by teacher training institutions to help foster and record student teachers' progress in developing teaching skills over the course of their training. A study by Hobson et al. (2006) asked student teachers to rate the importance of eight different types of knowledge and skills that beginning teachers needed to develop. The student teachers' ratings of these in order of importance were:

- ability to bring about pupil learning

- ability to maintain discipline in the classroom

- ability to use a range of teaching methods

- knowledge about their teaching subject(s)

- ability to deal with pastoral issues

- staff supervision/management skills

- knowledge/understanding of education policy

- awareness of research findings about effective teaching methods.

Of particular significance in this respect is the attempt by government agencies to specify the list of skills to be developed during initial teacher training or as part of teachers' continuing professional development. For example, the Department for Education (2012) published a list of standards that teachers are required to display during their initial teacher training programme, during their induction year as a qualified teacher in their first school, and during their subsequent career as an experienced teacher. These standards require teachers to:

- set high standards that inspire, motivate and challenge pupils

- promote good progress and outcomes by pupils

- demonstrate good subject and curriculum knowledge

- plan and teach well-structured lessons

- adapt teaching to respond to the strengths and needs of all pupils

- make accurate and productive use of assessment

- manage behaviour effectively to ensure a good and safe learning environment

- fulfil wider professional responsibilities.

These standards are used to monitor the quality and effectiveness of initial teacher training courses, the successful completion of the induction year, and the degree to which each teacher is able to improve their practice as their career progresses. Indeed, the Department for Education (2016) issued guidance to the effect that the continuing development of such skills through your career is an essential part of good practice and professional leadership in a school.

Evidence-based classroom practice

Another set of increasing literature on teaching skills comes from the attempts to provide an evidence base to inform developments in policy and practice in education (Hattie, 2011; Petty, 2009). This approach includes both original research studies and systematic reviews that look at the existing research literature on a particular topic and synthesise the research evidence in order to assess what impact different types of teaching approaches and intervention strategies have on pupils' learning. Such research often highlights particular aspects of teaching skills that are crucial in determining the extent to which a particular approach has had a positive impact on pupils' learning. For example, a systematic review looking at the impact of daily mathematics lessons (the numeracy hour), introduced as part of the National Numeracy Strategy in primary schools, highlighted the need for many teachers to develop the skills necessary to sustain the interactive aspect of whole-class 'interactive' teaching that was advocated in the National Numeracy Strategy (Kyriacou, 2005).

In the USA, a number of authors have used a synthesis of the evidence base for 'what works' to identify the key sets of teaching skills (Marzano, 2003; Stronge, 2006). These focus on five sets of key teaching skills:

- the teacher as a person

- classroom organisation and management

- instructional strategies

- monitoring pupil progress and potential

- classroom curriculum design.

Both Marzano (2003) and Stronge (2006), however, illustrate how the expert teacher differs from the beginning teacher in the extent to which they display a high level of these skills.

A list of essential teaching skills

Overall, the essential teaching skills involved in contributing to successful classroom practice can be identified and described as follows:

- *Planning and preparation:* the skills involved in selecting the educational aims and learning outcomes intended for a lesson and how best to achieve these.

- *Lesson presentation:* the skills involved in successfully engaging pupils in the learning experience, particularly in relation to the quality of instruction.

- *Lesson management:* the skills involved in managing and organising the learning activities taking place during the lesson to maintain pupils' attention, interest and involvement.

- *Classroom climate:* the skills involved in establishing and maintaining positive attitudes and motivation by pupils towards the lesson.

- *Behaviour management:* the skills involved in maintaining good order and dealing with any pupil misbehaviour that occurs.

- *Assessing pupils' progress:* the skills involved in assessing pupils' progress, covering both formative (i.e. intended to aid pupils' further development) and summative (i.e. providing a record of attainment) purposes of assessment.

- *Reflection:* the skills involved in evaluating your own current teaching practice in order to improve future practice, including mentoring and being mentored by others effectively.

- *Self-management:* the skills involved in managing one's time efficiently and in dealing effectively with challenges, pressure and stress.

These eight sets of essential teaching skills are further developed in the table on the next page, and form the basis of the chapters of this book.

Essential Teaching Skills

Planning and preparation

- The lesson plan has clear and suitable aims and objectives.
- The content, methods and structure of the lesson are appropriate for the pupil learning intended.
- The lesson is planned to link up with past and future lessons.
- Materials, resources and aids are well prepared and checked in good time.
- All planning decisions take account of the pupils and the context.
- The lesson is designed to elicit and sustain pupils' attention, interest and involvement.

Lesson presentation

- The teacher's manner is confident, self-assured and purposeful, and generates interest in the lesson.
- The teacher's instructions and explanations are clear and matched to pupils' needs.
- The teacher's questions include a variety of types and range, and are distributed widely.
- A variety of appropriate learning activities are used to foster pupil learning.
- Pupils are actively involved in the lesson and are given opportunities to organise and develop their own work.
- The teacher shows respect and encouragement for pupils' ideas and contributions, and fosters their development.
- The work undertaken by pupils is well matched to their needs.
- Materials, resources and aids are used to good effect.

Lesson management

- The beginning of the lesson is smooth and prompt, and sets up a positive mental set for what is to follow.
- Pupils' attention, interest and involvement in the lesson are maintained.
- Pupils' progress during the lesson is carefully monitored.
- Constructive and helpful feedback is given to pupils to encourage further progress.
- Transitions between activities are smooth.
- The time spent on different activities is well managed.
- The pace and flow of the lesson are adjusted and maintained at an appropriate level throughout the lesson.
- Adjustments to the lesson plan are made whenever appropriate.
- The ending of the lesson is used to good effect.

Classroom climate

- The classroom climate is purposeful, task-oriented, and with an established sense of order.
- Pupils feel supported and encouraged to learn, with high expectations conveyed by the teacher.
- Teacher–pupil relationships are largely based on mutual respect and rapport.
- Feedback from the teacher contributes to fostering pupil self-confidence and self-esteem.
- The teacher's mentoring of pupils enhances their learning.
- The appearance and layout of the classroom are conducive to positive pupil attitudes towards the lesson, and facilitate the activities taking place.

Managing behaviour

- Good order is largely based on the positive classroom climate and on good presentation and management.
- The teacher's authority is established and accepted by pupils.
- Clear rules and expectations regarding pupil behaviour are conveyed by the teacher at appropriate times.
- Pupil behaviour is carefully monitored and appropriate actions taken by the teacher to pre-empt misbehaviour.
- The teacher's mentoring of pupils helps them to maintain good behaviour.
- Pupil misbehaviour is dealt with through the appropriate use of investigation, counselling, academic help, reprimands and punishments.
- Confrontations are avoided, and skilfully defused.

Assessing pupils' progress

- The marking of pupils' work during and after lessons is thorough and constructive, and work is returned in good time.
- Feedback is diagnostic, corrective, encourages further effort, sustains pupils' self-confidence, and supports and helps their future work.
- A variety of assessment tasks are used, covering both formative and summative purposes.
- A variety of records of progress are kept.
- Opportunities are given for pupils to assess their own work and progress.
- Assessment of pupils' work is used to identify areas of difficulty and address these to enable a firm base for further progress.
- Assessment is made of study skills and learning strategies employed by pupils in order to foster their development.

Reflection

- Lessons are evaluated to inform future planning and practice.
- Current practice is regularly considered to identify aspects for useful development.
- Use is made of a variety of ways in which to reflect upon and evaluate current practice.
- Benefit is derived from mentoring by colleagues.
- Support is given to colleagues to benefit from mentoring.

Self-management

- The teacher regularly reviews how time and effort can be organised to better effect.
- The teacher regularly reviews the strategies and techniques used to deal with sources of stress.

Two important points, however, need to be borne in mind when considering these skills. First, there is clearly an interplay between these eight areas, so that the skills exercised in one area may simultaneously contribute to another area. For example, smooth transition between activities is included within lesson management, but at the same time will also contribute to maintaining discipline. Second, all the skills involved in lesson presentation, lesson management, classroom climate and discipline, are interactive skills. In other words, exercising these skills involves monitoring, adjusting and responding to what pupils are doing. Unlike acting on a stage, where you can perform without an audience, your skills cannot be considered in isolation from your interaction with pupils. So when giving an explanation, for example, a teacher would, at the very least, be attentive to the faces of pupils to judge whether it was being pitched appropriately for their needs, and might elaborate, alter the pace of delivery, tone of voice, content, or even stop and ask a question, in light of the what the facial expressions indicated.

Further reading

Cooper, J.M. (Ed.). (2014). *Classroom Teaching Skills* (10th ed.). Belmont, CA: Wadsworth. A detailed and critically informed analysis of key teaching skills, with contributing chapters by experts in the field.

Hattie, J. (2011). *Visible Learning for Teachers: Maximizing Impact on Learning*. Abingdon: Routledge. An excellent and authoritative analysis of the key teaching skills underpinning effective teaching based on research evidence.

Kyriacou, C. (2009). *Effective Teaching in Schools: Theory and Practice* (3rd ed.). Oxford: OUP. This book looks at the aspects of teaching and learning that are crucial for effective teaching, and provides a sound framework for an understanding of classroom teaching skills. The framework for exploring effective teaching in terms of pupil engagement outlined in Chapter 3 is the key message running through this book.

Petty, G. (2009). *Evidence-Based Teaching: A Practical Approach* (2nd ed.). Oxford: OUP. An excellent analysis of effective teaching that draws upon research evidence concerning the effectiveness of different teaching methods. You will find his treatment of 'what the best teachers do' (Chapter 22) and 'reflection and experimentation' (Chapter 23) are particularly helpful.

You should also look at descriptions of teaching skills in recent reports by government agencies dealing with the quality of teaching. As these descriptions change, from time to time it is advisable to use the Internet to identify the most up-to-date sources. Recent reports by teacher unions and teacher associations are also helpful in outlining – and critiquing – current developments in teaching skills.

At the end of each chapter, you will find a list of questions that are there to guide your reflection on the key issues covered in the chapter. To some extent, these questions can act as a checklist, but their primary purpose is to ask you to consider how you can develop your classroom practice.

Key questions

1   How do I view the characteristics of effective teaching?

2   What is a teaching skill and which processes are involved in displaying a skill?

3   Which teaching skills are involved in effective teaching?

4   What areas of knowledge and understanding underpin teaching skills?

5   How might the teaching skills I am expected to display change as my career develops?

6   Which teaching skills have government agencies highlighted as important?

7   What role can my mentor play in helping me think about the nature of teaching skills?

8   How can I best mentor colleagues to help them to develop their teaching skills?

9   Do I attend training workshops on effective teaching?

10 What teacher associations and organisations that are involved in developing good practice in schools are available to me locally, nationally or online?

Chapter 2

Developing skills

In defining teaching skills in Chapter 1, three elements were highlighted: knowledge, decision-making and action. Almost all beginning teachers will have had considerable experience of being taught as pupils themselves in a school. In all likelihood, this will be the single most important influence on their knowledge about teaching and the models they have of how to conduct a lesson. Numerous studies, however, have indicated just how inadequate a base this is for attempting to teach one's first few lessons. Long experience of being taught certainly provides a broad framework for thinking about how to teach, but once you have taken on the role of teacher, it becomes very evident that a whole range of teaching skills needs to be developed (Bentley-Davies, 2010; Day and Gu, 2010; Pollard et al., 2014).

Common problems experienced by beginning teachers include:

- not knowing what to do when, having given an explanation, the pupil does not understand, other than repeating the same explanation

- not knowing how to cope with pupils working at different rates, ranging from those who finish early to those making little progress

- not knowing which curriculum elements require more attention and emphasis in teaching

- not knowing what to do with pupils they cannot control.

Some studies have explicitly compared beginning teachers (either student teachers or newly qualified teachers) with experienced teachers to highlight the development of teaching skills. These indicate that beginning teachers more often became engrossed in private exchanges with pupils so as to lose overall perception of what was going on elsewhere. Experienced teachers, on the other hand, are more often able to split their attention between the pupil and the rest of the class, and can break off and comment on what is happening elsewhere, as and when appropriate. When it comes to planning lessons, experienced teachers are more selective in using the information provided by others, and prefer to rely on their knowledge of what they could typically expect from pupils of the age and class size given. In effect, the experienced teachers are able to use their repertoire of how to set up and deliver learning activities, whereas this is largely denied or non-existent for beginning teachers.

Monitoring your own teaching

Another source of information about how teaching skills develop concerns the efforts of experienced teachers to monitor and develop their own skills or to assist with developing those of colleagues. Such work has taken place either as part of formal schemes of teacher appraisal and staff development or simply as part of your own concern to monitor and develop your practice.

Of particular interest, as an example of the latter, has been the growth of teacher action research (Baumfield et al., 2013; McAteer, 2013). This involves a systematic procedure in which teachers look at some aspect of their own or the school's practice that is giving rise to some concern, identify the precise nature of the problem, collect some data concerning the problem, and then devise, implement, and evaluate a solution. Many teachers have used this approach to develop some aspect of their teaching skills, ranging from dealing with new approaches to teaching and learning (such as the use of more small group work) to simply improving skills that are already well developed (such as the quality of giving individual help). Studies reporting the efforts of experienced teachers to develop their teaching skills well illustrate that all teachers, not just beginning teachers, are continually involved in such development. Indeed, it is the sense that teaching skills continually need development to improve one's own practice and to meet new demands that makes teaching such a challenging profession.

Stages of development

The journey from being a novice teacher to becoming an expert teacher requires you to develop a wide variety of skills (Lange and Burroughs-Lange, 2017). The development of skills can range from considering a set of skills covering a broad area (such as communication skills) to considering a quite specific skill, such as the way you follow up a pupil's answer to a question when the answer is wrong.

The maxim that 'practice makes perfect' is mistaken. What is crucial in the development of skills is practice plus feedback. Perrott (1982), in her analysis of how quite specific teaching skills are acquired and developed, focuses on three stages. The first stage is cognitive and involves developing an awareness, by study and observation, of what the skill is, identifying the various elements of the skill and their sequencing, knowing the purpose of using the skill, and knowing how it will benefit your teaching. She identifies the second stage as practice, normally in the classroom, but occasionally in a controlled setting as part of a training course in which there is a short practice of the specific skill. The third stage is feedback, which enables the teacher to improve the performance of the skill by evaluating the relative success of its performance. Such feedback can range from simply an impressionistic sense of its successful performance to detailed feedback given by an observer, the use of audio-visual recording, or systematic data collected from pupils concerning their work, behaviour or opinions. Perrott sees this three-stage process as a cycle, in which the third stage feeds back into the first stage as part of an ongoing development of the skill.

The interplay between developing each quite specific skill and developing the broader set of skills is where high-quality mentoring by a more experienced teacher can be helpful. The role of mentoring, however, is not just simply a matter of coaching but one that also requires developing an understanding of pedagogy.

Having the ability to develop your skills

While it is clear that teachers are continually reflecting upon and developing their skills, it is also evident that this does not automatically lead to skilled performance. There are many teachers who, after years of experience, still have evident shortcomings in some teaching skills. In part, this reflects the fact that skilled performance also depends on ability and motivation. The teacher needs the ability to profit from reflection and practice, and the motivation to do so. If we consider questioning skills as an example, clearly all teachers need to develop such skills. However, while some teachers have built up great skills in the variety and range of question types they use and the skill with which they target pupils and elicit and elaborate pupils' responses, other experienced teachers may still show shortcomings in these respects. Why should this be so?

Teaching skills involve knowledge, decision-making and action. All three of these elements are subject to the various general abilities of teachers. The teacher may simply not have built up the knowledge about the effective use of questioning skills, or have difficulty in making the appropriate decisions which use that knowledge, or have difficulties in carrying out the actions required in a skilled manner.

If we extend the example of questioning skills further, an example where the fault lies with inadequate knowledge would be a teacher who is simply unaware of the educational importance and benefits of using 'open' questions

(questions where a number of correct answers are possible) as well as 'closed' questions (questions where only one correct answer is acceptable). An example where the fault lies with decision-making would be deciding to repeat the same question to a pupil having difficulty answering, rather than phrasing the question in a different way or providing a hint. An example where the fault lies in action would be a teacher who is unable to ask a question in a clear and unambiguous way. The relevant general abilities of the teacher involved here may not simply be intellectual ones, since much skilled performance depends on aspects of the teacher's personality or even acting ability. Some teachers find it easier than others to continually ask questions that sound as though they are genuinely curious and interested in the replies, and be comfortable with the longer pauses of silence required to give pupils time to think when being asked a more complex question.

Figure 2.1: Practise your exposition

Being motivated to develop your skills

Developing teaching skills also depends on your motivation. Teachers vary immensely in the extent to which they are prepared to invest time, energy and effort to reflect upon, evaluate and improve their teaching skills. This is particularly a problem once a teacher has developed a sufficiently adequate range of teaching skills to give satisfactory lessons. Teaching often then becomes a matter of routine. This can become even more confirmed once various materials, examples and strategies have been prepared and practised.

In addition, to some extent, teachers' approaches to lessons tend to play to their own strengths. Thus, for example, a teacher who finds lessons generally work well if based on worksheets, close monitoring of progress, and one-to-one help, but in contrast finds lessons involving group work and class discussion tend to become noisy and chaotic, is more likely to design lessons based on the former than to develop and extend the skills involved in making the latter type of lessons successful. One of the main reasons underlying the hostility against a particular curriculum innovation that may be felt by some teachers might relate to the changes in their general approach and teaching skills required by the innovation. It says much for the professional commitment and sense of vocation of teachers that the vast majority do spend much time and effort in continuing to develop their teaching skills and to develop new approaches to their teaching in the educational interests of their pupils.

Being open to new ideas and ways of doing things is crucial for developing teaching skills. Sometimes changes in practice can be imposed by government agencies and the framework used by Ofsted in its inspection of classroom practice. However, they can sometimes arise when powerful ideas gradually spread through the teaching community through key writings. A very good example of the latter is the work of Alexander (2008) on dialogic teaching, which has gradually led to a change in the way many teachers use language in the classroom to enhance the quality of pupils' thinking and understanding. Adopting new practices, however, requires the development of new skills and the courage to do so.

Professional development

One of the most important aspects of being a good teacher is being constantly open to new ideas about how to improve one's teaching; this will involve adopting new practices and the development of new skills. As such, continuing to review one's own teaching is essential to professional development (McGill, 2017). It is also important to note, however, that the responsibility to develop and extend teaching skills is not simply a teacher's personal responsibility. Rather, it is also the responsibility of those within the school and agencies outside the school to ensure that such development is facilitated as part of the teacher's professional development, and as part of staff development at the school as a whole.

School inspection, teacher appraisal, mentoring, and curriculum innovation all provide a stimulus for professional development. Equally important, however, is the climate that exists within the school to facilitate the development of teaching skills as an ongoing process. An important part of school improvement and the capacity of the school for self-renewal is the ability of the school to create a positive climate that facilitates staff developing their teaching skills. Moreover, schools that help a teacher to develop their sense of competence are also more likely to enhance their sense of well-being as a teacher (Hobson and Maxwell, 2017). The characteristics of schools that are particularly good at creating this type of positive climate tend to include the following:

- a sense of common ownership among staff for the educational aims to be achieved
- a constant generation of ideas
- sharing problems
- mutual support
- respect for each other's opinions
- an open and cooperative approach to dealing with conflicts and crises
- allowing styles to vary according to situations and needs
- encouraging anyone, not just leaders, to propose improvements
- an 'organic' rather than 'bureaucratic' management style (the former being more informal and flexible, with decision-making shared rather than directed from the top through a hierarchy, and with less emphasis on reports and record-keeping).

The term 'professional learning communities' (Watson, 2014) is often used to describe the many different ways in which the teacher can be part of a group that seeks to improve classroom practice and pupil learning. Such communities can be located within a particular school (such as a group of history teachers working together to explore how to enhance pupils' understanding of particular historical ideas), or across schools (such as through school curriculum subject associations and teacher development networks). Activities that occur as part of a professional learning community can have a particularly powerful impact on developing teaching skills, as working with colleagues in this way allows for practical considerations concerning skilled action to be shared and discussed.

Finally, it is worth bearing in mind that, despite the immense importance of developing sound teaching skills and seeing this as an ongoing process throughout your teaching career, teaching also involves a whole host of other important demands, both inside and outside the classroom. The reality of life as a teacher requires a prioritising and monitoring of the whole range of skills in doing the job effectively, and it will be both normal and sensible to find that skills other than those considered here will occasionally need attention. Perhaps it is best to view the development of your teaching skills as a process that is always in operation, but which varies in intensity depending on the situation and context you find yourself in. If your teaching is to retain the sharpness, freshness and cutting edge that characterises the most effective teaching, it is crucial that your skills are never allowed to rest for too long on the back burner.

Further reading

Bentley-Davies, C. (2010). *How to be an Amazing Teacher*. Bancyfelin: Crown House. A very helpful and readable account of the skills teachers need to develop to be effective in the classroom.

Lange, J., & Burroughs-Lange, S. (2017). *Learning to be a Teacher*. London: Sage. An excellent overview of the learning environment for beginning teachers. Chapter 2, on the skills involved in becoming a professional, is particularly helpful.

McGill, R.M. (2017). *Mark. Plan. Teach.* London: Bloomsbury. This book provides excellent guidance on how to develop key aspects of your classroom practice. While the book is very practical, the ideas are embedded in a sound understanding of the nature of teaching and learning.

Pollard, A., Black-Hawkins, K., Cliff-Hodges, G., Dudley, P., James, M., Linklater, H., Swaffield, S., Swann, M., Turner, F., & Warwick, P. (2014). *Reflective Teaching in Schools* (4th ed.). London: Bloomsbury. This book provides a comprehensive overview of reflective teaching regarding the key aspects of classroom practice, and highlights a range of reflective activities for the development of teaching skills.

Key questions

1 How have my skills developed over the last year?

2 Which of my teaching skills am I happiest with, and why?

3 Which of my teaching skills am I least happy with, and why?

4 How can I best improve my teaching skills?

5 Which skills do I think are the most important ones to develop, and why?

6 Are there new ways of teaching I need to make better use of?

7 How well do my teaching skills align with how I would like them to be, and what is expected by others, and does this matter?

8 What use do I make of feedback on my teaching from others to develop my teaching skills?

9 How can I help colleagues to improve their teaching skills?

10 Do I make use of opportunities to collaborate with colleagues on developing teaching skills?

Chapter 3

Planning and preparation

There is much to take into account in planning and preparing lessons. If you are a beginning teacher, rest assured that this will get much easier with experience. One word of advice at the outset: do not hesitate to make use of the experience of your mentor and other colleagues. Teaching is a team effort, and your more experienced colleagues are there to help you, share ideas with you, and give advice.

Two terms commonly used in planning lessons are 'educational objectives' and 'learning outcomes'. Educational objectives refer to the educational goals that the lesson is intended to bring about. Learning outcomes refer to what each pupil has actually achieved by the end of the lesson. This distinction is important in reminding you of the need to be constantly aware that what you intend may not actually occur, and that adjustments may need to be made to your lesson plans while the lesson is in progress in order to bring about your intentions.

The key task facing you is to set up a learning activity that effectively achieves the learning outcomes you intend for each pupil. At the start of a lesson, you need to have a clear idea of what learning you wish to take place (your educational objectives) and how the lesson will facilitate these. While student teachers on teaching practice are usually required to make explicit lesson plans, experienced teachers more often rely on their extensive experience to form a mental framework of how they want the lesson to proceed. This does not necessarily mean that the lesson plans of established teachers are any less detailed than those of beginning teachers, simply that the lesson plans have become internalised through repetition.

The elements of planning and preparation

Much has been written over the years about the planning and preparation of lessons (Beere, 2016; Brunn, 2010; Savage, 2015). This has identified four major elements involved in planning a lesson:

- *A decision about the educational objectives for the lesson* that includes the learning outcomes the lesson will be designed to foster.

- *A selection and scripting of a lesson*, which involves deciding on the type and nature of the activities to be used (e.g. exposition, group work, reading), the order and timing of each of these activities, and the content and materials to be used.

- *A preparation of all the props to be used*, including materials, worked examples, checking that apparatus is ordered, delivered and in working order, arranging the layout of the classroom, and, on occasion, even a rehearsal (such as when a new experiment or demonstration is involved).

- *A decision regarding how you will monitor and assess pupils' progress and attainment* during and after the lesson to evaluate whether the intended learning has taken place.

Meeting the needs of learners

Ofsted (2014), in its evaluation of lessons, typically focuses on two crucial aspects in relation to planning and preparation. First, is it clear what the purpose of the lesson is? Second, has the lesson taken adequate account of the learners' needs? The former question addresses the issue of how clearly specified the educational objectives of the lesson were. The latter question addresses the extent to which the educational objectives take adequate account of the range and type of pupils' abilities, their previous learning, and their progress towards future educational attainment. It is interesting to note here that during a school inspection, Ofsted does not normally wish to see lesson plans, but is primarily interested in the effectiveness of the planning.

It is perhaps your sensitivity to pupils' needs that is the most important of all the skills involved in effective teaching. This refers to the ability of the teacher to plan lessons and adapt and modify their delivery by taking account of how the lesson will be experienced by different pupils and foster their learning. It is impossible and meaningless to attempt to evaluate the quality of a lesson plan without taking into account how well it meets the needs of the pupils in the context in which it will take place.

A particular challenge you face in planning lessons is catering for pupils with a range of learning needs, which includes pupils who have special educational needs and disabilities (SEND), pupils who are gifted academically, pupils who may be learning with English as their second language, and pupils who may differ markedly in their aspirations and motivation to learn. The fact that there may be pupils from all these categories in the same class adds to this challenge. Ofsted (2014) is clear in its view that outstanding teaching requires all pupils in the class to have made at least the expected level of progress. In order for the lesson to be successful, you thus need to prepare differentiated materials to meet the needs of the different pupils in your class. The various forms of differentiation that can take place in the classroom will be discussed in Chapter 4, together with the notion of personalised learning. In effect, the central message here is that each pupil's learning experience needs to be tailored to their particular needs.

Skills in planning

As noted in Chapter 1, an additional source of information concerning essential teaching skills comes from an examination of the attempt to list the skills that should be developed during a course of initial teaching training. These focus on:

- planning for progression across the age and ability range
- designing effective learning sequences within lessons and across a series of lessons
- designing opportunities for pupils to develop literacy, numeracy and IT skills
- planning homework and other out-of-class work to sustain pupils' progress
- incorporating a range of teaching strategies and resources, including e-learning
- taking practical account of diversity, and promoting equality and inclusion
- building upon pupils' prior knowledge.

Educational objectives

Selecting the educational objectives for a lesson is no mean task (Skowron, 2006; Waugh and Gronlund, 2012). At the very least, they must contribute to broad educationally worthwhile aims. However, fashions change, and what is regarded as worthwhile at one time (e.g. rote memorisation of the ten longest rivers in the UK) may now be considered inappropriate. Many schools list a number of educational aims in their prospectuses. The aims of the school's curriculum in each country provide a key framework within which teachers' planning needs to operate. In general, such aims typically cover three areas:

- promoting the pupil's personal and social development
- promoting the pupil's academic progress

- instilling in pupils attitudes and values that will enable them to lead fulfilling lives as adults and contribute to the betterment of society.

Countries differ in the degree to which the content of the school curriculum is specified in terms of the subjects and topics that should be covered, and the particular attainment targets that should be addressed during the pupils' school careers. Even in those countries that have adopted a national curriculum that schools are required to follow, this only provides a broad framework within which teachers still need to plan individual lessons.

Another important part of the framework that will shape your planning is the regime of national examinations. To the extent that the success of pupils, teachers, and schools is judged in terms of pupils' grades in national examinations, preparing pupils to do well in what will be tested will clearly have a huge influence on what is taught and how. The notion of 'teaching for the test' can sometimes undermine the quality of education, if what is taught and how becomes so test-focused that the teaching becomes too narrow, and hitting attainment targets comes at the expense of developing pupils' genuine understanding and interest in the topics being taught.

In selecting educational objectives, you are obliged to specify clear learning outcomes that can usefully be analysed in terms of the development of pupils' knowledge, understanding, skills and attitudes. This planning is extremely complex, because a teacher inevitably has a range of learning outcomes in mind for a particular lesson, and indeed, the learning outcomes intended may differ markedly between the pupils in the class. In addition, all lessons involve an interplay between intellectual development (defined primarily in terms of a growth in pupils' knowledge, understanding and skills) and social development (defined primarily in terms of a growth in pupils' self-esteem and self-confidence in themselves as learners, an increased positive attitude towards the subject, and a greater maturity in their behaviour and interactions with others in the class). A teacher may, therefore, have the development of an understanding of the concept of area as a major educational objective for a particular lesson. At the same time, there may be an overlay of other objectives in operation, such as the intention to give an able pupil the opportunity to do some extended work on this topic, the intention to help and encourage a pupil who has been showing a lack of interest, and the intention to use this topic to show that learning is fun and relates to important real-life applications. Being aware of such differing intentions can help an observer make better sense of the teacher's behaviour in the lesson.

You also need to think about the amount of progress that pupils can be expected to make over a given period. It can come as a great surprise to a beginning teacher to plan a one-hour lesson only to find the work planned is completed within 30 minutes, or that they are only halfway through the work planned by the end of the hour. There are many factors that you need to take into account in determining the speed at which certain types of tasks can be completed and the speed with which progress may occur. You can usefully make use of data recorded by the school on the amount of progress by pupils that can be expected for each scheme of work.

Teachers' use of objectives in planning

While the notion of setting educational objectives is widely agreed to be an essential aspect of planning (Marzano, 2009; Tileston, 2004), some research on teachers' planning appears to indicate that many teachers do not start their planning of lessons by identifying educational objectives and then designing a lesson to deliver these objectives. Rather, they approach the task of planning in a more problem-solving manner by addressing the problem of how best to structure the time and experience of pupils during the lesson. This would suggest that many teachers may plan lessons without having clear learning outcomes in mind. I think, however, this is a misinterpretation based on the fact that if you ask a teacher to talk about their planning of a lesson, the educational objectives for the lesson are often left implicit, and greater attention is devoted to their description of the activities to be employed. Indeed, there is clear research evidence that teachers do think about educational objectives in planning their lessons, and that this is often made explicit by teachers when they talk about the thinking that occurs during and after the lesson. Overall, it appears that part of the problem in identifying how and when teachers specify the educational objectives for a lesson simply concerns how they articulate their thoughts to others.

The purposes and functions of planning

There are a number of important purposes and functions to the planning of lessons that are worth noting (Butt, 2008; Haynes, 2010). First and foremost, it enables you to think clearly and specifically about the type of learning outcomes you wish to occur in a particular lesson, and to relate the educational objectives to what you know about the pupils and the place of the lesson in the general programme of study.

Second, it enables you to think about the structure and content of the lesson. This includes, most importantly, thinking about how long to devote to each activity. One of the most important skills in teaching is that of judging how much time should be spent on each activity in a lesson and the best pace of progress through the activities.

Third, planning quite considerably reduces how much thinking you will have to do during the lesson. Once the lesson is in progress, there will be much to think about in order to maintain its effectiveness. The fact that the lesson as a whole has been well planned means that you can normally focus your attention on the fine-tuning of the lesson, rather than trying to make critical decisions on the hop. Indeed, many decisions about a lesson can only adequately be taken in advance. For example, if it becomes evident that a map is needed during a lesson, there may be little you can do about it if you had not realised this during your planning and had one available in case the need arose. A related point to this is that being under pressure is not a good state to be in when trying to make sensible decisions about teaching. You can all too easily find that trying to direct or alter the course of a lesson while teaching can lead to difficulties, until you have developed with experience a good sense of what will work and how, in the circumstances you face.

Fourth, planning leads on to the preparation of all the materials and resources in general that will be needed. For example, having some work already prepared for any pupils who might finish the intended work for the lesson well ahead of the majority, or a summary of some key points you wish to review between two activities, all enable the lesson to progress more smoothly and effectively.

A fifth important purpose of planning is that keeping your notes will provide a useful record for your future planning, particularly in relation to giving a similar lesson to another group of pupils and in your planning of future work with the pupils that will extend what they have done in that particular lesson. Indeed, it is very useful, particularly in the early years of teaching, to make a brief note at the end of each lesson of any point you want to draw to your attention at some future time when you need to refer to the lesson notes again.

Time spent planning

The time you spend planning is an area of your workload where you need to think carefully about how to make the most efficient use of your time (DfE, 2018). The amount of time spent planning varies immensely between teachers and for the same teacher between lessons. While beginning teachers will certainly need to spend more time planning, some of the differences between teachers at the same level of experience seem to relate to their general style or approach to planning. In essence, some teachers feel more secure and relaxed about the tasks of teaching if a lesson has been well planned. Others, to some extent, need the pressure generated by the close onset of a lesson to concentrate their minds to the task at hand. Certainly, the ideal approach will be one in which the teacher is able to devote some time, well in advance, to the planning of each lesson. The reality of life as a teacher, however, is that there are many competing demands on your time. The amount of time for planning is thus somewhat constrained. As a result, more extensive and formal planning is likely to focus on those lessons where something new or more demanding will take place.

Flexibility

Another very important aspect of planning is the need to be flexible about the implementation of your plans. Effective teaching depends on your ability to monitor, adapt and develop what goes on in the classroom in light of how pupils behave during the lesson. No matter how careful and well thought out the planning of the lesson is, once it starts the immediate demands of how things are going take complete precedence.

It may become apparent that some of the ideas you intended to introduce and discuss at length appear to be well understood by pupils already or are much more difficult for them to understand than you envisaged; or you may notice that a large number of pupils are having difficulties in carrying out a task you had set and had planned to allow them to undertake largely uninterrupted for most of the lesson. In such circumstances, a change in your original plan would be appropriate to ensure that the pupils' needs are being met.

Figure 3.1: Be flexible in your lesson planning

Unfortunately, beginning teachers are occasionally in the position of reaping the worst of both worlds. They invest a great deal of time and energy in preparing their plan for a lesson and at the same time have a greater need to be flexible and adapt their plan in light of ongoing feedback. Thus, for example, a worksheet may have been carefully prepared by a teacher who then finds the tasks set are too difficult, and a swift change to whole-class teaching may be required. For experienced teachers such a situation is less likely to occur, but if it did, changing to another activity would pose little problem. For the beginning teacher this situation is more likely, and the difficulty of switching to an unprepared activity is more demanding. Because of this, student teachers are particularly likely to persist with their original plan unless the problems arising are much more acute and, until they build up experience, are more often than not wise to do so. In contrast, a quick change of plan, to switch from one activity to a more appropriate one, is almost a skill of delight for the experienced teacher, in the extent to which it calls upon their professional knowledge and experience to be able to do so successfully. It is worth remembering here that, as a beginning teacher, you will be supported by a mentor who can advise and help you to make adjustments to your plans when possible and appropriate.

Developing lesson planning skills

A major difference between beginning teachers and experienced teachers is the latter's ability to take a longer view of how a whole sequence of lessons will fit together. Experienced teachers tend to be much more aware of the end point of learning that they want pupils to have reached after dealing with a topic over several weeks, whereas beginning teachers tend to focus much more on the short term learning outcomes for a particular lesson. This is well illustrated in a detailed case study of a secondary school English teacher reported by McCutcheon and Milner (2002) that reveals the way the teacher was able to draw upon his rich content knowledge in planning lessons, the way he viewed the planning of individual lessons, as well as his thinking about interconnected themes and which curriculum materials and activities to employ, as being very much subordinate to his overall long term perspective on planning.

Another major difference is the degree of pedagogical content knowledge (knowledge about how to teach particular topics) that experienced teachers are able to draw upon when planning lessons. Having taught a particular topic several times, experienced teachers are very much aware of the difficulties involved in teaching that topic, and the areas where the pupils' understanding may need to be developed and strengthened. They are also more aware of what aspects of the topic are the key elements that need to be grasped, and how much time needs to be devoted to doing this.

It is sometimes claimed that an experienced teacher should be able 'at the drop of a hat' to teach an acceptable lesson on any topic in their area. They would probably first of all want to know something about the pupils' age, general ability and motivation; they would then want information on what the pupils already knew about the topic (this would probably also be checked at the start of the lesson by having a question and answer session). After that, the teacher's experience of having taught this topic before with different groups of pupils would be enough to provide the teacher with a clear idea of how to organise the lesson. Beginning teachers lack this wealth of pedagogical content knowledge. A study by Van Der Valk and Broekman (1999) explored student teachers' pedagogical content knowledge by asking student teachers to prepare a lesson plan about a topic as if they had to teach it, and then interviewed the student teachers about their lesson plans. These interviews provided a very useful way of exploring their pedagogical content knowledge, and indeed, feedback from tutors and mentors on lesson plans provides a very important learning experience for beginning teachers in developing their lesson planning skills.

Lesson planning

As noted earlier, there are four major elements involved in lesson planning:

- deciding on educational objectives
- selecting and scripting a lesson
- preparing the materials and resources to be used
- deciding how to monitor and assess pupils' progress.

The preparation of materials and resources will be considered in the final section of this chapter. The other three elements will be the focus of our attention in this section.

Deciding on educational objectives

The most important aspect of an educational objective is that it is a description of an aspect of pupil learning. Examples of educational objectives for a lesson contributing to pupils' *intellectual development* are: to gain knowledge about prime numbers, to understand the nature of causality, to acquire the skill of drawing a river's path to the sea through contour lines, and to feel empathy for the victims of the slave trade. Examples of educational objectives for a lesson contributing to pupils' *social development* are: to develop the skills involved in cooperating with other pupils, to become better able to listen attentively to other pupils' statements during class discussion, and to feel more confident about one's own capabilities in the subject.

Educational objectives cannot be stated in terms of what pupils will be doing, such as working through an exercise, drawing a map, or small group discussion. These are activities used to *promote* learning. The educational objectives must describe what is to *constitute* the learning (the learning outcomes). One of the major pitfalls in teaching is to neglect thinking precisely about educational objectives and to see planning as simply organising activities. While the two go hand in hand, it is all too easy to think that a lesson that went well logistically was effective (i.e. the pupils did what you intended), until you ask yourself what the pupils actually learned (the learning outcomes).

In selecting your educational objectives, a great deal of thought needs to be given to how these objectives relate to previous and future work the pupils are involved in, and how appropriate they are to extending their current abilities, attitudes and interests. For example, in deciding to introduce the notion of prime numbers, do the pupils already have an adequate grasp of what it means for numbers to have factors? Linking new learning to previous learning is immensely important and particularly effective if the new learning can be seen to grow out of the previous learning. Thus, a lesson on prime numbers may first of all utilise an activity in which pupils can apply their previous knowledge and understanding of factors (this will check that all is well on that front). They may then identify numbers only divisible by one and itself, which are then given a special name (prime numbers). This would combine a linking of previous learning with a sense of discovery and growth, and also extend the previous learning.

Selecting content

Selecting the content for a lesson involves a number of considerations. Even working within the framework of a detailed curriculum, this still leaves the teacher with a great deal of choice. The selection of content will clearly need to relate to the overall programme of study for pupils, but the decision concerning how much emphasis to give to particular topics will depend on the teacher's view of its importance and difficulty.

A very important teaching skill is that of separating a topic into distinct elements or aspects, and designing a sequence or progression through these elements that makes coherent and intellectual sense and effectively facilitates learning. One of the most demanding aspects of planning for beginning teachers is to decide how best to do this in a way that satisfactorily meets the pupils' needs. This demands good subject knowledge by the teacher, an awareness of how to separate and sequence the elements of the topic, and an awareness of pupils' needs. Beginning teachers tend to rely somewhat on established practice in the school, particularly if a scheme of work is in use (such as that based on a textbook or worksheets). With experience, however, teachers become much more confident and authoritative in deciding on the nature and structure of the content they wish to use, and also better able to judge the pace of progress to expect through the content elements and the likely areas of difficulty or misunderstanding that may arise. The problem for experienced teachers becomes that of keeping abreast of developments in the teaching of their subject and topics in line with changes in required educational attainment.

Selecting learning activities

The selection of learning activities offers much scope and choice for teachers. The decision about which activity or combination of activities to use within a lesson depends on the teacher's beliefs about the relative effectiveness of the different activities for the type of learning intended. This decision, however, also needs to take account of a range of factors concerning the context of the lesson.

First, will the activities selected meet the needs of this particular group of pupils, taking account of their abilities, interests and motivation, and the way they are likely to respond to these activities? You may feel that because a particular class seems to work well when group work tasks are used, that you will incorporate group work into their lesson. Equally, you may decide to incorporate group work into the lesson because the class has not worked well with this activity, and you feel more practice and experience with this activity will be of value to them in developing associated skills and benefits. Indeed, the fact that an activity has not worked well may suggest a need to use it more often rather than to avoid using it.

A second important factor concerns when the lesson takes place. The type of activities that might be effective on a Friday afternoon, or following morning assembly, or extending work done in a previous lesson when a number of learning difficulties were encountered, may be influenced by this context.

Third, such planning decisions are also influenced by logistics, other demands and time pressures facing the teacher. A lesson that requires a lot of planning effort and preparation is perhaps best avoided in the middle of a week in which you have to mark a heavy load of examination scripts, or when you know that the particular equipment needed is in great demand for other activities.

The variety and appropriateness of learning activities

When thinking about the learning activities to be used, you also need to think of the lesson as a coherent whole, such that the total package of experience provided for pupils achieves your intended learning outcomes. As such, not only must the activities deliver the appropriate intellectual experience for this learning to occur, but also facilitate the ease with which pupils can engage, and remain engaged, in this experience. This is a challenging task for both beginning teachers and experienced teachers.

The activities must thus elicit and sustain pupils' attention, interest and motivation. Even when interest and motivation are high, pupils will find it difficult to listen to a teacher's exposition for a long period, doubly so if they are young or the exposition is difficult or unclear, or if it is a hot day. To counter this, most lessons will involve some variety of activities. The initial phase of the lesson may be designed to set the scene and elicit interest, the major part of the lesson may involve the main learning experiences, and the ending may involve some review or general comments about the importance, relevance or quality of the learning that took place.

While a variety of activities is important, each activity must be appropriate to the learning at hand. For example, developing pupils' ability to articulate and communicate their ideas orally is much more likely to be achieved through practice, feedback and critiquing others, rather than by extensive reading about how to do it (although the latter may play a useful part). A variety of activities also provides pupils with an opportunity to learn in different ways, and thereby to build up and develop the skills to do so effectively. At the same time, however, this does not mean that every lesson must involve a variety of activities. It is just as important to provide extended periods of work based on one type of task in order to allow pupils to develop the skills of organising and sustaining their concentration and effort, particularly in relation to a task where the quality of what is produced depends on the marshalling and development of the work undertaken (in contrast to a simply repetitive task).

Using information technology (IT)

When using IT, you need to take extra care to check the educational purpose for its use. Is it to help develop pupils' IT skills? Is it to illustrate to pupils how

IT can be used to explore the topic in hand? Is it to motivate the pupils? Is it to encourage pupils to work in a particular way, e.g. individualised work or small group work? Is it to develop a deeper understanding of the topic? All of these different purposes are valid, but you need to be sure what you intend for the use of IT in this particular lesson.

The type of IT and the way you use it might need to be quite different if you are primarily using it to motivate pupils compared with when you are trying to foster a higher quality of understanding of the topic. Research on the impact of IT on pupils and their learning indicates that teachers need to develop two sets of skills when using IT: (i) being able to use the IT with adequate technical competence; and (ii) being able to use the IT in a way that promotes higher quality pupil learning. Teachers need to master the first set of skills before they can develop expertise in the second set of skills (this is also true for pupils). Recognising the purpose you have for using IT will enable you to check that you have developed the necessary skills that go hand in hand with the particular purpose you have in mind for its use (Leask and Pachler, 2014; Wheeler, 2005).

Of particular importance when planning to use IT is being able to move beyond the stage of using IT simply as a means of engaging pupils in the work (the so-called 'whizz-bang' approach) to being able to use IT to enhance pupils' deeper understanding of the subject matter. While using IT can act as a powerful motivator for pupils in the short term (and that's fine as far as it goes), it is only when pupils use IT in a way that promotes their learning more effectively that a sustained impact on their self-confidence and attainment can be realised. This, of course, places demands on you to develop your IT skills to support your teaching. This is recognised by the emphasis given to the development of IT skills for beginning teachers to support their teaching and wider professional activities.

Planning for formative assessment

One of the major tasks involved in planning lessons is to build in opportunities for formative assessment (Dann, 2018). Formative assessment will be discussed further in Chapter 8, but broadly speaking it refers to the way in which the feedback that pupils receive when they engage in learning activities is geared towards enhancing their learning and progress. The point being made here is that incorporating formative assessment into your lesson needs careful planning, particularly when it may involve an extended dialogue with the pupil, or whole-class discussion, or the use of supplementary or follow-on learning activities and materials designed to exemplify or consolidate the formative feedback that the pupil has just received.

Monitoring and assessing pupils' progress

Once the lesson has begun, you will need to monitor and assess pupils' progress and attainment to ensure that the lesson is being effective and is likely to deliver the pupil learning intended. At the same time, this will also give you feedback on what aspects of the lesson, as originally planned, need ongoing modification and adaptation to maintain effectiveness. This requires more than just being responsive and reactive to feedback, such as waiting for a pupil to say they do not understand how to approach the task set. Rather, it requires you to be active, and to probe, question, check, and test whether the progress and attainment is occurring as intended.

While there is much feedback available to the teacher simply by looking at pupils' facial expressions or responding to those who confess to having difficulties, all too often most pupils will adopt strategies and techniques which indicate superficially that they understand and can do the work set. Only when exercise books are collected in, or questions asked at the end of the lesson, or subsequent tests are given, might it become evident that much less learning was going on than appeared to be the case.

Figure 3.2: You should regularly assess your pupils' progress

Unfortunately, it is all too easy to avoid active probing of progress and attainment; if the lesson appears to be going well, you naturally feel that to do so will be making problems for yourself that will need to be dealt with. It requires a great deal of integrity on the teacher's part to, in essence, look for trouble. However, that is in fact the very cutting edge of the skill involved here. Simply approaching a pupil who appears to be working well and asking the question 'How are things going?' and probing with a few telling questions, can often reveal difficulties that either the pupil was not aware of, or was even deliberately trying to avoid you noticing. It is important to be aware of just how well some pupils manage to avoid being noticed by teachers, by avoiding eye contact and appearing to be working well whenever the teacher is nearby. The 'ripple effect' refers to the way pupils appear to be working hard at the task in hand when the teacher walks around the room, with those pupils the teacher is approaching having their eyes glued to their work, while those pupils whom the teacher has just passed start to relax, and, in some cases, resume talking to their neighbour.

Such active monitoring and assessment of pupils requires some forethought and planning. At what stages during the lesson, and how, are you going to get the necessary feedback? For example, one may usefully use a transition period between one activity and another for some quick whole-class questioning and discussion about what was covered and whether any problems have arisen. This does not mean that every lesson must have some in-built testing of attainment; rather, a subtle form of ongoing probing and reviewing should be employed which will be sufficient to enable you to feel confident that your intended learning is occurring. Nevertheless, there is a role here for formal tests from time to time, and also the use of homework to explicitly probe the learning covered as well as to generate new learning.

Working with others

When you plan a lesson you also have to give careful thought to what use you will make of support that will be offered by other personnel in the classroom, which can include support staff, teaching assistants, learning mentors, student teachers, and volunteer helpers (Huddleston and Bills, 2012). Depending on their expertise and role, such support can enable you to enhance the lesson in a number of ways, and also to personalise the quality of the learning experience for each pupil to a greater extent. A number of activities designed to enhance the quality of pupils' learning experience involve teaching assistants or others requiring prior training, so this has to be built into the planning. The importance of making effective use of teaching assistants, learning mentors, and other support staff has been highlighted in a range of policy and practice documents (e.g. Ofsted, 2014), and in research studies looking at how one-to-one or small group activities run by support staff can enable pupils who are falling behind in literacy and numeracy to make faster progress, often referred to as 'catch-up activities' or 'interventions' (e.g. EEF, 2018).

However, working with others requires additional skills on your part, in particular the ability to rethink how a lesson can be organised to be more effective by making use of additional personnel. In planning learning activities that take place out of the classroom, and out of the school, you will also need to plan carefully with other personnel involved how the learning experience for pupils will be organised to best effect. When working with others, it is important to remember that other personnel can make a major contribution to your planning, and they will also be able to carry out their role more effectively if what is expected of them is made clear at the planning stage.

Homework is an area where good links between the teacher and parents are important. Parents can play a very important role in emphasising the importance of homework and ensuring that it is done. There is also a variety of home-based tasks set by the teacher that require parental support and participation, such as parents listening to their children reading aloud. Sylva et al. (2010) have reported data on homework based on a questionnaire completed by 1,752 14-year-old pupils, about their experiences in secondary school. The pupils reported that homework had a positive impact on their learning, but they also highlighted the importance of teachers' marking and returning homework promptly. Another important point made was that of parents checking homework was completed. Considering how to use homework as part of your lesson planning enables learning at school to be enhanced at home, and enables you to build on your partnership with parents, which is something that can usefully be discussed at meetings and other communications with parents.

Lesson preparation

Preparation primarily refers to the preparation of all the resources and materials to be used in the lesson, including the writing and printing of worksheets, the ordering, delivery and checking of equipment, arranging desks and chairs in the required layout, and making notes about the content of the lesson to be presented. Clearly, planning and preparation go hand in hand, and many planning decisions are taken while preparation is going on. Nevertheless, there are a number of important skills involved in preparation that are worthy of attention and may be crucial to the effectiveness of the lesson.

Showing you care

The care and effort that teachers take over preparation can have a major positive impact on pupils' sense that the teacher cares about their learning and that the activities to be undertaken are worthwhile and important. In contrast, a lack of preparation may not only simply disrupt the flow of the lesson, but may also be perceived by pupils as insulting to their sense of worth as learners ('If our learning were really important, the teacher would have prepared better!').

While such problems will occur from time to time even in the best-prepared circumstances, and pupils will tolerate these, the regular occurrence of poor preparation must be avoided. To be able to say in the middle of a lesson, 'I have already prepared for you ...', and then reveal some materials or equipment, or use a slideshow to display a diagram or set of key questions, can have a marked rousing effect on pupils' self-esteem, enthusiasm, and sense of purpose for the next part of the lesson.

Rehearsal, checking, and back-up

The use of any sort of equipment always poses potential problems for the teacher. Three key words are relevant here: rehearsal, checking, and back-up. If you are going to use equipment or materials for any sort of practical work, you will often find it useful and worthwhile to have a rehearsal of some sort before you deliver that lesson for the first time. Practical work that appears to be virtually problem-proof can have surprises in store for you. For example, you may find that the length of time it takes for a particular effect to be visible takes much longer than you had planned for; or that connecting to the Internet is particularly slow.

Another problem can arise if the equipment available is different in some form from that which you have used in the past. Some lessons will also require checking that equipment, facilities, and the setting are all fit for purpose. For example, if you are going to take pupils pond-dipping, you may want to check on the type of creatures currently in the pond and whether the jars, nets, or whatever is needed, are available. Another aspect of rehearsal involves trying to experience the use of the equipment and materials from the pupils' perspective; for example, is what is being projected onto the screen clear and readable from the back of the classroom? In using an audio file, is the sound clear at the back of the room? In making a construction from card, is the card too flimsy or too hard for its purpose? Is the visual display of material on a computer screen sufficiently clear for the task in hand?

Checking simply refers to the need to ensure, shortly before the lesson is due to start, that the resources needed are to hand and in good working order. For anything electrical, this is almost mandatory. Such checking is made easier if you have starred on your lesson notes those items that need a check in this way. Nevertheless, even with adequate rehearsal and checking, things will happen that require a change in your lesson plan. It is here that some thought to back-up can be extremely helpful. While you cannot have a back-up for every piece of equipment, as a matter of regular practice, it is always worth considering what you could do if a particular piece of equipment fails, or if the lesson grinds to a halt for some other reason. In planning a lesson, some thought, even if only limited, can be usefully devoted to how another part of the lesson or some alternative activity can be used to good effect if problems arise.

Teaching materials

Worksheets, task cards, and IT software packages are commonly employed in schools, and their design and use involve a number of preparation skills. Often it is important to regard such preparation as a team activity, shared with colleagues, rather than something you do in isolation. Resources of this sort can be used many times over and, as such, if they can be designed to fit well into the programmes of study, are also used by colleagues, and can be linked carefully to assessment tasks, then the time spent in producing high-quality items will be well worthwhile.

However, before embarking on such preparation, it is a good idea to explore whether such resources are already available and can be purchased, borrowed or copied. Some textbook schemes provide a set of parallel worksheets that can be used. Websites often contain a whole host of well-prepared resources of high quality that can be adapted and used for your purposes. Some schools have gone to great lengths to develop and catalogue materials into a resource centre, either school-wide or subject-specific, and some teachers have similarly indexed materials (including pictures and various artefacts) that they have in their personal possession or have easy access to.

There are many excellent resources and activity packs now published, including games, facsimile documents for historical analysis, and IT simulations, all of a quality well beyond that which you can normally produce. However, there is a danger in using such materials, particularly ones that have been commercially produced and which look very attractive: one can be misled into thinking that because such materials have been produced at a high level of quality in appearance, then effective learning is likely to follow from their use. In fact, it is extremely important for you to carefully consider what learning will actually follow from their use, in order to ensure that the educational outcomes you intended are realised.

In preparing worksheets, task cards, or similar types of materials, the quality of presentation is of the highest importance. They need to be well laid out, not contain too much information, and should attempt to elicit pupils' interest. Particular attention needs to be paid to the language used; you need to be sure it is neither too simple nor too difficult for the range of pupil ability for whom it is intended. You also need to give careful thought as to whether such materials are going to be introduced by you and supplemented with various instructions, or whether they are to be self-explanatory.

Worksheets and task cards can range from simple exercises and tasks aimed at extracting facts from what is given to answer the questions posed, to quite sophisticated materials aimed at giving pupils an opportunity for creative analysis and discussion. An example of the former is a worksheet on percentages containing cutout adverts from a newspaper concerning the prices of various items with percentage reductions; questions here involve calculating which items are the best buys. An example of the latter is a series of line-drawn pictures (as in children's comics) about which pupils have to write a story. As well as examples designed to be used by individual pupils, other materials can be designed for small group work, such as using a facsimile of a letter written by a king as a source of evidence to interpret an event (also taking account of when and to whom the letter was written as part of the discussion of the letter as valid evidence); here the use of small group discussion may highlight the extent to which the interpretation and validity of evidence involve personal judgements.

It will come as no surprise to you that preparing near perfect materials can take up hours of time. You therefore have to be realistic in thinking about how much time you have available for such preparation, and the very important notion of what is 'good enough'.

Assessment materials

Preparation skills also include the need to prepare assessment materials. The monitoring of pupils' progress and attainment throughout their school careers requires a formal and regular record to be kept. While some of this will involve formal tests given at the end of periods of study, much assessment is also based on observing performance during normal classroom activity. This is particularly so in relation to monitoring the development of various pupil skills. This requires that appropriate assessments are prepared and built into the planning of lessons, and a formal note made of pupils' performance. This means that some activities in the lesson will be deliberately planned with a view to an assessment being made. As such, the activity must offer a fair opportunity to monitor the performance being examined. Two important planning decisions are involved here. First, how many pupils will you attempt to assess in a particular lesson? (One, several, all?) Second, what procedures will you adopt? (Will you tell pupils that a formal assessment is being made? Will you help pupils having difficulties during the assessment and, if so, how will you take this into account in your recording?)

In designing assessment materials to be used during normal classroom activity, particular care needs to be taken to ensure that they validly explore the learning you intend to examine. This involves not only assessing what it purports to assess, but assessing it in the way and to the degree required. Before being able to even begin to prepare for the assessment of pupils' performance in this lesson, the teacher needs to be clear about what exactly is being assessed and how the assessment will be recorded. In addition, for such assessments to be fair, the assessment materials and procedures adopted will need to be standardised so that each pupil is assessed in the same way. For example, the teacher might prepare a set of levels of success criteria, and then identify the extent to which each pupil's performance matched a particular level of success criteria.

Record-keeping

Advanced thought and planning about how records are to be made and kept is also required. These will almost certainly need to be developed and agreed with other colleagues, so that the school's records will be consistent and coherent as the pupil progresses through their school career. A variety of assessment materials needs to be used and types of responses given (based on direct observations of pupils' behaviour, questioning in verbal and written form, paper and pencil tests, and derived from normal coursework, including homework). This includes IT designed to track pupils' progress against attainment targets and programmes of study. Good record-keeping is essential not only to inform your future work, but also for the external assessment of the quality of your teaching.

Preparing yourself and pupils

Another aspect of preparation is the need to prepare yourself. While most teachers can teach most topics most of the time with little need to stimulate their subject knowledge, there will be some topics where you will need to learn about the topic in advance of teaching about it. In that sense, you need to stay one jump ahead of the pupils. Indeed, in areas of rapid curriculum development, you may be hard-pressed to do this. This means that private study of particular topics will be needed, ranging from making use of appropriate teacher guides that are available, to attending formal courses or workshop activities for teachers. At its best, the need to do this can add a sense of freshness and curiosity for these topics that you can share and delight in with your pupils.

In addition, you need to consider whether pupils need to be prepared in any way. You may need to give them advance warning of certain topics, particularly if they will need to do some preparatory reading, revise some previous work, or bring certain equipment or articles with them. In such circumstances, you also need to check that they are prepared as required, and you may need to have spares of the equipment available. In some schools, having spare pens to hand is almost essential for the smooth running of lessons.

Preparing pupils to use IT, such as interactive whiteboards, laptops and graphic calculators, is particularly important, in order to ensure that pupils do not feel threatened or marginalised by lacking the required IT skills when using such equipment during the lesson. Indeed, a whole-class interactive style of teaching using IT will generate a lot of pupil frustration if the necessary IT skills have not been developed and practised first.

Further reading

Beere, J. (2016). *The Perfect Lesson* (3rd ed.). Carmarthen: Independent Thinking Press. This book makes clear and helpful links between the qualities involved in effective teaching and the key features of good lesson planning.

Haynes, A. (2010). *The Complete Guide to Lesson Planning and Preparation.* London: Continuum. A very helpful guide to how decisions about planning and preparation need to be embedded into effective teaching and learning.

Savage, J. (2015). *Lesson Planning.* Abingdon: Routledge. An excellent and practical overview of the key issues involved in lesson planning. You will find Chapter 8, on the 'performance' of teaching, is especially helpful in considering the important interplay between your planning and your teaching.

Waugh, C.K., & Gronlund, N.E. (2012). *Assessment of Student Achievement* (10th ed.). New York: Pearson. A very readable book that considers good practice in the areas of planning and assessment that enables teachers to enhance the quality of teaching and learning.

Key questions

1   Are my educational objectives for this lesson clear, and do they take appropriate account of pupils' needs, particularly in terms of their abilities, interests, motivation, the context of the lesson, and the work they have previously done and will do in the future as part of their programme of study?

2   Does my plan for the lesson make good use of support teachers, teaching assistants, and other adults who are involved in the lesson, and are they properly briefed about their roles?

3   Does the content matter of the lesson and the learning activities selected, together with the structure of the lesson, appear appropriate to maintain pupils' interest and motivation, and deliver my intended learning outcomes, and how were my learning objectives for the lesson achieved?

4   What type of pupil performance during the lessons can I expect, and how do I monitor and explore pupils' progress to ensure that the lesson is effectively promoting the intended learning outcomes?

5   Are all the materials, resources and equipment I require well prepared and checked?

6   Does my lesson plan contain all the notes I need to refer to, including, for example, worked examples or a note about extension work to be used if the need arises?

7   Have I adequately prepared pupils for this lesson, by alerting them in advance to any revision that may be required or preparation they should do beforehand?

8   Am I prepared for this lesson, in terms of my subject matter knowledge about the topic to be covered?

9   What types of assessment will I be using during the lesson, and are these well planned and prepared?

10   Are there any particular concerns that I need to bear in mind regarding this lesson, such as pupils with special educational needs and disabilities, or a particular aspect of the topic, or a learning activity that will require careful monitoring?

Chapter 4

Lesson presentation

Lesson presentation refers to the learning experiences you set up so that pupils achieve the intended learning outcomes. As a result of the many different types of teaching methods that have been developed, there is now a staggering range of learning activities available that can be deployed to good effect. These include, by way of example, exposition, practicals, worksheets, e-learning, role play, and small group discussion. Moreover, you are actively encouraged and expected to make use of a variety of teaching methods in your programme of lessons. Your teaching skills need to be continually developed to take account of the changing context of what is required in terms of good practice regarding teaching and learning (Capel et al., 2016; Cremin and Arthur, 2014; Dymoke, 2012; Hayes, 2012; Muijs and Reynolds, 2017).

In considering learning activities that you can use, a useful distinction can be made between those activities largely dependent on teacher talk and those that can proceed with little or no direct teacher participation. The former include teacher exposition, teacher questioning and, to a greater or lesser extent, classroom discussion channelled through the teacher. I shall call the former *teacher talk activities*. The latter include, for example, practicals, problem-solving activities, and worksheets. I shall call these *academic tasks*. These two classes of activities will be discussed later in this chapter. Before doing so, however, it is important to consider first of all another aspect of lesson presentation: the teacher's manner.

The teacher's manner

When it comes to lesson presentation, the *way* that you do it is just as important as *what* you do. Asking a question with interest conveyed in your tone of voice and facial expression, as opposed to sounding tired and bored, makes a world of difference to the type of response you will get, no matter how appropriate the actual question was. Similarly, circulating around the room to monitor progress and help anyone having difficulties, rather than sitting at your desk at the front marking work from another lesson, also conveys an attitude to pupils about the importance of the lesson. All such cues together create a general impression regarding how much effort you feel it is worthwhile to put into the lesson to ensure pupil learning takes place. To elicit and sustain effective learning by pupils, in general your manner needs to be confident, relaxed, self-assured, purposeful, and should generate an interest in the lesson. In addition, you need to exude positive expectations concerning the progress you expect to occur during the lesson.

Positive cues about your manner

There are a number of skills involved in conveying to pupils that you are confident, relaxed, self-assured and purposeful. However, the most crucial aspect of doing this is that you *are* in fact confident, relaxed, self-assured and purposeful! The starting point is not one of being nervous and anxious, and then thinking how you can convey that you are relaxed and confident. Rather, the starting point should be that by sound planning and preparation, and with developing experience, you will quite naturally and unconsciously convey these positive cues. Nevertheless, there are times, particularly when beginning a career in teaching, or occasionally when things are going wrong, that you will feel anxious. In such circumstances, it is helpful to try to consciously induce a sense of relaxation as far as possible, and also to be aware of the aspects of your behaviour involved in conveying this.

Positive cues are largely conveyed by your facial expression, tone of voice, speech, use of eye contact, gestures, and positioning. When you feel nervous, you will naturally tend to look and sound nervous, avoid eye contact, and make awkward or repetitive gestures. As such, when feeling nervous, consciously make an effort to ensure that your speech is fluid, clear and audible, that you maintain regular eye contact with pupils and scan around the classroom, and that you spend time standing centre stage at the front when appropriate.

For the vast majority of beginning teachers, such skills develop fairly quickly; for others, it takes somewhat longer. Some student teachers appear to feel at home in the classroom from the very first lesson; others only start to feel really relaxed and confident during their first year or two of teaching. It must be recognised, however, that there are some for whom the act of teaching will always be anxiety-provoking. Most of those who are unable to feel at home in the classroom will not pursue a career in teaching for long. This largely reflects the fact that although much of the teacher's manner can develop through training and experience, it is in part also bound up with the person's personality. This is why it is so important for teachers to capitalise on their strengths and mitigate their shortcomings, rather than attempt to model themselves on any particular style of teaching they have witnessed or is being advocated to them.

Other important aspects of your manner

Over the years there has been much discussion and research concerning other aspects of the teacher's manner that contribute to effective teaching, and it must be said that no clear and consistent picture has emerged (Borich, 2013; Kyriacou, 2009). Undoubtedly, this is because it is possible to be effective through different means. For one teacher, the key to success may largely stem from being firm; for another teacher, it may stem from a warm and caring attitude. Nevertheless, in general, it does appear that the quality of conveying enthusiasm and interest for the subject matter at hand is important. Less consistently supported by research evidence, although widely advocated, are the qualities of patience and a sense of humour.

Teacher talk activities

Teachers spend a great deal of their time talking, whether it be lecturing, explaining, giving instructions, asking questions, or directing whole-class discussion. As such, it is not surprising that the quality of teacher talk is one of the most important aspects of effective teaching. Indeed, many would claim that it is the most important quality of effective teaching. Communicating effectively with pupils and, in particular, the teacher's effective use of language when using explanations, questions, discussions and plenaries, feature as an important element of the competency standards expected of teachers (DfE, 2012).

Exposition

There is a wealth of research evidence to support the claim that clarity of explanation (often referred to as 'teacher clarity') makes a major contribution to greater educational attainment. Teacher clarity certainly enhances teacher talk activities, and also makes a contribution to the effectiveness of a variety of academic tasks, for example in briefing and debriefing role-play activities, or in the content and layout of a worksheet.

Periods of teacher exposition (i.e. informing, describing and explaining) typically occur throughout a lesson. In schools, it rarely takes the form of a lecture for any great length of time, nor should it, as pupils will find it difficult to pay attention to a lecture, except for a short length of time. Indeed, for this reason, many teachers use a series of questions and the development of pupils' replies to trace out what they want to say, rather than an uninterrupted exposition. This not only involves the pupils more, but also enables you to check on pupils' understanding.

Starting the lesson

What you say at the start of the lesson can be particularly important as it serves a number of functions. First, it must elicit and sustain pupils' attention and interest in the lesson. Establishing a positive attitude at the start of the lesson provides a good springboard for what follows. To create a positive mental set among pupils, it is important to ensure that pupils are paying attention when the lesson begins.

Second, it is useful to indicate what the purpose or topic for the lesson is, and its importance or relevance. You will also need to outline the main structure for the lesson (for example, will there be a starter session or a plenary at the end?). A short warm-up or starter activity can usefully function as a quick recap of a previous lesson or be linked to the topic for the current lesson. In introducing the main part of the lesson, a question to the class, rather than a statement, can usefully arouse their curiosity and induce a problem-solving thrust towards what follows. A fairly quiet but audible voice level is best, as it encourages listening, discourages background noise, and makes varying the tone and volume of your delivery easier.

Third, having gained attention and indicated the purpose of the lesson, your introduction can alert pupils to any links with previous lessons that they need to be aware of, or any particular problems or aspects of this lesson they should be alert to, in order to best prepare them for what is to follow. Such preparation may include practical matters concerning the equipment they will need to use or the pace at which they will be expected to work.

Finally, you can discuss and share with pupils how the main learning intentions will be linked to success criteria and targets for learning, and whether the lesson will be linked to subsequent lessons and to a homework activity.

Effective explaining

Explaining often goes hand in hand with questioning, with the teacher switching from one to the other as and when appropriate. Often this switch is influenced by whether the teacher feels it is appropriate to pull ideas together swiftly to facilitate a move to the next phase of the lesson, using a synthesising statement, or whether the teacher feels more involvement and probing of pupils' ideas is needed. For both explaining and questioning, it is particularly important to ensure that the nature and complexity of the language used by the teacher is at an appropriate level for pupils to understand. Indeed, the skill of the teacher to pitch language use appropriately by taking account of pupils' current level of understanding is one of the most important skills the beginning teacher needs to master.

Writings and research on explaining (Kerry, 2002; Wragg and Brown, 2001a, b) have highlighted seven key aspects that are involved in enhancing the effectiveness of an explanation:

- *Clarity:* it is clear and pitched at the appropriate level.

- *Structure:* the major ideas are broken down into meaningful segments and linked together in a logical order.

- *Length:* it is fairly brief and may be interspersed with questions and other activities.

- *Attention:* the delivery makes good use of voice and body language to sustain attention and interest.

- *Language:* it avoids use of over complex language and explains new terms.

- *Exemplars:* it uses examples, particularly ones relating to pupils' experiences and interests.

- *Understanding:* the teacher monitors and checks pupils' understanding.

Perhaps the most important aspect of explaining, however, is the skill in deciding the size of step that pupils can take in going from what they know at the start of the lesson to the learning you intend will take place by the end of the lesson. This decision about the size of step has crucial implications for the type and sophistication of the explanations offered.

In summary, explanations should, by and large, be grammatically simple, make good use of examples, define any technical terms and, most importantly, should not go on for too long!

Questioning

Questioning skills are also central to the repertoire of effective teaching (Kerry, 2002; Walsh and Settes, 2005; Wragg and Brown, 2001c, d). There can be few professions to compare with teaching where you spend so much time every day asking questions to which you already know the answer. Research studies looking at the teachers' use of questioning have identified the various reasons given by teachers for asking questions as follows:

- to encourage thought and the understanding of ideas, phenomena, procedures and values

- to check understanding, knowledge and skills

- to gain attention to task; to enable the teacher to move towards teaching points; as a 'warm-up' activity for pupils

- to facilitate review, revision, recall, reinforcement of recently learned points; as a reminder of earlier procedures

- for management: to ensure settling down, to stop calling out by pupils, to direct attention to teacher or text, to warn of precautions

- specifically to teach whole class through pupil answers

- to give everyone a chance to answer

- to prompt bright pupils to encourage others

- to draw in shyer pupils

- to probe a pupil's answer to a question and, when appropriate, to redirect the same question to another pupil

- to allow expressions of feelings, views and empathy.

Types of questions

A useful distinction can be made between 'open' and 'closed' questions. Open questions can have a number of right answers, whereas closed questions will only have one right answer. Another useful distinction can be made between 'higher order' questions and 'lower order' questions. Higher order questions involve reasoning, analysis and evaluation, whereas lower order questions are concerned with simple recall or comprehension.

Much research indicates that teachers overwhelmingly ask more closed and lower order questions than open and higher order questions. While in general, open and higher order questions are more intellectually demanding and stimulating, and research does indicate that more of these question types should be used, one does need to bear in mind the range of purposes behind asking questions, as indicated earlier. Given that open and higher order questions are more time-consuming, it would be difficult to use these very frequently without constraining other intentions, such as the need to maintain an appropriate pace to the lesson, or to involve most of the pupils. As with all aspects of teaching skills, a balance is required in meeting a range of different intentions at the same time.

Effective questioning

It is useful to think about the different types of questions, and when, how and why you might use a particular type of question. You also need to think about the skills involved in asking a question effectively. Kerry (2002) has highlighted seven questioning skills:

- pitching the language and content level of questions appropriately for the class

- distributing questions around the class

- prompting and giving clues when necessary

- using pupils' responses (even incorrect ones) in a positive way

- timing questions and pauses between questions

- learning to make progressively greater cognitive demands through sequences of higher order questions

- using written questions effectively.

When asking questions there are two extremely important points to bear in mind. First, answering a question, particularly in front of classmates, is an emotionally high-risk activity. As such, it is essential that the classroom climate during questioning is one of support and respect for the pupil's answer (both by the teacher and by pupils). Second, do not allow some pupils to opt out of questioning. It is evident that some pupils are adept at avoiding being noticed and will do whatever they can to terminate quickly any interaction with the teacher. Such pupils need to be involved and helped to contribute to the lesson.

A number of features characterise skilful questioning. It is a useful technique not to name the pupil whom you want to answer the question until you have finished the question. This helps to ensure that all pupils are attentive. When asking the question, try to ensure that it is as clear and unambiguous as possible. If the pupil is in difficulties, it can be useful to rephrase the question in a different way or guide the pupil towards an answer through the use of scaffolding (see later in this chapter for a description of scaffolding). Allowing pupils some time to talk to partners and to share answers can be useful in promoting higher quality thinking.

Most importantly, ask the question in a manner that conveys you are interested in the reply, maintain eye contact with the pupil, and ensure that other pupils have the courtesy to listen in silence. When prompting or helping a pupil, remember that the object of this is to assist the pupil's thinking, not to enable the correct answer to be guessed from the clues given. It is often worthwhile to check how a pupil arrived at the answer given (whether right or wrong), as this can give you some useful insight into the thinking involved.

Questioning is an area of teaching skills that has received a great deal of attention, as it lies at the heart of three key areas of development in teaching: dialogic teaching, personalised learning, and assessment for learning. These three areas are discussed elsewhere in this book, but in essence they have one central theme, which is how to use questioning to enhance the pupil's learning.

Directing classroom discussion

The third area of teacher talk activities to be considered here is that of classroom discussion channelled through the teacher: a mixture of teacher and pupil explanations, views and questions (Wassermann, 2017). Classroom discussion begins at the point when pupils ask questions and when one pupil responds to what another pupil has said.

When classroom discussion takes place, there are two key decisions you need to take. First, you need to consider how best to lay the room out (for example, is it appropriate to organise pupils so that they can see and hear each other?). Second, you need to consider the extent to which you are going to direct the discussion and make a leading contribution to shaping the flow and development of what is said.

Figure 4.1: Directing classroom discussion

In using classroom discussion to good effect, it is useful to indicate the purpose of having such a discussion, to indicate how long the discussion is intended to last, and to summarise at the end what conclusions can be drawn. It is particularly important to remember that one of the prime reasons for having classroom discussion is to give pupils the opportunity to develop and express their ideas. This will need encouragement, and a tolerance to allow badly formed and incorrect notions to be expressed (ensuring that any errors become apparent as the discussion develops, rather than interrupted or shot down immediately).

Whole-class interactive teaching

A style of teaching referred to as whole-class interactive teaching has been widely advocated (Hayes, 2006; Moyles et al., 2003; Wassermann, 2017). This style of teaching involves the skilful use of exposition and questioning to engage pupils in higher level thinking about the topic in hand. This is often characterised as being done with pace, in order to sustain a lively and buoyant feel to the lesson, but the teacher also needs to give pupils adequate thinking time when appropriate, in order to allow higher quality responses to questions to occur. A teacher will typically also give pupils short tasks to do or ask them to talk in pairs for a few minutes before asking for answers. Unfortunately, in unskilled hands, this style of teaching can regress back into a more conventional whole-class (exposition-based) teaching. Indeed, a study by Smith et al. (2004) looking at the quality of interactive whole-class teaching, reported that traditional patterns of whole-class interaction have not been dramatically transformed by efforts to improve classroom practice. The skills needed lie in being able to sustain pupils' engagement and contributions, and in particular to ensure that less able pupils and more socially reserved pupils in the class do not feel intimidated by this style of teaching. At its best, pupils will be encouraged to argue with and comment on both what the teacher says and on what other pupils have said. Generating high-quality pupil talk in this way is perhaps one of the most challenging and important tasks facing teachers (Myhill et al., 2006).

Classroom dialogue

There has been increasing recognition of the importance of high-quality teacher-pupil and pupil-pupil dialogue as a means of promoting pupils' understanding and engagement (Lyle, 2008; Wassermann, 2017).

Alexander (2008) has written about 'dialogic teaching', which is characterised by:

- structuring questions to provoke thoughtful answers

- using pupils' answers to establish dialogue

- developing a strand of thinking through the use of dialogue.

The essence of such an approach lies in creating a collaborative dialogue. Alexander argues that such an approach can have a powerful effect in enhancing the quality of pupils' thinking. This theme has also been taken up by Mercer, where he refers to the teacher acting as a discourse guide in order to enhance the quality of classroom discussion. Mercer uses the term 'exploratory talk' to highlight the ways that teachers and pupils can use dialogue to co-construct knowledge and understanding in a purposeful manner (Mercer and Littleton, 2007).

This approach can be contrasted with what is often referred to as the Initiation–Response–Feedback pattern of classroom discourse, where you ask the pupil a question (Initiation), the pupil answers (Response), and you then give comments on what the pupil said (Feedback). This I-R-F pattern often generates low-level thinking, particularly if the teacher asks a question with just one right answer.

An example of a dialogic approach would be a teacher asking different pupils what method they used to solve a problem, asking them to discuss with each other (in pairs or in a small group of three or four pupils) which method might be best, and asking pupils in a whole-class discussion to comment on each other's viewpoint. What is crucial here is that the participation of the teacher is directed at stimulating and promoting a genuine dialogue about the issue being discussed.

Academic tasks

Academic tasks refer to activities set up by teachers to facilitate pupil learning, which can proceed with little or no direct teacher participation once they are up and running. Examples include doing experiments or other practical tasks, investigation and problem-solving activities, worksheets, e-learning, role play, and small group discussion. Almost all such activities tend to involve the teacher circulating around and monitoring progress, giving individual help as and when necessary. Nevertheless, some teachers prefer to maintain a high level of direction during such activities, while others see important educational benefits deriving from being less directive (this point will be developed further when we consider the notion of 'active learning' later in this chapter).

Setting up academic tasks

For academic tasks to be successfully employed, it is absolutely crucial that it is clear to pupils what they have to do, and to indicate the relationship between the task and the learning intended. It is easy to fall into the trap of thinking that the most important aspect is to get the pupils underway quickly with the task and then to deal with any problems as they arise. Doing so can lead to your having to dash from one desk to another throughout the lesson, or else having to interrupt the class as a whole on several occasions. In fact, the most important aspect for success is the careful preparation of the tasks and materials to be used (so that they are clear and, if necessary, self-explanatory) coupled with a clear briefing of what is required before the task is started. Some pupils may not pay attention during this briefing session if they know that you will simply give an individual briefing to anyone who wants one once the work has begun. If several pupils have this attitude, there will be many demands made on you at the start. As such, it is well worthwhile to ensure that as many pupils as possible are clear about the task in hand before the class is allowed to start the work.

Another aspect of academic tasks that is of great importance is to ensure that pupils possess the skills required to undertake the task successfully, or, if not, that they are helped to develop those skills. All tasks, whether it be extracting information from a set text, using a worksheet, extracting data from the Internet, carrying out an experiment, or participating in small group discussion, involve a number of skills. It is all too easy to assume that pupils already have appropriate skills or can develop these by trial and error. In fact, a lot of pupils get into difficulties simply because they are unsure about how to proceed and what is expected of them.

A good example of this is that of a teacher asking pupils to spend a lesson writing a poem about winter. Now, for some pupils the processes involved in writing a poem are rather mysterious, and little headway may be made. However, if the teacher were first to spend a lesson composing a poem from scratch on the board in front of the pupils, and demonstrate by thinking aloud, showing how one can start from some ideas and phrases and rework these and change words, the whole process for pupils can then be demystified. This demystification is essential for almost all academic tasks. How do you extract information from a set text? How do you make successful use of small group discussion? What steps are involved in conducting an investigation? Paying explicit attention to pupils' learning skills before, during and after academic tasks can have a major impact on the quality of learning that takes place.

The advantages of setting work for individuals include: allowing pupils to work at their own pace; helping them to organise and take responsibility for their own effort; the work can be structured and tailored to each pupil's own level of difficulty (including the provision of extension and enrichment materials and tasks for more able pupils in the class). Where pupils are working individually on an extended piece of work or project, or through a work scheme, careful and regular monitoring of progress is essential.

Cooperative activities

Cooperative activities, such as small group discussion or collaborative problem-solving, enable pupils to share ideas, to develop the skills involved in cooperative interaction, to communicate clearly, and to work as a team. Generally speaking, a group size ranging from two to six seems to be best for most cooperative tasks. Pairs are most commonly used, in part for logistical reasons and in part because both partners will get more contribution time than when in a larger group. However, it is important to make use of larger groups, which will enable pupils to develop wider communication and organisational skills.

Some teachers, however, are reluctant to make use of cooperative tasks because they fear that by relinquishing tight control over the learning activities, it will be harder to sustain good order. There is little doubt that such activities do depend on good teaching skills, but fortunately with the increasing use of such activities, pupils are more familiar and more skilled at using such activities to good effect than when such activities were relatively novel in schools.

It is important to note that pupils require help and support to use small-group cooperative activities effectively. Research indicates that the way the activity is structured can have a positive impact on the quality of leaning that takes place. A study by Gillies (2004) identified three key elements of a structured activity:

- The pupils understand what they are expected to do and how they are expected to work together.

- The task is established so that all group members realise they are required to contribute to completing it and to assist others to do likewise.

- Pupils are taught the interpersonal and small-group skills needed to promote a sharing and respectful attitude towards others.

Gillies found that pupils in structured groups (as described above) worked together much better and more effectively than pupils working together in unstructured groups.

Active learning

Active learning refers to any activities where pupils are given a marked degree of autonomy and control over the organisation, conduct and direction of the learning activity. Usually such activities involve problem-solving and investigational work, and may be individualised (such as an extended piece of work or project) or involve small group collaboration (such as small group discussion, games, a role-play simulation or collaborative project).

In essence, active learning may usefully be contrasted with expository teaching, in which pupils are largely passive receivers of information that is tightly under the teacher's control. A number of educational benefits have been claimed for active learning:

- Such activities are intellectually more stimulating and thereby are more effective in eliciting and sustaining pupil motivation and interest in the activities.

- Such activities are effective in fostering a number of important learning skills involved in the process of organising the activities, such as when organising their own work during individualised activities, and interaction and communication skills during cooperative activities.

- Such activities are likely to be enjoyed, offer opportunity for progress, are less threatening than teacher talk activities, and thereby foster pupil attitudes towards themselves as learners and more positive attitudes towards the subject.

- Cooperative activities in particular enable greater insights to occur regarding the conduct of the learning activities through observing the performance of peers and sharing and discussing procedures and strategies.

In considering active learning, however, you need to be aware that this term has not been used by teachers with any consistency. As well as referring to teaching methods or learning activities, it is sometimes used to refer to the mental experience of learning by discovery. Nevertheless, in the sense of activities such as small-group work, teachers are generally expected to make use of such activities as well as teacher talk activities. The message, in effect, is that how pupils learn is as important as the content of what they learn.

In addition, active learning can sometimes offer a much more powerful experience or insight into what is to be learned than expository teaching. For example, in a mathematics lesson, a teacher could ask pupils to guess how many pupils fit into a one cubic metre box, and then bring one in and see. Pupils having this experience are left with a very strong image of what this unit of volume means.

Academic tasks versus teacher talk activities

Much discussion has taken place over the years concerning the relative merits of teachers using whole-class teaching methods based on teacher talk activities compared with the use of academic tasks, particularly those characterised by active learning. Comparisons of educational attainment in different countries coupled with a whole host of research studies of effective teaching suggest that an approach described as 'direct teaching' is probably the most effective approach to promoting higher levels of pupil attainment. Direct teaching essentially consists of lessons that follow five main stages:

- The teacher sets clear goals for the lesson.

- The teacher teaches through exposition of what is to be learned.

- The teacher asks questions to check pupil understanding.

- The teacher provides a period of supervised practice.

- The teacher assesses pupils' work to check that the goals have been achieved.

Nevertheless, one should not use such findings to call for teaching to become predominantly based on whole-class teaching methods employing teacher talk activities. It is widely accepted that teachers need to make use of a variety of teaching methods. Doing so helps pupils to develop the skills of learning in different ways and also provides for a greater variety of learning outcomes. What is needed is the right mix of activities.

Teaching styles and learning styles

Discussion of the skills involved in lesson presentation has sometimes made reference to the way in which some teachers seem to adopt a typical approach to their teaching, and also the way in which some pupils seem to have strong preferences about how they prefer to learn. This has given rise to consideration of whether certain teaching approaches may be particularly effective, and whether an attempt should be made by teachers to take account of differences between pupils in their preferences for certain learning activities.

Teaching styles

Studies of classroom practice have attempted to categorise teachers in terms of their teaching styles, which refers to their tendency to make frequent use of certain types of learning activities in their teaching (Carpenter and Bryan, 2016; Cohen et al., 2010). For example, some teachers tend to make much greater use of teacher-centred, exposition-dominated activities, together with teacher-directed seatwork tasks. At its most traditional, this approach may be coupled with the organisation of desks into rows and a great deal of guided practice. This approach has often been described as a 'formal teaching style'. In contrast, some teachers make much greater use of student-centred activities, involving small group work and giving pupils' more control over the direction of their work. This may be coupled with arranging desks together to form groups of pupils seated together, and the use of more open-ended tasks negotiated with pupils. This approach has often been described as an 'informal teaching style'.

Attempts to identify and describe teaching styles, however, have been problematic, because there is a wider variety of styles than can be described (a simple dichotomy between formal and informal, for example, is too simplistic), and most teachers use a mix of styles and also vary their mix of styles from lesson to lesson and from class to class. Nevertheless, some consistent differences between teachers in terms of their general approach to teaching do seem to be discernible.

Learning styles

Similarly, attempts have also been made to describe pupils in terms of their learning styles (Buckler and Castle, 2014; Pritchard, 2018; Reid, 2005). This refers to pupils' preferences concerning the types of learning activities and tasks they prefer to experience and which they feel are more effective in promoting their own learning. It also includes their preferences about the types of strategies for learning they prefer to adopt when given a choice, and their preferences regarding the physical and social characteristics of the learning situation. For example, some pupils prefer to read (rather than listen), work alone (rather than in a group), find things out for themselves (rather than be given a digest by the teacher), and have tasks tightly prescribed (rather than be left to their own decision-making).

The point is sometimes made that if pupils were taught more often in their preferred learning style, more learning would take place. As such, teachers should try to match learning activities to pupils' preferences. While I agree that it is important for teachers to be aware that pupils differ in their learning styles, I think the idea of matching work to pupils' preferred learning styles involves a number of problems. First of all, it is important to help pupils to develop the skills to learn effectively in their non-preferred learning styles. Pupils who are taught overwhelmingly in their preferred learning style may not be able to develop a full range of learning skills. Second, pupils' learning styles are not easy to determine and also vary from lesson to lesson and from subject to subject. Third, the logistics of classroom life would make it extremely difficult to cater differentially for the variety of pupils' learning preferences in the same class.

Personalised learning

The debate about the relative effectiveness of different teaching methods and learning activities is a complex one, and what works best will vary from situation to situation, depending on the type of class taught and the particular type of learning outcomes being fostered. However, one important implication of research on teaching styles and learning styles is that teachers do need to make use of a variety of learning activities in their teaching. In addition, teachers can use their awareness of the differences between pupils in their learning preferences to help sustain each pupil's motivation by making use of their preferred activities when appropriate, and also by providing additional support and encouragement when making use of their non-preferred activities.

The consideration of how teachers can best meet pupils' learning needs by taking careful account of each pupil's circumstances, ability and motivation, and preferred learning styles, has given rise to the notion of 'personalised learning'. This refers to how a school can tailor the curriculum and teaching methods to the specific learning needs of each pupil, and offer each pupil the type of personalised support that will enable them to develop the skills needed to access learning activities to better effect.

The genesis of personalised learning was initially seen to be a way of combating disaffection among lower attaining pupils, but it gradually began to be conceived in terms of being good practice to better meet the needs of all pupils. As such, personalised learning features heavily in a range of educational policy statements produced to improve the quality of education and to raise the level of pupil attainment.

Personalised learning also needs to be based on the regular assessment of pupil progress to identify each pupil's learning needs in order to teach them accordingly ('assessment for learning'). The essence of personalised learning is for the pupil to experience learning as something that is relevant to their needs and that they can readily engage in with success. Some attempts have also been made to indicate how the development of personalised learning in schools can be informed by research evidence (Pollard and James, 2004). A study by Prain et al. (2013) in Australia looked at the experience of secondary school pupils of personalised learning in four schools committed to adopting this approach. They reported that the pupils felt motivated as a result of the personalised support they received from teachers, but there were ambiguities involved concerning issues such as shared control between teachers and pupils in guiding learning and how well the differentiation of learning tasks met pupils' personalised needs.

The importance of developing teaching skills related to personalised learning is reflected in its common occurrence as part of initial teacher-training courses and in continuing professional development courses. The agenda here typically covers the need for teachers to have knowledge and understanding of a range of teaching, learning and behaviour management strategies and to know how to use and adapt them in order to provide opportunities for all pupils to achieve their potential.

A number of writers have highlighted the ways in which the skilful use of IT can support personalising learning (Hammond, 2012). These include:

- personalising content sources and resources
- providing pathways through content that are personalised to an individual pupil's needs
- presenting a range of interfaces appropriate to an individual pupil's level and ability
- facilitating effective assessment and reporting tools
- providing flexibility regarding when, where and with whom pupils learn.

Matching work to pupil ability and needs

Matching the learning experience to the ability level and needs of each pupil in the class is one of the most skilful aspects of teaching. The difficulty of doing this successfully is in part a reflection of the complexity of the teacher's task: namely, that the class may well have about 30 pupils in it, comprising a wide range of ability and needs.

One of the problems facing teachers is that there is a tendency to pitch the lesson towards meeting the needs of the broad middle range of ability within the class, and then to provide additional material, demands or help for those at the extremes. Part of the problem with this approach is that more able pupils need more enriching and more stimulating demands, not simply more of the same or more difficult work. Similarly, less able pupils also need more enriching and stimulating demands, not simply less of the same or easier work. A number of work schemes based on individualised programmes of work have been particularly successful in enabling this match to occur across a broad range of ability.

The notion of matching work to pupils does not mean setting work at a level that pupils can already do fairly successfully. Rather, it deals with the idea of what pupils of a certain level of ability are able to achieve in the way of new learning. 'Matching the work' thus refers to deciding how much progress pupils can make in a given lesson or over a course of lessons, and then pitching the work to achieve the optimal progress the pupils appear to be capable of.

Studies looking at the school factors influencing pupil progress have indicated that a key factor contributing to greater progress was intellectually challenging teaching (McNeil and Sammons, 2006). However, many studies have noted that the match of task demands to pupils indicated that a majority of tasks were not well matched to pupils, in the sense of promoting optimal progress: in some cases the tasks were too easy, while in other cases they were too difficult.

Setting and streaming

Another approach used to help match work to pupils is that of grouping pupils into narrower ability bands. This can be done by streaming, where pupils in a particular ability band stay together as a group for all lessons and topics, or setting, where pupils are put into a separate ability group for each subject or topic. Research on the advantages and disadvantages of grouping pupils by ability (Ireson and Hallam, 2002, 2009) indicates that such grouping can be very helpful in terms of:

- allowing pupils to make progress in line with their ability

- making it easier for the teacher to set work that meets the needs of the whole group

- more able pupils not being held back by the less able

- less able pupils not being discouraged by the more able.

At the same time, research has indicated that there are also dangers here, most particularly that pupils grouped together into a low ability band or set may get caught up in a vicious circle of lowered teacher and pupil expectations concerning what they are capable of.

Mixed ability groups and differentiation

In some schools, mixed ability group teaching is used. This may occur because the small size of the age group or the small number of pupils doing a particular subject or topic does not allow setting. Additionally, some schools wish to make use of the advantages of having mixed ability groups in allowing pupils from different backgrounds to mix socially and academically, and to avoid having to teach low sets. It is also important to note that all classes of pupils, even those where some selection has occurred in terms of attainment, will involve a range of ability.

Differentiation refers to the ways in which a teacher can adapt how the work is set and assessed in order to meet the needs of a range of abilities within the same class. Seven types of differentiation have been highlighted:

- *differentiation by task*, where pupils cover the same content but at different levels

- *differentiation by outcome*, where the same general task is set, but they are flexible enough for pupils to work at their own level

- *differentiation by learning activity*, where pupils are required to address the same task at the same level, but in a different way

- *differentiation by pace*, where pupils can cover the same content at the same level but at a different rate

- *differentiation by dialogue*, where the teacher discusses the work with individual pupils in order to tailor the work to their needs

- *differentiation by support*, where the degree of support is tailored to the needs of individual pupils, with less support offering more challenge and opportunity for initiative

- *differentiation by resource*, where the type of resource used (worksheets, Internet, graphical calculator) is tailored to the pupil's ability and skills.

These seven types of differentiation are not mutually exclusive, but rather a matter of emphasis. The teaching skills involved in using differentiation successfully involve bringing into play a good understanding of the nature of teaching and learning (Sellars, 2017).

Inclusive teaching

Inclusive teaching refers to the way in which teaching and learning in schools is organised such that it enables the school to cater for pupils with a broad range of ability and needs. Some pupils with moderate or severe special educational needs, including those whose behaviour can be regarded as challenging to deal with, are now being taught in mainstream schools, who might in the past have had their special educational needs catered for in special schools. You need to be skilled at handling a wide range of pupils' needs in the classroom, and this may often involve being able to plan and teach with the help of a support teacher (Knowles, 2011; Lewis and Norwich, 2005). The importance of the skills involved in doing this is well recognised, covering key areas such as:

- knowing and understanding the role of colleagues with special responsibility for pupils with special educational needs and disabilities and other individual learning needs

- knowing how to make effective personalised provision for those they teach, including those for whom English is an additional language or who have special educational needs or disabilities, and how to take practical account of diversity and promote equality and inclusion in their teaching.

In addition, inclusive teaching refers to the ways in which the teacher's classroom practice enables all pupils to feel engaged and involved as valued participants. A study by Florian and Black-Hawkins (2011) explored the practice of teachers at two primary schools in Scotland to explore how eleven teachers in their study perceived inclusive teaching and how this was evident in their classroom practice. Florian and Black-Hawkins view the essence of inclusive teaching as employing strategies that avoid the need to mark some pupils as different. Of particular interest here is their observation that successful inclusive practice stems from teachers holding inclusive beliefs, such as taking the view that learning difficulties are a professional challenge for the teacher rather than deficits in the learners; believing that all pupils will make progress; and believing that teaching activities need to be accessible to all pupils rather than viewing some pupils as needing something different.

The growth of inclusive teaching in schools means that you need to be adept at developing teaching skills to meet a diversity of learning needs in a range of different contexts and settings. This is not simply a matter of trial and error practical learning on your part, or even looking at how more skilful colleagues approach inclusive teaching. Rather, it means that you need to develop an understanding of the diversity of learning needs, so that the activities and practices you adopt in the classroom are appropriate. Fortunately, the broader knowledge base that underpins the teaching skills involved in inclusive teaching is much better understood these days and has shaped improved classroom practice (Holliman, 2014).

Skilful matching

One of the useful ways in which teachers can help ensure that a match is occurring is through careful monitoring of pupils' progress and questioning to check understanding. Unfortunately, many pupils are reluctant to confess to difficulties and instead are likely to do little work in silence, or else to use various strategies to get the required work done with little or even incorrect understanding. Therefore it is of crucial importance that you take the initiative in monitoring progress, rather than wait for difficulties to be drawn to your attention.

Expectations also play a role in sometimes obscuring what pupils are capable of. Most pupils will do slightly less than is typically demanded of them. This can easily result in a downward spiral of teacher demands, if what the teacher demands of each lesson is the level of work that was produced in previous lessons. Therefore you need to be consistently conveying expectations of a higher quality of work and progress in each lesson than is typically achieved. This will create an impression of encouraging and expecting a standard just higher than the norm previously produced, but not so much higher that pupils feel discouraged or that you are dissatisfied with genuine effort on their part.

Matching work to pupils also concerns the need to take account of pupils' interests and needs. This includes taking advantage of examples and topics and their applications that are likely to be of interest or relevance to the pupils in your class. In addition, as noted earlier in this chapter, it includes providing a variety of ways of working, using both teacher talk activities and a range of academic tasks, so that pupils can build up the skills involved in working successfully in these different ways.

Some pupils will have particular needs that need to be met. These may range from a pupil who is rather shy and needs encouragement to participate, to a pupil who has difficulty producing legible handwriting. Some pupils will require individual attention for their needs to be met. Some pupils may well have a marked learning difficulty and be identified as having a special educational need. In such cases, the teacher may be able to meet these needs, or else there may be additional help or resources available. Indeed, all teachers need to be alert to the possibility that a pupil may have a special educational need and to ensure that such needs are identified and met. Learning difficulties may stem from a physical disability of some sort, a long period of absence from school, very low general ability, or social and emotional problems.

Tutoring

Another aspect of matching work to pupils is the use of one-to-one teaching, sometimes referred to as tutoring. As well as whole-class teaching and the monitoring of progress on academic tasks, teachers also spend much of their time helping individual pupils on a one-to-one basis. This type of help is a crucial part of effective teaching, not only because of the academic help offered, but also because it is a personal and private encounter between you and the pupil. As such, it offers an important opportunity to emphasise your care, support and encouragement for the pupils' progress. It also provides an important opportunity to assess the pupil's general ability and motivation, and to identify any particular needs.

One of the most important aspects involved in skilful tutoring is that of *scaffolding.* The notion of scaffolding deals with how skilful tutoring can involve helping the pupil with a task by directing their attention to the key elements necessary for applying and developing their current understanding, and thereby enabling them to carry out the task successfully. A number of studies of classroom practice have shown that the teacher's ability to scaffold effectively requires a sensitive awareness of both the pupil's current level of understanding and the subject matter in hand.

The effectiveness of tutoring has long been recognised, and some schools now make use of parents as helpers in the classroom or use other pupils, either the same age or older, to provide additional opportunities for one-to-one help in the classroom. The use of pupils as tutors, often referred to as 'peer tutoring', is fairly widespread and a number of studies have indicated that where pupils are asked to help other pupils in this way (usually with reading or number work), both pupils seem to benefit. Of particular importance in using other adults or pupils as tutors in this way is that they are carefully briefed about their role and the need to offer encouragement to pupils during the interactions.

Using resources and materials

There is a vast range of resources and materials available for use in the classroom, including interactive whiteboards, laptops, slideshows, worksheets, and simulation materials. Perhaps the golden rule concerning their use is always to check their quality and appropriateness for the lesson. It is all too easy to think that because such resources are going to be used, that is an excuse for accepting a somewhat lower quality or something not quite appropriate for the intended learning. As a result, pupils all too often have to watch videos with poor sound quality or work through a software package that is unclear or even inappropriate to the topic being investigated. While the desire for pupils to acquire a familiarity with such materials may be important enough to warrant this on the odd occasion, you must be rigorous in your appraisal of the suitability of such materials for the learning outcomes you intend.

Figure 4.2: A wide variety of resources is available

It is also important to familiarise yourself with the content of such materials if you have not used them before or for some time, since it may prove difficult to deal with any problems that may arise unexpectedly. In addition, since many resources may be used by pupils with little or no help from the teacher, difficulties may arise that you may not be aware of until after the lesson, or at all, unless you carefully monitor progress.

Electronic resources and e-learning

The expansion of electronic resources is transforming the ways in which teaching and learning take place (Beetham and Sharpe, 2013; Younie and Leask, 2013). This is widely referred to as e-learning. Work can be submitted and feedback received electronically. Online forums can be used to post comments and share ideas. Resources and materials are widely available online to which teachers can direct pupils, or which pupils can discover for themselves. Changes in social media are occurring so rapidly that pupils are engaging in learning activities that the teacher may be unaware of (Poore, 2012). In this context, some writers have produced useful guidance on 'blending learning' that combines IT activities with face-to-face non-IT activities.

The pace of change in e-learning is occurring so fast that identification of the teaching skills that underpin effective teaching is underdeveloped, particularly as the skills can be very specific to the particular type of e-learning being considered. A study by Asterhan et al. (2012) illustrates this well. Their study focused on how teachers were able to improve the quality of online discussion between pupils that took place as a classroom activity. The role of the teacher in supporting online discussion between pupils is a challenging one, in that it needs to support pupil autonomy while at the same time scaffold reasoning and interaction. The study took place in a middle school in Israel, and looked at how the type of online contribution made by a teacher influenced the chain of reasoning (e-argumentation) developed by the pupils in their response to a question they were asked to discuss online. The authors of the study concluded that the skilful online guidance from the teacher can enhance both the argumentative quality of the contributions from an individual pupil and the collaborative quality (participation and interaction) of the collective dialogue.

Using the whiteboard and projectors

The whiteboard is still the most widely used teaching aid and the quality of your board use will be a major indicator of your teaching. Well-prepared and clear use of the whiteboard is not only effective as a teaching aid, but is also an example to the class of the standard of quality of work and presentation you expect. The whiteboard can also usefully be used as a reminder or record of important points: for example, the spelling of new or difficult words, a note of the task pupils are to undertake when the present task has been completed, or a list of pupils' ideas to be used for later analysis. One pitfall for beginning teachers to note is talking while facing the whiteboard: when you are writing on the whiteboard and have something important to say, you must turn your head to face the class as you speak.

Similar points can be made about the use of interactive whiteboards and data projectors, although here it is possible to produce materials in advance to good effect. Always ensure that the projection onto the screen is clearly visible from all parts of the classroom, and check that you are not obscuring the view yourself (an occasional fault, even among some experienced teachers!).

Individualised schemes of work

One marked area of development in the use of resources and materials has been the widespread use of individualised schemes of work based on software packages. One of the skills involved in their effective use concerns the organisation of how and when pupils use these, and how and when they receive feedback on their progress.

Many studies have indicated that one of the key factors in promoting greater pupil attainment is the ability of the teacher to maximise the time that pupils spend educationally benefiting from the learning activity in hand. The more time they spend waiting to use resources or waiting for help when they are in difficulties, the less time they spend making progress in their attainment. The procedures used by teachers to ensure good organisation in using such resources are thus of great importance.

One advantage of some software packages is that they are designed to be self-explanatory and often provide feedback concerning correct answers and help for pupils in difficulties. Nevertheless, most of these kinds of resources do still require teacher assistance from time to time, and for teachers to be involved in assessing progress. You therefore need to ensure that the arrangements you make allow such time to be given. One particularly useful strategy, more commonly employed in primary schools, is to organise a lesson so that different groups are working on different tasks, ranging from tasks involving minimal teacher contact to those involving a great deal of contact. By dividing the class up in this way, you will be able to spend more time with those pupils needing your help without this being to the detriment of other pupils.

Another useful strategy is to establish routines or procedures that pupils are required to follow, so that they do not waste time wondering what to do next in a particular situation. A simple rule concerning what pupils are expected to do if they get into difficulties or have finished a piece of work can help to ensure smooth running of classroom activities, and enables you to check whether the activities set are causing problems, are too easy, too difficult, or are unclear in any respect.

Treating resources and materials with care

Finally, when pupils use resources and materials that will be used again by others, it is worth emphasising that the resources must be handled with care and respect. This is important, not only because loss or damage may be costly and also inconvenience other pupils, but also because it highlights that in life everyone will be sharing resources and that such common ownership and use imposes responsibilities and obligations on each user. What is true in this respect within the community of the school is also true for society in general.

Further reading

Dymoke, S. (Ed.). (2012). *Reflective Teaching and Learning in the Secondary School* (2nd ed.). London: Sage. This book considers how our understanding of teaching and learning helps teachers to improve their classroom teaching skills. You will find the material dealing with lesson presentation in Chapter 3 on 'learning and teaching contexts' and Chapter 4 on 'classroom management' is particularly helpful.

Hayes, D. (2012). *Developing Advanced Primary Teaching Skills.* London: David Fulton. Looks at the development of effective teaching skills within the context of what it means to be a caring and competent teacher.

Muijs, D., & Reynolds, D. (2017). *Effective Teaching: Evidence and Practice* (4th ed.). London: Sage. A good overview of effective teaching that takes careful account of research evidence.

Wassermann, S. (2017). *The Art of Interactive Teaching: Listening, Responding, Questioning.* Abingdon: Routledge. This is an excellent overview of how the effective use of questioning skills can enhance pupils' engagement and understanding. Chapter 7 on the different types of questioning techniques is particularly helpful.

 Key questions

1   Are the learning activities appropriate to the type of learning outcomes I intend?

2   Do the learning activities take adequate account of pupils' abilities, interests and needs, and of their previous and future learning?

3   Do I audit the frequency of the different types of learning activity I use for a scheme of work?

4   Are my instructions, explanations and questions clear and appropriate for pupils' needs?

5   Do I use a variety of question types and distribute these widely throughout the class?

6   Is my general manner confident, relaxed, self-assured and purposeful, and one that is conducive to generating an interest in the lesson and providing support and encouragement for learning?

7   Does my lesson take account of any particular needs of individual pupils, including any special educational needs and disabilities?

8   Are resources and materials used to good effect?

9   Do I carefully monitor the progress of the lesson and the progress of pupils' learning to ensure that the learning activities are effectively fostering the learning outcomes I intend?

10   Does my general standard of presentation indicate to pupils my respect and care for their learning?

Chapter 5

Lesson management

Teaching a class of 30 pupils requires a wide range of management and organisational skills if there is to be sufficient order necessary for pupil learning. In many ways, I think the task of teaching is rather like the act one sometimes sees on a stage where a person has to spin plates on top of several canes simultaneously. To do this successfully requires the performer to set new plates spinning while occasionally returning to those plates that have slowed down and are near to falling off, for a booster spin. In the same way, successful lesson management requires you to keep switching attention and action between several activities to ensure that pupils' learning proceeds smoothly.

The key task facing you is to elicit and sustain pupils' involvement in the learning experience throughout a lesson in such a way that will lead to the learning outcomes you intend. At any one time you are likely to have several demands pressing on you for action. For example, you may be dealing with a pupil having problems with the task in hand, then become aware that another pupil needs an item of equipment, notice another pupil is staring out of the window apparently daydreaming, and be approached by another pupil who wants some work checked.

Lesson management essentially refers to those skills involved in managing and organising the learning activities such that you maximise pupils' productive involvement in the lesson as much as possible (Brooks et al., 2012; Dean, 2008; Kyriacou, 2009). Given the large size and range of ability of most classes, this is no mean task! Research based on classroom observation and interviews with beginning and experienced teachers has identified how a successful lesson hinges on certain key lesson management skills.

Paradoxically, watching expert teachers in action tends to provide student teachers with little explicit guidance on successful lesson management skills, since such teachers make everything look too easy. It is only when such teaching is contrasted with that of teachers where problems arise, that the differences in what they do become evident, and the skills used by successful lesson managers can be described.

Beginnings, transitions and endings

One of the key areas of lesson management concerns the skills used in beginning a lesson, handling the transitions within the lesson between activities (say, moving from group work to whole-class discussion), and bringing a lesson to a successful ending.

Beginning punctually

The two most important aspects concerning the beginning of the lesson are punctuality and mental set. Punctuality refers to the importance of the lesson starting fairly soon after the time formally timetabled for its start. This requires that both you and your pupils have arrived for the lesson in good time. Ideally, it is a great help if you can be in the classroom first, to greet pupils as they arrive and to ensure that pupils enter the classroom in an orderly fashion and settle down quickly. Certainly you should convey to pupils that lateness is not acceptable without good excuse.

For the first few minutes of a lesson, there is usually a period of dead time during which pupils settle down, books may be distributed, or you may check material or notes. If possible, you can usually use this time to good effect by having a social exchange with one or two pupils, or deal with some matters outstanding from a previous lesson, such as a pupil's overdue homework. Once you are happy that everyone has arrived, you need to indicate that the lesson itself is ready to begin. This is probably the most important moment in the lesson. It signals the exact point that pupils are to pay attention and begin their involvement in the lesson. A clear explicit signal, perhaps saying 'Okay everyone' or 'Pay attention now', is required. It is immensely important for pupils to start paying attention immediately. If you are not happy that all pupils are paying attention, you should indicate this. Trying to continue with the start of a lesson when a few pupils are not paying attention often acts as a signal for others to do likewise in future.

Establishing a positive mental set

Most lessons begin with the topic in hand or with some short activity that needs to be dealt with first, such as comments on homework, or some comment about equipment or materials that everyone should have ready. Whether you start with the topic itself or some other activity, it is important to stand centre stage at the front of the room, and to use a clear voice, eye contact and scanning, to ensure everyone is paying attention. A pause followed by a stare at someone not paying attention is often sufficient to signal this.

Once you begin to introduce the topic in hand for the lesson, you need to think about how to elicit and sustain pupils' interest. The best way to do this is to convey in your tone of voice and general manner a sense of curiosity and excitement, and a sense of purposefulness about what is to follow. Two useful techniques are to establish a link with previous work (e.g. 'Now, you remember last week we looked at ...') or to pose some questions (e.g. 'Can anybody tell me what the word "energy" means?'). Such techniques help to establish a positive mental set towards the lesson, i.e. an attitude of mind in which the pupil prepares to devote attention and mental effort towards the activities you set up. A successful introduction to a lesson, which establishes a positive mental set, makes it far easier to sustain learning as the lesson unfolds.

Another aspect of establishing this mental set is to check that every pupil is ready and prepared for the start of the lesson. Are there still pupils with bags on the desk, or standing up talking to each other, or looking for an exercise book that was not handed back? One of the skills involved here is deciding whether to hold up the start of the lesson and chivvy pupils to settle down quickly (e.g. 'Hurry up now, I can still see bags on desks') or whether simply by starting, pupils will quickly pay attention.

Once a routine for a quick and smooth start to lessons has been well established, you can normally relax the formality of the start, as pupils will quickly respond. However, it is useful from time to time to re-emphasise the procedure and expectations, to ensure that they continue to operate well. At the same time, you also need to check that you are ready and prepared for the start of the lesson. Are the materials you intend to use readily to hand? Has the diagram you wish pupils to talk about been drawn on the board? Are the copies of the worksheets to be used ready for distribution? A state of readiness on your part will contribute to your own mental set, and this will in turn influence the mental set of pupils.

It has been well established that giving pupils 'advanced organisers' at the start of a lesson can be helpful. Advanced organisers refer to ways in which the teacher alerts pupils to how the content and activities of the lesson can be organised and related to their previous knowledge and understanding. However, it appears that explicitly sharing with pupils the educational objectives for the lesson at the start of the lesson can also have a positive impact on the quality of their work. A study by Seidel et al. (2005) indicated that in lessons where the pupils were given a clear idea of the lesson goals, the pupils characterised the lesson as providing a more supportive classroom climate for their learning and pupils made greater progress in their learning, as was indicated by their subsequent attainment test scores. However, it is important for the teacher to engage with pupils concerning the educational objectives through some discussion, as there is a danger that if these are simply stated by the teacher without any such engagement, pupils may fail to recognise their significance for their learning outcomes.

Smooth transitions

The notion of 'smoothness' is helpful when considering whether a lesson has started smoothly and whether there has been a smooth transition between activities (Kounin, 1970). This can best be described by contrasting it with the notion of 'jerkiness'. Jerkiness would be evident if the teacher had to repeat instructions because pupils had not heard or were confused by what was said, or if, having begun a new activity, the teacher keep referring back to the previous activity.

The worst form of jerkiness is attempting to start an activity only to find that some prior activity needed to be undertaken first, and as a result of this needing to stop the activity and change to the prior activity. An example of this would be having to tell pupils who had started working through a worksheet that they should have been told to read a passage in their textbook first. This not only interrupts the pupils, but makes them feel that their efforts have been wasted through the teacher's poor planning and lesson management. Effective beginnings and transitions are smooth in the sense of lacking jerkiness. Clearly, from time to time, such jerkiness is inevitable and occurs for good educational reasons, such as if it becomes evident that an unforeseeable learning difficulty has arisen. Nevertheless, skilful teaching tends to be characterised by a minimum of unnecessary and avoidable instances of jerkiness.

In looking at smooth transitions, two other aspects contribute to smoothness. First, the teacher needs to be sensitive to how a lesson is progressing in deciding when to initiate a transition. For example, if pupils seem to be working fairly well at a task but somewhat slower than anticipated, the teacher may decide that it is better to allow more time for the task to continue, rather than interrupt the activity before it is completed to move them on to another activity. In some cases, this may be crucial. For example, a transition to discussion following group work may be harder to set up effectively if the group work has not continued long enough for the issues or ideas to develop that were to form the basis for the discussion.

The second aspect of transitions worthy of note is deciding when to give instructions to the class as a whole, rather than to individuals. All too often a teacher interrupts a class embarking on a new activity simply to issue a further or elaborated instruction that is only of use to two or three particular pupils. It may well have been better and less disruptive for the teacher to talk to each of those pupils privately. The same pitfall can relate to issuing a reprimand, which again may disrupt the working of a whole class when simple and silent eye contact might have been more effective and less disruptive.

The key point to bear in mind concerning transitions is that care and attention in setting up a sequence of activities in which pupils are working steadily are just as important as the effort you put into dealing with the content of the learning activities.

Ending the lesson

The ending of a lesson can usefully include a few words of praise concerning the work covered and some conclusions or summary about what was achieved. Three important issues of management concern endings. First, a lesson should end on time, neither early, nor (except for special reasons) late. Good time management is one of the skills that pupils will expect you to have. Ending early can imply a lack of concern about the worthwhileness of using all the time available. Should some time be available at the end of the lesson, this time can be usefully spent reviewing or probing the topic covered. Ending late can imply that you lack the organisational skills to marshal the activities together, and will deprive you of the opportunity to finish the lesson in a well-ordered and unhurried fashion. Most pupils will naturally resent lessons running over time on a regular basis.

A second management issue concerns the procedure for getting pupils ready for the end of the lesson. This may involve collecting books and equipment, giving feedback on the work done, and setting homework or other action needed before the next lesson. While this should occur in good time, you also need to ensure that some pupils do not start to pack away too early or before you have signalled this.

Third, the exit from the classroom should be well ordered. If necessary, it should be controlled, with you dismissing groups of pupils at a time, rather than allowing a rushed exit, until such time as pupils are used to making a well-ordered exit from the classroom without your explicit control.

Maintaining pupils' involvement

Once the lesson is underway, your main task is to maintain pupils' attention, interest and involvement in the learning activities. The task is *not*, however, one of simply keeping pupils busy. There may be a number of activities that you could set up that would effectively keep pupils busy, but they may not be effectively promoting the learning you intend.

What makes lesson management skills so sophisticated is the task of setting up activities that are both educationally effective and maintain pupils' involvement. While the two should go together, it is easy to find some activities erring too far towards only the latter. Skilful lesson management is primarily a question of getting a good balance between the learning potential of an activity and its degree of sustaining pupils' involvement. Since learning cannot occur without involvement, a danger facing teachers is to be uncritical about the quality of learning that occurs when they have successfully maintained a high level of pupil involvement. Nevertheless, at the same time, it is important to bear in mind that the learning outcomes that teachers try to achieve include the development of study skills, organisational skills, and sustained concentration by pupils. These can usefully be fostered by lengthy periods of working without interaction with the teacher. As such, a teacher may well choose to use an activity that can sustain high pupil involvement for a long period, primarily as a means to foster such skills.

Skills in lesson management

There are a number of skills involved in effective lesson management (e.g. DfE, 2012; Muijs and Reynolds, 2017; Ofsted, 2014), although some of these clearly overlap with issues of lesson presentation covered in Chapter 4. In particular, these focus on the need to be able to use teaching methods that sustain the momentum of pupils' work and keep all pupils engaged, through:

- stimulating pupils' intellectual curiosity, communicating enthusiasm for the subject being taught, and fostering pupils' enthusiasm and maintaining their motivation

- structuring information well, including outlining content and aims, signalling transitions, and summarising key points as the lesson progresses

- clear instruction and demonstration, and accurate well-paced explanation

- effective questioning that matches the pace and direction of the lesson and ensures that pupils take part

- listening carefully to pupils, analysing their responses, and responding constructively in order to take pupils' learning forward

- providing opportunities for pupils to consolidate their knowledge and maximising opportunities, both in the classroom and through setting well-focused homework, to reinforce and develop what has been learned

- setting high expectations for all pupils notwithstanding individual differences, including gender, and cultural and linguistic backgrounds

- managing the learning of individuals, groups and whole classes

- modifying the teaching to suit the stage of the lesson.

Monitoring pupils' progress

Overall, the most important skill involved in maintaining pupils' involvement is that of carefully monitoring pupils' progress. You should do this actively, through circulating around the room and asking probing questions, and passively, by having well-established routines whereby pupils are encouraged to ask for help. Both active and passive monitoring is important. As a result of such monitoring, key decisions may be made about how best to sustain pupils' involvement. Such decisions may relate to the needs of one or two particular pupils or to the needs of the class as a whole.

Monitoring pupil progress is a key aspect of Assessment for Learning (AfL). This deals with strategies and activities that enable the teacher to assess the pupil's progress and then use the results of such monitoring to enhance the pupil's learning, so as to provide the pupil with a better understanding of how their performance in an assessment task can be improved (Dann, 2018). AfL is discussed further in Chapter 8.

You can also make use of school data on pupil progress to get a good sense of what amount of progress you can reasonably expect your pupils to make over a given period. Such yardsticks are important in ensuring that work is not rushed and that pupils do not dwell for too long on covering a particular scheme of work.

Pace and flow of the lesson

If pupils' attention or interest in the lesson seems to be on the wane, a number of possible reasons may account for this. It may be that a particular activity is being employed for too long (most commonly a long exposition). Alternatively, it may be that the general pace and flow of the lesson is either too fast or too slow.

If the pace of activities (be it exposition, group work, worksheets, or reading tasks) is too fast, pupils will simply wilt or find that they are missing important points or ideas. If the pace is too slow, pupils' minds can easily start to wander. Indeed, an important aspect of maintaining the correct pace during exposition involves having a sense of how long to dwell on each particular point for understanding to occur and not spending too long dwelling on minor points or points already well taken.

In addition, maintaining a good pace also involves avoiding unnecessary interruptions to the flow of the lesson. For example, if while explaining a task, you stop in order to get a pencil for a pupil, or to find a map you need to refer to, or to reprimand a pupil, the flow of the lesson will be interrupted. A useful lesson management skill is that of dealing with the demands that arise, or postponing dealing with them, so that they are not allowed to interrupt the flow of the lesson. For example, if while explaining a task you notice two pupils talking, you may continue your explanation while looking at the two pupils concerned or, if necessary, move towards them. This would enable the flow of the lesson to continue while dealing with the problem. This skill is sometimes referred to as 'overlapping', i.e. dealing with two or more tasks at the same time.

Another example of overlapping is the teacher's ability to monitor pupils' progress and behaviour while giving individual help to a particular pupil. A skilful teacher is able to listen to a pupil reading aloud or give help with some number work, for example, while at the same time periodically scanning the classroom and listening to the background noise to pick out any behaviour giving concern. This involves quickly switching attention between your interaction with the particular pupil and what else is going on in the classroom. Indeed, a particular pitfall for beginning teachers is to become so engrossed in giving individual help and attention, so as to fail to monitor what else is happening. In contrast, experienced teachers are much more skilful in their attention switching.

Figure 5.1: You have to be able to do a wide variety of things at the same time

Withitness

The general awareness of what is going on in the classroom is commonly referred to as 'withitness' (Kounin, 1970). Experienced teachers are adept at picking up cues and signals that indicate to them what is going on. A quick downward glance by a pupil in the back row, or a furtive look at a neighbour, or simply taking slightly too long to walk to a seat, can all be picked up by a teacher as signalling the onset of possible misbehaviour.

Beginning teachers are often so overwhelmed by all the demands of classroom life that they find it difficult to pick up such signals. With increasing experience, which gradually makes the unfamiliar familiar, the teacher becomes better able to pick up and monitor subtle cues of this type. As such, it is useful for beginning teachers to consciously make an effort to scan the classroom periodically and monitor general behaviour, to see if anything gives concern. It is also useful to bear in mind the times when such monitoring is vulnerable to being interrupted: for example, when giving individual help, when your back is turned to the classroom while writing on the board, or when looking in cupboards. A useful technique when writing on the board is to face sideways or to glance back at the class regularly, and to listen carefully to any background noise.

The importance of lesson managing skills concerning transition, overlapping and withitness, was highlighted in a seminal study by Kounin (1970), in which he compared the videotaped classroom behaviour of teachers who were regarded as having few discipline problems with teachers having frequent problems. What was particularly noticeable was that the former's relative success largely stemmed from them simply being more effective lesson managers, rather than anything to do with how they dealt with pupil misbehaviour itself. Research on teaching skills, including my own (e.g. Kyriacou and McKelvey, 1985), indicates that experienced teachers are generally very skilful in transition, overlapping and withitness.

Managing pupils' time

Pupils' involvement in the lesson can also be facilitated if they are given a clear idea of how much time and effort they are expected to devote to particular tasks or activities. For example, if you ask pupils to copy a map into their exercise books and answer three questions related to the map, some pupils may rush the task, anticipating that 10 minutes should be sufficient time, and others may assume the task is intended to last half an hour. If you indicate that the task should take about 20 minutes, this will help pupils to tailor their effort to the time available.

There can, of course, sometimes be a danger in encouraging pupils to perhaps take longer than they need. In general, however, it helps to ensure that some pupils do not work slowly only to find they are halfway through a task when you want to move on to another activity. It also helps to maintain attention and interest, since they have a clear sense that another activity is shortly to follow. This also helps to break the lesson up into more attractive chunks of time.

Giving supportive feedback

Constructive and helpful feedback also needs to be given to pupils to support and encourage further progress (Black et al., 2003; Gardner, 2011). Such feedback is not only of practical use to pupils in identifying problems or indicating successful work, but also conveys to them that their progress is being carefully monitored and that you care about such progress. Such regular feedback thus offers a periodic boost to pupils' motivation and effort.

The skill of offering such feedback is a fairly complex one that needs time and practice to develop. You need to be able to identify the nature of the pupil's problem. Simply indicating a 'correct' method or answer may not be enough to give the pupil the insight required. You also need to be able to offer feedback in a way that is unthreatening, since once a pupil feels anxious, it is harder for them to follow what is being said. This requires the use of a sympathetic tone of voice, and locating the problem in the task or activity, rather than in the pupil. In other words, it is better to say, 'In this type of question, it is a good idea to start by taking careful note of the information given in the diagram', rather than 'You should have been more careful in your approach.' The former statement is task-focused, whereas the latter locates the fault or blame with the pupil. This sensitivity to pupils' feelings is now widely appreciated as being an important aspect of the skill involved in providing supportive feedback. Indeed, in a number of studies of pupils' views of their teachers it was reported that the teacher's capacity to empathise was one of the most valued teacher qualities cited (Cullingford, 2003).

Giving individual feedback privately to each pupil in a fairly large class is clearly going to be demanding, and attempting to do this will almost certainly distract you from other important tasks. Therefore you need to maintain a good balance between giving individual feedback and other strategies, including giving feedback to the whole class, or enabling pupils to correct their own or each other's work. These other techniques help to ensure that feedback occurs regularly and with sufficient speed to improve the quality of work and learning. However, you do need to ensure that such techniques are used sensitively, given the emotional consequences of identifying failure.

It is a good idea to circulate around the classroom while pupils are engaged in a task, and to give them ongoing feedback on their work in an informal manner. You can take these opportunities to use the technique of 'scaffolding': this is where the teacher helps a pupil who is in difficulty by drawing their attention to the key features of the task, and through dialogue with the pupil, gradually guides them towards the understanding they need in order to complete the task successfully.

Adjusting your lesson plans

Careful monitoring of pupils' progress and giving feedback also enables you to consider how best the lesson ought to proceed in the light of its success to date and any problems encountered. While lesson plans are important, all teachers will need to tailor the development of the lesson to the needs of the moment. As such, part of successful lesson management involves making whatever adjustments to your original plans for the lesson that are necessary. In doing so, however, always ensure that you have a good feel for how the class as a whole is progressing. Clearly, just because one or two pupils are finding the work too easy or too difficult or lacking interest, this should not be taken as a signal that this is generally true for most of the class. Once you get to know a class fairly well, however, it becomes possible to make useful inferences from the behaviour of just a handful of pupils. If, for example, two or three pupils who normally find the work in hand difficult are suddenly racing through a particular task, you may well be fairly certain that most pupils in the class are going to complete the task quickly without the need for you to check too widely for confirmation.

Handling the logistics of classroom life

Lesson management skills are essential if the learning activities you set up are to take place with sufficient order for learning to occur. Almost any task or activity can lead to chaos, unless you give some thought to the organisation of how and when pupils are to do what is required of them. Organised control over the logistics of classroom life, whether it be how pupils answer questions, collect equipment from cupboards, or form themselves into small groups, requires explicit direction from you – at least until the procedures you expect are followed as a matter of routine.

Social demand tasks

Research on teachers' management effectiveness indicates that every learning activity involves a 'social demand task'. This social demand task concerns, for example, who can talk to whom, about what, where, when, in what ways, and for what purpose. Such research highlights the importance of how teachers indicate to pupils what is required of them, and facilitate the smooth and effective running of the activity. Indeed, with the increasing variety of learning activities used, effective lesson management skills need to be applied to a host of very different types of activities to deal with the social demand task involved in each. This has become increasingly evident in looking at the different ways in which IT use in the classroom has generated new types of social demands that teachers have to manage skilfully.

Group work

Setting up group work activities involves a number of decisions about the logistics of their organisation (Jaques, 2000; Kutnick and Blachford, 2013). First, there is the question of the size of the group and how groups are to be formed. If you have a task which, ideally, involves four pupils, you need to think about how the groups of four are to be created, and what to do if there are one or more pupils left over, or indeed, one or two pupils that no one wants in their group.

A second question concerns the nature of the task. Is it clear exactly what the task involves, who will undertake which roles, and how and what is to be produced? A clear instruction, such as 'At the end, each group will give a list of the four most important factors involved, in order of importance', is clearer than simply getting each group to discuss the factors involved. Often, it is useful to write the task on the board or on a briefing handout issued to each pupil or group. You may wish to let each group decide who should report back at the end, or name a pupil from each group to do this (the latter is useful in ensuring that certain pupils are given the experience of doing this).

A third aspect of group work concerns your monitoring role. While close monitoring is usually desirable, particularly in checking that everyone is clear about the task, your presence may have an inhibiting effect on group discussion. As such, it is often better to spend only a short while with each group to check that everything is in order, rather than to sit in for any length of time.

Fourth, clear time-management directions are crucial to most group work activities. Not only is it useful to say how long each group has for the task as a whole, but also how much time they may spend on any stages that make up the task. One last aspect concerning group work is the need to help pupils develop the skills involved in successful group work. Pupils need to develop a number of skills to use group work to good effect, and feedback and guidance from you concerning good practice can help such skills to develop.

Fifth, and perhaps most challenging of all, is the need for the teacher to interject from time to time in a manner that serves to facilitate and promote high-quality dialogue between pupils, while at the same time ensuring that pupils do not feel that their sense of being self-directed learners is undermined (Mercer and Littleton, 2007; Watkins et al., 2007). One useful technique here is to switch backwards and forwards between whole-class teaching and group work, so that the type of conversational interaction that takes place during the whole-class teaching helps shape the quality of the dialogue that occurs during group work.

Of particular interest here is a study by Tolmie et al. (2010) that looked at the social effects of collaborative learning in primary schools. The question they addressed concerns what impact the use of group work tasks in the classroom has on pupils' social relations. In a study involving 575 primary school pupils in Scotland, aged 9 to 12 years, their findings indicated that group work had a beneficial effect on both pupils' learning and social interaction. However, they also concluded that what was crucial to this dual beneficial effect was that the teacher spent some time building up pupils' group work skills, particularly in the area of being able to resolve the tensions and disagreements that occur during group work.

Practicals

Practicals of any sort present a number of logistical problems, in part because you need to co-ordinate your management of pupils and materials with the sequence and speed of the practical itself. In a science practical, for example, there may be a 20-minute period during which some effect is developing; this period can be actively used to explore with pupils what is going on and to probe their thinking and the care they are taking to observe and record any changes.

Another common problem regarding practicals may arise if certain equipment needs to be shared. Again, a strict rota for the use of such equipment, or a procedure to ensure its speedy use and return, can make a large difference to reducing unproductive time. During practicals there are often times when bottlenecks can occur, such as when everyone wants to collect or return equipment, or perhaps wash apparatuses. Simple rules, such as only allowing one pupil from each group to collect apparatuses, can help prevent problems occurring.

Using IT

The plethora of IT-based teaching and learning activities presents you with a host of challenges in your management of the learning experience and the IT equipment being used (Younie and Leask, 2013). This includes fixed hardware and portable hardware, and equipment that is owned by the school and by the pupil. This often requires you to spend quite a bit of time in instructing pupils on how to use electronic equipment in order to tackle the particular task, such as asking a small group to produce a slideshow presentation, or asking individual pupils to contribute to a discussion board.

Unless you can arrange all pupils to have ready access to the IT equipment they need to use at the same time, such as booking an IT suite, you will need to organise a rota of some sort. One point about pairs, or occasionally a small group of three pupils, working together when using IT, is that it is useful in most cases to group together pupils of similar ability, unless you explicitly wish one pupil to act as a tutor. With other types of group work, friendship groupings seem to work well, unless there is a clear educational rationale for forming the groups on the basis of similar ability or in some other way.

Managing pupil movement and noise

Two of the most important aspects of effective management skills concern maintaining adequate control over the movement of pupils around the classroom and keeping the degree of noise generated at an appropriate level. In both cases, part of the difficulty lies in there being no fixed acceptable standard; what may be acceptable to one teacher in one context may not be regarded as acceptable to another teacher in another context. Furthermore, problems over movement and noise can arise simply as a result of pupils being actively engaged in the tasks at hand and not because of any deliberate attempt by them to be troublesome.

Figure 5.2: You need to be able to manage pupil movement and noise

Pupil movement

We have already touched on some aspects of pupil movement in the classroom earlier in this chapter, such as entering and leaving the room, and collecting equipment. In addition to these, there are some occasions that require particular attention. The first of these involves giving out books at the start of or during the lesson. It is certainly important to issue books rather than allow pupils to collect them from a central point. Often, it is more efficient for you to ask two or three pupils to issue books, rather than do it yourself, unless you feel that distributing books yourself will provide a useful social function or enable you to have a few pertinent words with some pupils. If pupils are issuing the books, ensure that they do so sensibly and with care.

The second aspect concerns any mass movement of pupils; this always requires careful control. While useful routines can be established, there are occasions when you need to organise a somewhat unusual or novel arrangement. For example, you may wish to devise a role-play activity that requires all the classroom furniture, apart from eight chairs, to be moved towards the edge of the classroom. Any complicated manoeuvre of this sort requires prior thought if it is to proceed smoothly; a clear sequence of tasks and instructions on who needs to do what are essential.

The third aspect involves establishing your expectations concerning when pupils may leave their seats. Most pupils will spend the majority of their time in their seats in the majority of lessons. The management of pupils being out of their seats during periods of work when pupils are expected to work at their desks is important. The normal expectation during such activities is that pupils remain at their desks until given explicit permission to move, unless certain well-established routines that allow movement without explicit permission are followed. In such circumstances it is useful to ensure that only a handful of pupils at any one time are out of their seats or away from their work area; it becomes much harder to monitor pupils' progress if several pupils appear to be wandering about, even if their purposes are legitimate. This is one reason why teachers often set an upper limit on how many pupils are allowed to queue up at the teacher's desk. Being out of one's seat for some pupils also acts as a break from their work, and they may feel like extending this break longer than necessary, and, as a result, may also start to disturb others. This needs careful monitoring.

Pupil noise

Managing the general level of noise is also an important management skill. Every teacher develops their own standard of acceptable level of noise. The key thing here is to be reasonably consistent, so that pupils have a clear idea of your expectations. If the level of background noise during an activity appears to be too high, it is useful to give specific feedback on the work practice you require, rather than a general complaint that the noise is too high. For example, saying 'You can talk to your neighbour, but not to other pupils' or 'Try to ensure that only one person in each group is speaking at a time' is better than simply saying 'The noise level is too high' or 'Less noise please.'

It is also worth planning the activities to ensure that noise levels are not disruptive. For example, in a science practical looking at sound as a form of energy, clear instructions on how the apparatus or equipment is to be used can prevent problems occurring through unnecessarily high noise levels. Indeed, the opportunity to make a lot of noise legitimately is too tempting for many pupils to resist. At the same time, it must be recognised that a certain level of noise is, of course, acceptable and desirable, and that enthusiastic and excited contributions by pupils need to be harnessed to good effect rather than squashed. Clearly, a balance that ensures sufficient order is what is needed.

Some studies, however, have indicated that the teacher's management of noise can sometimes become an end in itself. Given that the noise level of a class is often taken as an indicator of the teacher's level of control, many teachers are very sensitive about their classroom noise level, particularly if they feel it may be heard by colleagues or interfere with colleagues' lessons. Indeed, beginning teachers often feel themselves to be under particular pressure to control the noise level of their classes lest it conveys that they lack control to colleagues. As a result, some teachers make more frequent use of certain learning activities because they help sustain periods of quiet work by pupils, despite the fact that other learning activities might be more effective for the learning outcomes intended (but have more potential to generate noise). Indeed, the reluctance that some teachers have to make greater use of group work is related to the greater level of noise such activity typically generates.

Movement and noise as constraints on your teaching

While the management of movement and noise is important, you do need to be on your guard concerning whether, as indicated above, you are allowing management considerations to have too great an influence on your choice of effective learning activities. Skilful lesson management involves an interplay between the different constraints within which you operate. Clearly, you need to ensure that a role-play activity involving a lot of movement and noise does not disturb another class, or that one pupil's excitement does not lead to other pupils being constantly interrupted when they are speaking. At the same time, you need to ensure that the learning activity facilitates and encourages pupils' attention, interest, and involvement in the lesson, and that this is not unduly inhibited by management strategies that could be usefully relaxed to good effect.

One of the dilemmas facing teachers is that they may feel better able to manage certain types of lessons, and as a result are reluctant to use other types of learning activities. This reluctance may persist, despite the fact that certain curriculum developments have made the need for such change essential. This is evident, for example, in studies of how teachers' classroom practice has been influenced by the introduction of the National Curriculum, with many teachers expressing hostility and resistance towards the need for them to change their established practice. Indeed, senior managers in some schools welcomed the National Curriculum because it made it easier for them to put pressure on colleagues to change certain aspects of their classroom practice by externalising the source of the need for change: 'Your practice has got to change, not because it's my idea, but because the National Curriculum requires it.' This type of pressure for change was also very evident when the National Numeracy Strategy and the National Literacy Strategy were introduced.

In thinking about your own classroom practice, you should not be wary of setting up activities that may involve more than the usual movement or noise, as long as this is well managed and to good purpose. Some years ago, a well-known head teacher remarked that effective teaching could sometimes be described as 'organised chaos'. On the one hand, I think that there is some truth in this description, insofar as some effective lessons may well appear to have such a quality. On the other hand, there can at times be a danger in thinking that certain activities are so worthwhile in their own right, particularly in terms of the extent to which they may offer pupils a fair measure of control over their work, that the need to maintain sufficient order and control for effective learning can be relaxed. While I am a strong advocate of using a variety of learning activities, particularly active learning methods, there is always a need to ensure that effective learning is occurring, and to provide the conditions that will facilitate this. Again, what is required here is an appropriate balance between the management strategies used and the type of learning outcomes you intend, most notably if the learning outcomes are in terms of developing pupils' own skills to organise themselves.

Further reading

Brooks, V., Abbott, I., & Huddleston, P. (Eds). (2012). *Preparing to Teach in Secondary Schools: A Student Teacher's Guide to Professional Issues in Secondary Education* (3rd ed.). Milton Keynes: Open University Press. The chapters dealing with teaching and learning provide an informative overview of issues in skilful lesson management.

Dean, J. (2008). *Organising Learning in the Primary School Classroom* (4th ed.). Abingdon: Routledge. A readable overview of effective teaching, with some useful points on lesson management.

Mercer, N., & Littleton, K. (2007). *Dialogue and the Development of Children's Thinking: A Sociocultural Approach.* Abingdon: Routledge. An excellent analysis of the importance of high-quality dialogue in the classroom and how teachers can promote and manage this skilfully. You will find Chapter 4, on the role of productive teacher–pupil dialogue in fostering high-level pupil thinking, to be extremely powerful in shaping your ideas about your classroom practice.

Younie, S., & Leask, M. (2013). *Teaching with Technologies: The Essential Guide.* Milton Keynes: Open University Press. A very helpful guide to a range of lesson management issues that underpin the effective use of IT in the classroom.

Key questions

1 Does my lesson start smoothly and promptly, and induce a positive mental set among pupils?

2 Does the management of the lesson help to elicit and maintain pupils' attention, interest and motivation?

3 Are the pace and flow of the lesson maintained at an appropriate level and are transitions between activities well managed?

4 Do I carefully monitor the progress of pupils so that the effectiveness of the lesson is maintained, for example, by giving individual help or making modifications and adjustments to the development of the lesson, as appropriate?

5 Do I give clear guidance and direction on what is expected of pupils during each activity? Do I manage their time and effort, in relation to their involvement in and the sequencing of the various activities, to good effect?

6 Do I make effective use of the various materials, resources and teaching aids, so that pupils' time is not wasted waiting for equipment to be set up or materials distributed?

7 Do I organise and control the logistics of classroom life, such as how pupils answer questions, collect equipment, or form into groups, so that the order necessary for learning to occur is maintained?

8 In particular, do I use effective management strategies in handling pupil movement and the general level of noise?

9 Is the feedback conveyed to pupils about their progress helpful and constructive, and does it encourage further progress?

10 Do my lessons end effectively, in terms of ending on time, drawing the topic of the lesson to an appropriate conclusion, and having a well-ordered exit by pupils from the classroom?

Chapter 6

Classroom climate

The classroom climate you establish can have a major impact on pupils' motivation and attitudes towards learning (Cullingford, 2003; Haydn, 2012). As such, the skills involved in establishing a positive classroom climate are of immense importance. Indeed, a study by Day et al. (2007) found that having the skills to establish a positive classroom climate, and in particular to establish a positive relationship with pupils, was seen by teachers to lie at the heart of their view of themselves as effective teachers. One of the most effective ways to understand how best to establish a positive classroom involves reading accounts of how pupils experience teaching and learning in the classroom (e.g. Hargreaves, 2017).

Establishing a positive classroom climate

The type of classroom climate generally considered to best facilitate pupil learning is one that is described as being purposeful, task-oriented, relaxed, warm, supportive, and with a sense of order. Such a climate facilitates learning, in essence, by establishing and maintaining positive attitudes and motivation by pupils towards the lesson. In analysing the skills involved in setting up a positive classroom climate, it is clear that the climate largely derives from the values that are implicit and pervade the lesson – simply that pupils and their learning are of immense importance. Interestingly, a study by Kaplan et al. (2002) found that the level of disruptive behaviour by pupils tended to be higher in those classrooms where the pupils felt that the demonstration of ability and doing better than others was the dominant value, compared with classrooms where the pupils felt that the dominant value was learning, understanding and improving over your past performance.

Purposeful and task-oriented

A purposeful and task-oriented ethos stems largely from the way in which the teacher emphasises the need to make steady progress with the learning in hand. An important aspect of this derives from the teacher's insistence that time must not be wasted. Hence, a prompt start to the lesson, close monitoring of pupils' progress, and careful attention to organisational matters, all help to ensure a smooth flow to the lesson and maintenance of pupil involvement. When you allow minor matters or avoidable organisational problems to interrupt the flow of the lesson, a message is conveyed to pupils that the learning is not of such immense importance that it warranted more care to ensure that it was not interrupted. Certainly conveying in your tone of voice a lack of enthusiasm for a topic will undermine creating a purposeful and task-oriented ethos. Ending a lesson early is likely to have the same effect.

Overall, a purposeful and task-oriented emphasis can usefully be described as a 'businesslike' style of presentation. This is characterised by pupils' acceptance of the teacher's authority to organise and manage the learning activities, and a pervading expectation by you and your pupils that pupils will make an effort to undertake the work in hand and that good progress will be made.

A very important aspect of establishing such positive expectations by pupils is the need to ensure that pupils have self-respect and self-esteem regarding themselves as learners. This can, in part, be fostered by providing realistic opportunities for success, and helpful support and encouragement, whenever pupils experience difficulties. Learning is an emotionally high-risk activity and failure is often extremely painful. Prolonged experience of failure or deprecating remarks by a teacher about pupils' low attainment can have devastating consequences for pupils' self-esteem. As a result, quite naturally, such pupils are likely to withdraw from making further efforts as a means of protecting themselves from further pain (in effect, if I am not trying, my lack of success is simply my choice).

Being relaxed, warm and supportive

A relaxed, warm and supportive ethos stems largely from the style and manner of the relationship you establish with pupils. Being relaxed yourself, and in particular, dealing with any pupil misbehaviour calmly, helps pupils to relax too. This type of atmosphere will enable pupils to develop curiosity and interest in the learning activities more easily.

Warmth can best be thought of as conveying to pupils a sense that you care for them and their learning personally, partly out of your affection for them as individuals. This is conveyed in the way you deal with individual pupils. Simply saying at the end of giving individual help, 'Have you got that now?' in a sympathetic and caring tone of voice (rather than in a harsh and admonishing tone), can do much to convey this sense of warmth. Pye (1988), in his analysis of skilful teaching, used the phrase 'solicitous tenderness' to describe the mixture of warmth, reassurance, kindness and tact shown by skilful teachers in how they handle interactions with pupils. At its best, this can work extremely well in contributing to a positive classroom climate, but care needs to be taken not to sound patronising.

Being supportive refers to the efforts you make to help and encourage pupils to meet the demands made on them and, in particular, to deal with the difficulties they encounter in a situation where they need further assistance rather than being reprimanded. However, you do need to be aware of the fact that too readily providing individual help and support may encourage some pupils to rely on such help rather than to make the appropriate effort to pay attention during whole-class teaching or to work things out for themselves. In giving supportive feedback you can usefully help pupils to develop study skills by indicating how paying attention earlier or using certain strategies in approaching their work will enable them to meet the demands made on them. In the context of establishing a positive classroom climate, such feedback can be a useful part of offering support.

It is interesting to note that a study by Koutrouba (2012), based on a survey of 340 secondary school teachers in Greece, noted that the most highly rated attributes of an effective teacher included being 'encouraging and supportive', 'tactful' and 'kind and open', which are widely regarded as key qualities that underpin the creation of a positive classroom climate.

A sense of order

A final aspect of a positive classroom climate is the need to establish a sense of order (Rogers, 2012). Clearly, a sense of order can be established in many different ways. What is advocated here is that to contribute to a positive classroom climate, such order needs to arise out of and complement the other features considered in establishing a purposeful, task-oriented, relaxed, warm and supportive ethos. Such order will thus be based on effective lesson presentation and lesson management skills, and on a relationship with pupils based on mutual respect and rapport.

Studies of classroom climate

A number of studies looking at effective teaching and effective schools have focused on the notion of climate or ethos (Muijs and Reynolds, 2017; Skinner, 2010). These include some particularly interesting research that has focused on the wider notion of the 'learning environment' of which the classroom climate is a part (Buckler and Castle, 2014). For example, Fraser (2002) identified several aspects of the learning environment that relate to classroom climate, such as:

- *involvement:* the extent to which pupils have attentive interest, participate in discussions, do additional work, and enjoy the class

- *equity:* the extent to which pupils are treated equally and fairly by the teacher

- *differentiation:* the extent to which teachers cater for pupils differently on the basis of ability, rates of learning, and interests

- *responsibility for own learning:* the extent to which pupils perceive themselves as being in charge of their learning process, motivated by constant feedback and affirmation.

A number of writers have also highlighted the importance of the classroom climate being 'inclusive' or 'incorporative': the extent to which all pupils in the class feel themselves to be a full participant in class activities and to be a valued member of the class (Campbell et al., 2004; Watkins, 2005). The opposite of this would be a class where some pupils feel marginalised and that the work they do in the class is not valued. The notion of inclusive teaching originally developed as part of a consideration of good classroom practice regarding the inclusion of pupils with special educational needs. It is now used much more widely to refer to the ways in which all pupils in the class can feel engaged and involved in classroom activities and tasks, as a way of combating the feelings of disaffection or isolation among pupils whose background or circumstances make them vulnerable.

Studies of classroom climate have provided a wealth of evidence to support the importance of a positive classroom climate in facilitating pupil learning, and are in line with the judgements expressed in a series of Ofsted reports dealing with aspects of skilful teaching and good classroom practice.

Interestingly, a number of studies have also noted how important the first few lessons with a new class are in establishing a positive classroom climate. Wragg (2005), for example, compared the behaviour of experienced teachers with that of student teachers during their first few lessons with a new class, and noted that experienced teachers:

- were more confident, warm and friendly

- were more businesslike

- were more stimulating

- were more mobile

- made greater use of eye contact

- made greater use of humour

- were clearer about their classroom rules

- better established their presence and authority.

These are all features that helped the experienced teachers to establish fairly quickly a positive working climate for the school year ahead.

There is also research evidence to indicate that a positive classroom climate is more likely to be established by the use of a learner-centred teaching style. A study by Opdenakker and Van Damme (2006) identified seven key features of a learner-centred teaching style that enabled teachers to develop a positive classroom climate:

- the use of differentiated activities and material

- undertaking activities to help problem pupils

- active pupil participation in lessons

- discussing pupil and class affairs with other teachers

- using the assessment of pupils to direct one's own teaching

- an orientation towards the development of the personality of the pupils

- establishing a personal relationship with pupils based on trust.

The use of whole-class interactive teaching 'with pace' has been advocated as a way in which teachers can establish a positive classroom climate. In addition, the use of IT has been viewed as a means of sustaining pupils' engagement in lessons. Thus many have seen the use of interactive whiteboards as offering the best of both worlds in combining interactive whole-class teaching with IT. A study by Smith et al. (2006), which looked at the quality of pupil–teacher interaction in lessons using interactive whiteboards, found that many teachers were using interactive whiteboards with a traditional type of whole-class teaching. It is clear that using interactive whiteboards 'interactively' requires a high degree of skill by both teacher and pupils.

Skills in establishing a positive classroom climate

Given the importance of establishing a positive classroom climate, it is not surprising that descriptions of the skills that need to be displayed by teachers often make a specific reference to this. For example, writing on teacher standards (e.g. DfE, 2012) typically includes elements that relate to establishing a positive classroom climate, such as the following:

- establishing a purposeful and safe learning environment conducive to learning

- having high expectations of pupils including a commitment to ensuring that pupils can achieve their full educational potential

- establishing fair, respectful, trusting, supportive and constructive relationships with pupils

- demonstrating the positive values, attitudes and behaviour expected from pupils

- supporting and guiding pupils to reflect upon their learning and identify their learning needs

- knowing how to identify and support pupils whose progress, development or well-being is affected by changes or difficulties in their personal circumstances, and when to refer them to colleagues for specialist support.

School climate

Of course, establishing a positive classroom climate needs to be seen in the context of the school climate as a whole. It is easier to establish a positive classroom climate in a school where other teachers are doing so, and where the school climate as a whole is also positive. A positive school climate can be viewed as one where pupils feel safe, valued, supported and encouraged to do well, and where both teachers and pupils have high expectations that pupils will do their best. A study by Voight et al. (2013) in California looked at middle and high schools where pupil attainment was identified as higher than expected, and compared the school climate in these with schools where pupil attainment was lower than expected. The 'beating-the-odds' schools on average scored higher on a variety of scales measuring school climate, such as academic support, connectedness (so pupils feel emotionally engaged with their learning), and social relationships.

Motivating pupils

An essential feature of the teaching skills involved in establishing a positive classroom climate concerns how best to foster pupils' motivation towards learning. In looking at pupil motivation, a useful distinction can be made between three major influences in the classroom:

- intrinsic motivation

- extrinsic motivation

- expectation for success.

Influences on pupil motivation

Intrinsic motivation concerns the extent to which pupils engage in an activity to satisfy their curiosity and interest in the topic area being covered or develop their competence and skills in dealing with the demands made on them, *for their own sake.* All human beings appear to have a natural drive of curiosity and wish to develop competence and skills in various tasks for their own sake, rather than as a means to some other end.

Extrinsic motivation involves engaging in an activity in order to achieve some end or goal that is rewarding and is external to the task itself. Engaging in the activity is therefore a means towards some other end (e.g. getting praise from parents or the teacher, an academic qualification, eliciting respect and admiration from fellow pupils, or avoiding some unpleasant consequences of being unsuccessful). Intrinsic and extrinsic motivation are often contrasted with each other, but are not in fact incompatible. Indeed, many pupils have high intrinsic and high extrinsic motivation for engaging in a particular task. For example, they may work hard in their mathematics lessons both because they enjoy doing mathematics and because it is important for them to attain well in order to realise their career aspirations.

Expectation for success concerns the extent to which pupils feel they are likely to succeed at a particular activity. Many pupils will not attempt to make strenuous efforts to succeed at a task they feel is far too difficult for them and with which they feel they therefore have little hope of success. Interestingly, however, not all tasks that pupils feel they can easily succeed at may be motivating; tasks that are far too easy may be seen by pupils as not being worthy of the effort unless there is some explicit reason to do so. Research evidence indicates that the tasks which best elicit pupil motivation are those seen by pupils to be challenging, i.e. difficult but achievable (Wertzel and Brophy, 2014).

Eliciting pupil motivation

The key strategies that teachers can use to elicit pupil motivation are concerned with building upon pupils' intrinsic motivation, extrinsic motivation, and their expectation for success. It is important to note, however, that there are large individual differences between pupils in how and when their intrinsic motivation, extrinsic motivation, and expectation for success are elicited.

Figure 6.1: Eliciting pupils' motivation

To a great extent these will be influenced by their experience at home (particularly how much encouragement they receive from parents to be interested in and value school learning and school-related attainment), by their experience in school (particularly their experience of success and failure to date), and how they perceive teachers' expectations of them and the demands of various tasks. In the context of skilful teaching, the most important factor is to ensure that pupils are supported and encouraged to learn, with high positive expectations being conveyed by the teacher. Such expectations need to be realistic but challenging; they need to convey that the activities are worthwhile and of interest, and, above all, they need to convey that each pupil's progress really does matter.

Building on intrinsic motivation

Strategies that build on pupils' intrinsic motivation include selecting topics that are likely to interest pupils, particularly if they relate to pupils' own experiences. For example, a task on drawing charts could be based on how pupils in the class travelled to school that morning.

Offering choice can also elicit interest. For example, in composing a school newspaper, those interested in sports could compile the sports page. Active involvement and cooperation between pupils also fosters enjoyment. The use of various games has much to offer. Novelty and variety also provide a more stimulating experience. For example, starting a lesson by producing a shoe box that purports to contain the belongings of a person, and then trying to build up as much information about the person as possible from these belongings, would do this effectively.

Because intrinsic motivation involves a drive towards increasing competence, as well as a curiosity drive, it can also be fostered by providing pupils with regular feedback concerning how their skills and competence are developing, and drawing to their attention what they can do and understand now compared with before the course of work began.

Building on extrinsic motivation

Strategies that build on pupils' extrinsic motivation include linking effort and success to material rewards and privileges. You must be extremely careful, however, to ensure that the reward or privilege offered is actually one desired by the pupils concerned and does not undermine their intrinsic motivation or alienate those who make an effort but who are not rewarded in this way. For example, offering the opportunity to those who work hard to start their break early seems to devalue the worthwhileness of the activity; offering a book token to the best piece of project work may again offer far more hurt to those unsuccessful than pleasure to the pupil who wins it.

Other strategies include esteem-related rewards, such as high grades or other forms of recognition for effort and success; although again, if such rewards are overtly competitive, you need to be aware of their possible effect on other pupils. Teacher praise is a very important and powerful motivation, although its effect depends on skilful use. Praise that is explicitly linked to the pupil's efforts and attainment, which conveys sincere pleasure on the teacher's part, and which is used with credibility, is more effective than praise simply offered on a regular basis but lacking these qualities.

Extrinsic motivation can also be highlighted by indicating to pupils the usefulness, relevance and importance of the topic or activity to their needs. These may be their short term needs, such as for academic qualifications or high test scores of attainment, or their long term needs, such as coping with the demands of adult life successfully or to help realise their career aspirations.

Building on expectation for success

Strategies that build upon pupils' expectation for success include ensuring that the tasks set are challenging and offer pupils a realistic chance of success, taking into account their ability and previous learning. In particular, you need to try to minimise any unnecessary frustration caused by setting up the activities poorly. This requires close monitoring of pupils' progress once the lesson is underway, together with quick and supportive feedback when a pupil has encountered major difficulties.

Your help and expectations must convey confidence in the pupils and your belief that with appropriate effort they will be successful. When dealing with pupils who lack confidence in themselves as learners, such help and expectations are of crucial importance. It is also important to convey that success lies in their own hands, and that they need to be aware of how they approach tasks, the degree of persistence they have to apply to be successful, and that there is no substitute for a willingness on their part to apply sustained effort.

An interesting study by Putwain et al. (2017) looked at the effects on secondary school pupils when the teacher gave feedback that warned pupils of the negative consequences of not improving their effort and performance (e.g. if you do not work harder, you will fail the examination). For pupils who are confident in their ability to do better, this tends be seen as challenging and may enhance their performance, but for those who are not confident in their ability to do better, this tends to engender fear and may depress their performance. This study indicates that it is important for you to tailor your feedback to individual pupils rather than to the class as a whole, in order to develop and sustain an expectation for success for all the pupils in your class.

Your relationships with pupils

A positive classroom climate very much depends on the type of relationship you establish with your pupils. Pupils' learning is most likely to flourish in a climate where this relationship is based on mutual respect and rapport.

Mutual respect and rapport

Mutual respect largely develops from the pupils seeing by your actions that you are a competent teacher, and that you care about their progress by planning and conducting effective lessons and carrying out your various tasks with commitment. In addition, you should convey in your dealings with pupils, both during whole-class teaching and in your interactions with individuals, that you respect each pupil as an individual who has individual and personal needs.

Good rapport stems from conveying to pupils that you understand, share and value their perspective, as individuals, on a whole range of matters and experiences, academic, social and personal; for example, sympathising that the local football team got knocked out of a cup competition, praise for a pupil who has performed well in a school play, concern that a pupil has a bad cold, and excitement that a school trip is near. The development of a positive classroom climate depends on this relationship being two-way; your respect for pupils should be reciprocated in their respect for you, and your understanding of their perspectives reciprocated in their understanding of yours. Nevertheless, as an adult, and given your role, it is up to you to have a major influence in establishing such a harmonious relationship in the classroom.

The skills involved in establishing a climate of mutual respect and rapport are highly prized in schools, as they also have a major impact on the general climate of the school as a whole. They also contribute to the pastoral care role of the teacher, and make it easier for pupils to come to you with their personal problems and difficulties. Indeed, a high proportion of outstanding teachers in inner-city comprehensive schools tend to be very skilful in developing good rapport with potentially difficult and demanding adolescents and, not surprisingly, many of these outstanding teachers have specific pastoral care responsibilities in the school as a result. Pye (1988), interestingly, noticed how skilful teachers were able to convey a personal manner in their interaction with an individual pupil during a private exchange, in which the mutual respect and rapport established was particularly evident. Pye described this as a situation in which the teacher and pupil were 'acknowledging' each other: they had established a personal relationship that was separate from, and yet still part of, the relationship that the teacher had with the class as a whole.

Acting as a good example

It is also important to be aware of the influence that your behaviour can have on pupils in acting as an example or model for their own behaviour. This identification with the teacher is evident in both the primary and secondary school years. Pupils will expect you to be a good example of the expectations that you convey. If you insist on neat work, your own board work should also be neat. If you expect pupils to act in a civilised manner, you should not lose your temper or use sarcasm to hurt their feelings. If you want pupils to find the work interesting, you should convey interest in the activities yourself. Indeed, in a number of their reports based on school inspections, Ofsted frequently reports on the particular importance of the example set by the teacher in establishing a positive ethos in the classroom.

The use of humour

One of the difficulties facing beginning teachers concerns knowing whether, how and when to use humour in the classroom, and the extent to which their relationship with pupils should be friendly. Judicious use of humour and conveying that you have a sense of humour can play a useful part in helping to establish good rapport and a positive classroom climate. Humour can be used to good effect in a whole range of situations, including introducing a light-hearted aspect of the work in hand or making a joke at your own expense (and, if done skilfully, making a joke at the pupil's expense but in a way that enables the pupil to share the joke rather than feel victimised).

Humour can also be used to reassure a pupil who is anxious or in difficulties, or to defuse a potential conflict with a pupil concerning misbehaviour. Conveying that you have a sense of humour is indicated in the way you respond to events that occur with good humour or share with pupils some amusement that they see in a situation. It might be something as simple as how you react to a pupil's humorous aside with your own humour and quick-wittedness.

Linked with the use of humour is the extent to which you try to establish friendly relations with pupils. Part of establishing good rapport with pupils involves sharing to some extent each other's understanding and perspective on the demands of classroom life and life outside the classroom in general. This will include valuing and respecting each other as individuals and valuing each other's viewpoints. Much of this forms the basis of friendship between individuals. Nevertheless, the classroom is a unique and, to a large extent, a very ritualised environment. To sustain order and control, your relationship with pupils, above all, must be one in which they respect and accept your authority to manage and control what happens in the classroom so that their learning may progress effectively. This means that your manner needs to be competent, businesslike and task-oriented. Frequent use of humour, particularly being 'jokey', and trying to act as a friend of equal status, tends to undermine your authority because it does not accord with the ritual of school life and how pupils typically see and react to different aspects of a teacher's manner.

As a result, beginning teachers who attempt to build their relationships with pupils on frequent use of humour, or on an over-friendly approach, often find that they are less able to establish and exert their authority when required to do so. The ability to establish mutual respect and rapport in the classroom, to use humour to good effect, and to establish a friendly ethos without being too friendly, involves very sensitive social awareness on the teacher's part. It is somewhat like a chef who uses taste while cooking to decide on the right amount of seasoning to enhance the flavour of the dish rather than spoil it. Use of humour and friendship in the classroom can be seen as 'flavour enhancers' to add to the generally businesslike and task-oriented manner you convey.

Enhancing pupils' self-esteem

Perhaps the single most important feature that has contributed to improving the quality of education provided in schools has been the increasing awareness among teachers of the importance of fostering pupils' self-esteem, self-confidence and self-respect as learners. Many writers have documented the ways in which schools can damage pupils' self-esteem by emphasising for many pupils their relative lack of success compared with that of high-attaining pupils. As a result, such pupils attribute a sense of failure to the work they do, even if it is their best. In consequence, they may then get caught up in a vicious downward spiral of under-achievement on their part and low expectations by teachers for their future work. Hargreaves (1982) famously referred to this process as involving the destruction of pupils' sense of dignity, in which they increasingly feel inferior, unable and powerless. He argues that this attack on their dignity stems not only from their experience of the 'formal curriculum', but also, and even more so, from their experience of the 'hidden curriculum'.

The formal curriculum refers to learning about the subject and topic being studied, whereas the hidden curriculum refers to all the messages conveyed to pupils by their experiences in school. These messages stem from the way they are treated, and the attitudes and values conveyed to them about their role and worth as individuals, and the worth of what they have accomplished. Many of the messages conveyed in the hidden curriculum may be unintended. For example, if during classroom discussion with pupils you never use or elaborate on pupils' contributions, but always judge them simply in terms of whether they have contributed what you wanted in a narrowly conceived view of their correctness, pupils may get the message that their thoughts and ideas are of little worth or value except insofar as they are correct as judged by you. This may undermine the degree to which they are then willing to contribute ideas, particularly exploratory or uncertain ones, which may be the opposite of what you would wish.

Many writers have emphasised that successful teaching involves catering for pupils who differ in ability and personal circumstances, and this includes pupils who are disaffected and lack confidence. Helping disaffected pupils to succeed at school involves building up their self-esteem and resilience, and this involves adopting approaches that focus on helping pupils to develop a more positive view of themselves and their capabilities (Tough, 2012).

One of the most important characteristics that you can help develop in your pupils is a sense of confidence. A study by Stankov et al. (2014) noted that pupils' level of confidence was an important predictor of academic achievement. In their study of nearly 600 secondary school pupils in Singapore, they found that a pupil's confidence about being able to answer mathematical questions correctly was a better predictor of their achievement in mathematics than their general level of academic ability. In other words, being confident in a particular subject domain tends to go hand in hand with actually performing well in that subject domain. In that sense, the skills you need to enhance pupils' confidence are important. If a pupil does well in a lesson, you can usefully take the opportunity to draw their attention to this as a way of enhancing and consolidating positive self-beliefs, thereby creating a virtuous circle between their self-beliefs and their academic achievement.

The need to enhance pupils' self-esteem and self-confidence is particularly evident with pupils who have special educational needs and disabilities (SEND), and who may be facing major challenges in trying to make progress with their learning due to the personal difficulties they face in their daily lives. SEND pupils comprise a whole range of diverse categories, so there is no one way of teaching SEND pupils. However, what they all need is encouraging and supportive learning experiences that enable them to sense that they are able to make good progress (Wearmouth, 2017).

The humanistic approach to teaching and learning

The increasing awareness of the importance of fostering pupils' self-esteem has been a major development over the years. This view of its importance has a long pedigree, and stems in part from its emphasis within humanistic psychology and its applications to education, notably through the work of Maslow and Rogers (e.g. Maslow, 1987; Rogers and Freiberg, 1994). They both argued that education must place an emphasis on the whole person, on the idea of personal growth, on the pupil's own perspective in terms of how they see themselves and see the world, and on the notions of personal agency and the power of choice. The key elements in applying such an approach to classroom teaching involve:

- seeing the teacher's role as essentially that of being a facilitator

- providing a significant degree of choice and control to pupils to manage and organise their learning

- displaying respect for and empathy with pupils.

Studies of the attitudes held by student teachers towards teaching and learning in schools typically show that student teachers tend to hold views consistent with the humanistic approach at the start of their initial training courses, but that by the end of their training they often report that such views are sometimes quite hard to sustain in their actual classroom practice, given the constraints they face in terms of the realities of classroom life (Kyriacou and Cheng, 1993). Nevertheless, despite such difficulties, the classroom climate in schools has become much more humanistic in tone over the years.

Fostering pupils' self-esteem is seen to lie at the heart of this approach. This perspective is evident, either explicitly or implicitly, in many important developments in classroom practice; in particular, the growth of active learning methods, as well as in the introduction of new forms of assessment, most notably that of records of achievement. Indeed, some lessons, such as those forming part of a personal and social education programme, are often designed specifically to help foster pupils' self-esteem in general, as well as their self-esteem as learners in particular.

Conveying positive messages

The need to foster pupils' self-esteem as learners is fundamental to establishing a positive classroom climate, and the most important influence on pupils' self-esteem in the classroom is your interaction with the pupils. If your comments to pupils are largely positive, supportive, encouraging, praising, valuing and relaxing, rather than negative, deprecating, harsh, attacking, dominating and anxiety-provoking, this will do much to foster pupils' self-esteem.

In addition, your body language also communicates to pupils how you feel about them, through messages conveyed non-verbally by your use of eye contact, posture and facial expression. It can be difficult to convey a message verbally about how you feel if your body language indicates to pupils something different. An awareness of how pupils are likely to perceive what you say and your body language can help you to develop the skills involved in establishing a positive classroom climate. Nevertheless, positive messages are much easier to convey if you genuinely do have the feelings you are trying to convey; that is to say, you genuinely do like and respect pupils, care for their learning, and feel relaxed and confident in your role.

Encouraging pupils is widely regarded as a key feature of effective teaching. A study by Gamlem and Munthe (2014), based on 56 video-recorded lessons in four lower secondary schools in Norway, found that teachers were in general very good at creating a positive classroom climate by emphasising encouragement in their feedback to pupils during classroom interaction. However, they warn that an emphasis on encouragement can sometimes be at the expense of providing more learning-oriented feedback in which pupils can gain a better understanding of the academic work at hand. The skill involved in giving high-quality feedback to pupils during classroom interaction that both encourages pupils and informs their learning is a challenging one for teachers. You need to ensure that you get this balance right in a way that takes appropriate account of the context for the learning at hand, so that both the affective and the cognitive needs of pupils are addressed. There will be times when you judge that what is more important is to be encouraging, and other times when you judge that promoting pupils' cognitive understanding is paramount.

Giving positive help

In your interactions with pupils the two areas that probably have the greatest effect concern how you treat pupils' errors and the extent to which you take a personal interest in their progress.

Pupil errors refer to any contribution that falls short of the standard of progress you desire. It includes a poor answer to a question, a poorly written-up project, or simply not being able to undertake a task you have set. In such circumstances you need to consider the type of feedback to give that will be helpful and supportive rather than admonishing. It is generally better to give specific help that relates to the task rather than critical feedback about performance or critical comments about the pupil. For example, pointing out that the pupil needs to remember that the hypotenuse is always the side opposite to the right angle is better than simply saying 'You can do better than this' or, even worse, 'This is the low standard of work I have come to expect from you'.

Also, when a pupil is having difficulties, you need to avoid sounding patronising. This can be difficult, because you are in authority and may, from time to time, be giving advice or diagnosing a difficulty that the pupil is already aware of. This should not be a problem, since the pupil should be willing to tolerate this if it only happens occasionally. The real problem arises if your tone is perceived by the pupil to be conveying an element of 'put down', sarcasm or unfair criticism. So, for example, telling a pupil whose diagram would have been much better if a sharpened pencil had been used that 'You should use a pencil sharpener because they're handy for sharpening pencils' would be considered unnecessarily hostile.

Taking a personal interest in each pupil's progress can be conveyed by relating what you say to each pupil and how you respond to their progress, and to their particular needs and previous work. Learning and using pupils' names with a new class as soon as possible is well worthwhile, and you should certainly know their names after the first few weeks. During personal interactions, indicating to pupils how they are making progress and linking your comments to previous interactions does much to convey to each pupil that you are taking a personal interest in them as individuals and, so far as possible, tailoring matters to meet their individual needs.

Mentoring your pupils

The term 'classroom climate' conveys a focus on the classroom as a whole – a set of values, an atmosphere, an ethos, that somehow summarises how that class functions and what it feels like to be a pupil in that classroom. However, the classroom climate is not only conveyed by your whole-class interaction with pupils, but also by your personalised dealings with each individual pupil. This is particularly the case when considering your role as a mentor for each pupil in your class.

In essence, mentoring your pupils refers to how in your personalised, one-to-one, private dealings with an individual pupil over a period of time you get to know and understand that pupil's needs, concerns, attitudes, strengths and weaknesses, aspirations, vulnerabilities and personal circumstances, and provide appropriate guidance, help and support to enable that pupil to make progress with their learning. There has been an increasing shift towards viewing the mentoring of pupils as being an important part of your everyday practice as a classroom teacher (Tolhurst, 2010).

There are many cases that adults can cite of a teacher who made a real difference to them during their schooldays. In such cases, they often refer to a teacher who seemed to be taking a personal interest in them at a time when they needed particular support. Many cases refer to troubled or vulnerable pupils who were making poor academic progress, had become disaffected, and were at risk of being excluded from school. However, there are also many cases where the pupil was not presenting any particular problems. In such cases, what was crucial was that their teacher believed in them as individuals who could do better than they were currently doing, and who managed, through mentoring, to enhance their self-belief and to offer them the advice, guidance and support that enabled them to achieve success.

Mentoring and coaching

Coaching refers to improving a pupil's performance at a task by providing advice, guidance and feedback on repeated practice at the task. Although the terms 'mentoring' and 'coaching' are often paired together, there are differences. In coaching, the focus is specifically on the pupil's performance.

So, for example, making clear to pupils what they have to do in a test to pick up the maximum marks, and then practising this with you, would be a good example of coaching. Another example might be repeated pronunciation of a phrase in French with modelling and feedback from you. There are times when your mentoring of a pupil may include coaching, as this may well be part of your providing more general support. However, the key difference is that mentoring looks at the wider picture of the pupil's needs and essentially seeks to empower the pupil to deal with the challenges they face in more general terms, while coaching is much more performance and task specific.

You will find, at times, that mentoring and coaching are complementary, but at other times you will find them in tension with each other. For example, your mentoring of a pupil may seek to increase a pupil's engagement with academic work through raising their intrinsic motivation (i.e. interest in the subject matter), but if you adopt a coaching-heavy style of teaching, this may well undermine their intrinsic motivation. A key part of developing your mentoring skills is to understand which of several different possible strategies will be the best one to adopt in a given situation.

The classroom teacher as mentor

There are many formal programmes of mentoring, which involve other adults or pupils acting as a mentor, often meeting with the pupil at a specific time on a regular basis (say once a week over a period of six months). Such programmes can be offered to all pupils, or to a specifically targeted group (e.g. gifted pupils, poor readers, pupils with a learning difficulty, disengaged pupils).

In contrast with formal programmes, the power of mentoring when undertaken by the pupil's normal classroom teacher, as and when appropriate, lies not only in the way it enhances the pupil's relationship with the teacher as a trusted and caring adult, but also the way it enhances the positive nature of the classroom climate.

Classroom appearance and composition

There are two important features of a lesson that have a major influence on the classroom climate that develops, although neither is part of the lesson itself. The first concerns the general appearance of the classroom, including its layout and even the appearance of the teacher and that of the pupils. The second concerns the composition of the class, whether in an ability set, mixed ability, or mixed age in composition. Both of these features convey strong messages through the hidden curriculum referred to earlier.

Classroom appearance

The general appearance of a classroom indicates to pupils the care that goes into providing them with an environment that is conducive to learning. A clean and well-kept room, with appropriate resources in evidence, which appears comfortable, light and well aired, helps to establish a positive expectation towards the lesson. A positive mental set is also provided by appropriate use of posters and other visual displays concerning the type of work done in the classroom. Displays of pupils' work also indicate a pride in the work achieved, as well as acting as a motivation for those producing display work. Everywhere a pupil looks should convey positive expectations. The degree of light, space and air in the classroom of many schools built in the last few years has been generally very good, and the atmosphere created is positive and uplifting. However, for schools more than twenty years old where wear and tear has taken its toll, and in schools where general repairs and refurbishment are evidently needed, this can have a depressing effect on both pupils and teachers.

While the ethos in the classroom will, in part, be influenced by that of the school in general, each teacher can do much to improve the appearance of their own room, assuming you – as most teachers do – have your own room. For subject specialists in secondary schools, your room should act as an invitation to the subject. For example, entering a foreign language classroom should immerse pupils into the atmosphere of the foreign countries, most notably through the use of posters, maps, and even objects from those countries. While primary school classrooms will be host to a variety of activities, it is often possible to create areas that are subject specific, and that can also act as a resource area or as a focal point for particular activities.

Layout

The layout of the room should be functional for the purposes intended. At the very least, you and the board should be clearly visible. There is much debate concerning the importance of using a layout to match the general style of teaching and learning that takes place. In 'open classrooms', characterised by more active learning methods (including frequent use of group work, movement of pupils between areas, the use of resource centres, and independent work using IT), the seating arrangements will almost certainly require desks to be grouped together and the use of activity-specific areas. In 'traditional classrooms', which emphasise didactic teaching, formal rows of desks are more appropriate.

Unfortunately, the large number of pupils in some classes compared with the physical size of the room itself often places severe constraints on teachers in creating the most functionally efficient layout. Fortunately, many modern primary schools were designed with open classrooms in mind. This has allowed functionally efficient layouts to be developed, some even making use of movable walls. Secondary schools have generally been much less flexible in this respect. Some schools have developed well laid-out resource centres housed in rooms of their own, where teachers can send a pupil or groups of pupils to undertake particular tasks, either unsupervised or supervised by a teacher based in the resource centre.

Tidiness

It is also very important to keep the classroom clean and tidy. This can have a marked impact on pupils when they first arrive at the classroom, whether at the beginning of the school day or after a break. In primary schools one can make efforts to ensure that pupils themselves help to keep things tidy and avoid making a mess. This tends to be more difficult in secondary schools, where you will be teaching many different classes, and may not always be using your own room. If on occasion you take over a room where desks and tables have been left disarranged, it is well worthwhile to tidy up quickly before your class arrives. You, of course, also have a responsibility to colleagues to ensure that any room you leave is fit and ready for the next user, which includes cleaning the whiteboard. This is all part of having a professional attitude towards your work.

Dress

Your appearance conveys messages to pupils about the care and attention you give to presentation in general. It is the case that, in our society, dress conveys signals about status and about your formal role. However, the norms that operate here are changing all the time. For example, in some schools, a school uniform is worn by pupils, female teachers are expected not to wear trousers, most male teachers wear a jacket and tie, teachers may be addressed as 'Sir' or 'Miss' and pupils addressed by their surnames. At the other extreme, there are schools where none of these apply. Whatever else, you will need to adapt to the conventions and expectations that operate in your school, as radical deviations away from these are likely to be misunderstood by pupils, although some degree of departure in the direction you feel is educationally worthwhile is acceptable and desirable. Nevertheless, your behaviour in the classroom must take account of your role in also contributing to a consistent and coherent attempt by staff in the school as a whole to operate as a team in developing and emphasising certain values and expectations.

Figure 6.2: Your appearance will convey a message about you

While you will have little control over pupils' dress, other than dealing with major departures from school conventions (such as wearing earrings or jeans), it is important to insist that they arrive at the lesson prepared for the tasks to be undertaken, with appropriate equipment, such as pens, pencils and rulers. Bags should not be left on desks and coats should not be worn. In some schools such apparently minor matters can involve a lot of time and effort by teachers. In such cases, well-developed routines are of immense value in helping to ensure that a prompt start to the lesson is not delayed.

Class composition

The pupil composition of the class also conveys important messages. A class composed of pupils set or streamed in terms of attainment will almost certainly have an influence on pupils' expectations about themselves and on your expectations about them. It is particularly important to ensure that those groups identified as average or below average in attainment are not discouraged and do not underachieve as a result.

Mixed ability groups are often used to convey a sense of equal valuing of all pupils, which in part explains their widespread adoption in comprehensive schools and in primary schools, although in the latter it is often simply the most convenient form of group given the size of the year group. In some primary schools and for some secondary school (morning registration) tutor groups, cross-age groups are used, and these may be composed of quite a wide age range.

Other aspects of pupil composition of importance include social class mix, ethnic origin mix, and the proportion of able pupils or pupils with learning difficulties. All such factors have an important bearing on teaching and learning. They also have an important bearing on the type of classroom climate that develops, and on the ways you can best facilitate a positive classroom culture. The key factor here is the skill involved in developing mutual respect and rapport that takes the composition of the class into account. Establishing your authority, being sociable and motivating pupils will require different shared understandings and points of reference dependent on the composition of each particular class. So, for example, the way in which pupils in general may react to your use of humour, how supportive your feedback needs to be, the way you exert discipline, and how you try to personalise interactions, may well be quite different for a group of racially mixed pupils in an infant class in a school serving a relatively deprived urban catchment, compared with a group of top set pupils at a sixth form college serving a prosperous rural catchment. An important aspect of your skill in establishing a positive classroom climate involves your sensitivity to the effect of your behaviour on the type of pupils that make up the class and the context within which this occurs.

Further reading

Hargreaves, E. (2017). *Children's Experiences of Classrooms.* London: Sage. This book provides insights into how pupils experience teaching and learning in the classroom that will inform your understanding of how and why some teachers are better able to establish a positive classroom climate.

Haydn, T. (2012). *Managing Pupil Behaviour: Improving the Classroom Atmosphere* (2nd ed.). Abingdon: Routledge. A very insightful, well-informed and helpful guide to establishing a positive classroom climate. You will find Chapter 8 on the 'working atmosphere in the classroom' is especially helpful.

Skinner, D. (2010). *Effective Teaching and Learning in Practice.* London: Continuum. Considers the skills involved in effective classroom practice and relates these to the task of establishing a positive classroom climate and the learning environment.

Wertzel, K.R., & Brophy, J.E. (2014). *Motivating Students to Learn* (4th ed.). Abingdon: Routledge. A very readable overview of the ways in which teachers can use a variety of strategies in order to foster and sustain pupil motivation in the classroom.

Key questions

1 Is the classroom climate purposeful, task-oriented, relaxed, warm and supportive, and does it have a sense of order?

2 Do my comments, particularly feedback on their progress, and use of rewards, help pupils to develop self-respect as learners?

3 Are the learning activities challenging and do they offer realistic opportunities for success?

4 Do I make good use of both intrinsic and extrinsic sources of pupil motivation?

5 Do I convey positive expectations and a personal interest and care for the progress of each pupil?

6 Do I use my mentoring skills to provide each pupil with personalised support?

7 Is my relationship with pupils based on mutual respect and rapport?

8 Do the messages conveyed by the nature and types of activities used and the way I interact with pupils contribute to establishing a positive classroom climate?

9 Do the appearance and layout of the classroom convey positive expectations and facilitate the activities that occur?

10 Do I take account of the influence of the composition of the class (for example, spread of ability, social class mix) on the way I can best establish a positive classroom climate?

Chapter 7

Behaviour management

Developing the skills needed to establish a well-ordered learning environment in the classroom is one of the major challenges facing teachers. Not surprisingly, this challenge frequently features in government policy documents (e.g. DfE, 2014), where behaviour management is typically described in terms of the skills involved in establishing a clear framework to manage pupils' behaviour constructively, promoting pupils' self-control and independence, and using a range of behaviour management strategies.

Behaviour management is a key area of concern for teachers. It refers to establishing the order that is necessary in the classroom for pupil learning to occur effectively. There is a massive amount of literature on behaviour management in schools. This includes a number of books offering sound practical advice (Dansie, 2016; Porter, 2014; Rogers, 2015), publications reporting the results of research studies dealing with the views and experiences of pupils and teachers, including student teachers (e.g. Evertson and Weinstein, 2006; Kyriacou et al., 2007; Riley et al., 2012), and a plethora of government reports (DfE, 2014; Steer, 2005).

Clearly, order is needed in the classroom if the activities that take place are to facilitate effective learning by pupils. The most important point to bear in mind in considering behaviour management is that creating the necessary order is more to do with the skills involved in effective teaching in general than it is to do with how you deal with pupil misbehaviour itself. If the learning activities are well planned and prepared, if the presentation elicits and maintains pupils' attention, interest and involvement, and if the activities are challenging and offer realistic opportunities for success, then the necessary order will be established as part of these qualities. In essence, skilful teaching, as outlined in the previous chapters, lies at the heart of establishing good behaviour. The term 'behaviour for learning' has been used to emphasise the need to think about how the experience of successful learning and engaging learning activities are effective in promoting good behaviour, rather than viewing good behaviour as something that arises out of how misbehaviour is dealt with (Garner, 2016).

Nevertheless, pupil misbehaviour will occur from time to time, even in the lessons of the most skilful teachers, and has to be dealt with. However, it is a mistake to view behaviour management as something concerned with how you deal with pupil misbehaviour, separate from your general teaching. It is an even worse mistake to try to establish order by focusing on how to dominate and engender fear in pupils as a strategy for minimising misbehaviour. Such a course of action is undesirable, not only because it will undermine you creating the positive classroom climate necessary to facilitate pupils learning effectively, but also because it directs your attention away from considering how to develop the quality of your teaching as the primary means of establishing good behaviour. The central message here is that you need to focus more on how you encourage good behaviour, rather than how you react to misbehaviour.

You also need to remember that as a teacher you are part of a team. Behaviour management is most effective in a school when teachers and support staff act together in a consistent manner framed by the school's policy and procedures. As such, you need to be familiar with and work within the school's behaviour management framework in order to ensure that how you interact with pupils is in line with this. Interestingly, almost all school policy documents for staff on dealing with behaviour management start with guidance on how to promote good behaviour, maintain pupil engagement in lessons, and create a positive and caring learning environment in which good behaviour is promoted and encouraged. Only after this does the guidance go on to outline the action and procedures you need to follow in dealing with pupil misbehaviour.

The nature of pupil misbehaviour

Most pupil misbehaviour is quite trivial. The types of pupil misbehaviour most frequently cited by teachers are:

- excessive talk or talking out of turn
- being noisy (both verbal, such as shouting to another pupil across the room, and non-verbal, such as dropping bags onto the floor)
- not paying attention to the teacher
- not getting on with the work required
- being out of their seat without good cause
- hindering other pupils
- arriving late for lessons.

To a large extent, such problems can be minimised by skilful teaching in general, and by developing conventions and routines for behaviour that are followed. More serious types of misbehaviour (verbal aggression to another pupil, bad language and cheek, disobedience, refusal to accept authority, and physical destructiveness) are much less frequent and are likely to occur if the lesser forms of pupil misbehaviour are allowed to become commonplace, or if pupils are reacting against personal and academic difficulties they are facing.

In thinking about pupil misbehaviour, we need to remember that there is a continuum of such behaviour ranging from quite trivial acts to very serious ones. Moreover, the standard of behaviour expected will vary from teacher to teacher. One teacher may insist on virtual silence in a lesson while pupils are working, whereas another might be happy with a marked degree of background talking. In addition, pupils will also vary in their attitudes towards good behaviour. Some pupils will be happy to wait quietly while a teacher looks for some equipment in a storeroom, whereas some pupils will be poised to take any such opportunity to engage in rowdy behaviour. Both teachers' and pupils' attitudes about good behaviour are also affected by their mood, such as if they are upset about something that has happened before reaching the classroom. The learning environment that prevails in your classroom will not only be influenced by your behaviour and expectations, but also by the expectations pupils bring with them and, importantly, by the prevailing ethos in the school. Nevertheless, a well-managed lesson coupled with a relationship based on mutual respect and rapport will do much to minimise pupil misbehaviour. Indeed, even in schools where it is recognised that there are a number of pupils with marked emotional or academic difficulties, skilful teaching can ensure that good behaviour in lessons will be the norm.

Causes of pupil misbehaviour

In general, you should start with the assumption that all pupils will be willing to engage in the work and are only likely to misbehave if there are specific reasons or motives for doing so. Your task is to make it as easy as possible for pupils to sustain good behaviour. Much has been written about the causes of pupil misbehaviour in the classroom (e.g. Evertson and Weinstein, 2006; Lewis, 2008; Rogers, 2015). The main causes are:

- *Boredom.* If the activities are presented in a manner that fails to elicit and sustain their interest, or if the activity lasts for too long and fails to be stimulating, or if the activity is too easy or is felt to lack relevance, then pupils are likely to become bored.

- *Prolonged mental effort.* Most academic work requires sustained mental effort, and this is demanding. Everyone finds that sustaining mental effort for long periods is difficult and, at times, unpleasant.

- *Inability to do the work.* Pupils may be unable to do the work set, either because it is too difficult or because they are unclear about the demands of the task.

- *Being sociable.* Pupils have a complex social life in schools, in which friendships are made, conflicts arise, and interests are shared. Aspects of these social relationships between pupils will often spill over into a lesson (e.g. pupils may resume a conversation started during the break period).

- *Low academic self-esteem.* Some pupils will lack confidence in themselves as learners, and may have experienced frequent failure in the past that makes them reluctant to engage in academic tasks for fear of further failure (failing because you did not try is much less painful than failing if you made the effort). Such pupils can become quite alienated from the academic expectations that form part of a positive classroom climate.

- *Emotional difficulties.* Some pupils may have emotional problems that make it difficult for them to adjust to and cope with the demands of school life and the academic demands of the classroom. It may be because they are being bullied in school, or because they are neglected at home. In many cases, such pupils may become attention seeking, and may actually enjoy the attention they provoke from you or their fellow pupils for misbehaving.

- *Poor attitudes.* Some pupils may simply not value doing well at school and, to the extent that problems arise such as finding the work boring or difficult, will switch off their effort. Moreover, some may try to avoid doing the work by arriving late to lessons, or by keeping a low profile while doing little. When challenged, they may be apologetic or hostile, but still do little. Some pupils may deliberately make a nuisance of themselves simply to cause excitement.

- *Lack of negative consequences.* Whenever a pupil misbehaves, your actions that follow in consequence must be aimed at getting the pupil involved in the work again as quickly as possible. Furthermore, your behaviour should act to dissuade such pupil misbehaviour occurring again in similar circumstances. If pupil misbehaviour is not picked up quickly and discouraged by the consequences that follow, it is likely to become more frequent.

Implications for teaching

It will be evident from looking at these main causes of pupil misbehaviour that they have different implications for how you can best deal with such incidents. For example, if a pupil fails to pay attention because they are finding the topic boring, your best course of action will be quite different than if the problem stems from worries and anxieties the pupil has because the work seems too difficult. Part of the skill of teaching involves being sensitive to the different causes of pupil misbehaviour. While most of the time sound management techniques and the most obvious assumptions about the cause of the misbehaviour are appropriate, skilful teachers are alert to circumstances where an exploratory probe in private is needed. This will be evident if a pupil's behaviour appears to be out of character or if the normal management techniques do not appear to be having their expected effect. Skilful teachers are also very adept at picking up subtle cues from a pupil's facial expression or tone of voice that might indicate an underlying cause for concern.

An important point to bear in mind about the causes of misbehaviour is that pupils are a captive audience. Unlike many activities in life, where we have some degree of choice over whether we participate and can often withdraw from a situation that we find unpleasant, pupils are required to attend lessons. Moreover, they are not allowed to opt out of learning. As such, all teaching has an implicit tension underlying the activities that if pupils do not engage freely in the activities set up by the teacher, they will be coerced to do so. Poor progress is not simply the concern of the pupil, but also the concern of the teacher and the pupil's parents. Most people will find, from time to time, that being trapped in a situation that is unpleasant and from which they cannot escape is extremely frustrating. If coercion to participate is also exerted, the sense of frustration can become unbearable. The most serious incidents of pupil misbehaviour are likely to occur when such a tension has built up, and when the pupil feels your attention is aggressive and coercive rather than sympathetic and supportive. A warning signal of this might be the pupil looking increasingly angry or tense, and perhaps claiming to be picked upon or treated unfairly in some way. The skills involved in being sensitive to whether a pupil is feeling tense in this way, and the ability to defuse such a feeling, is very important in preventing serious incidents occurring.

Establishing your authority

The key to establishing good behaviour in the classroom lies in pupils accepting your authority to manage their behaviour and their progress in learning. Learning activities cannot take place effectively in a full classroom of 30 pupils unless you are given authority to control, manage and direct what is going on, as and when appropriate. All pupils recognise this from their earliest days in school, but it is important to note that this authority is given to you to act as a manager of their learning rather than as a power relationship. A useful analogy is with the authority you give to a tour guide to show you around places of interest in a particular city: you obey instructions concerning where and when to go to different places and what to do there, because you trust and expect that in doing so you will get to see what is worth seeing efficiently; your trust largely rests on the expertise and skill you expect your tour guide to have. Similarly, establishing your authority as a teacher largely depends on four main aspects of your role:

- conveying your status

- teaching competently

- exercising managerial control

- dealing with pupil misbehaviour effectively.

Conveying your status

Much of your authority as a teacher derives from the status you have in that role, and the respect and esteem for teachers generally held in society; particularly conveyed to pupils by their parents and other sources of influence. You are also an adult, and will have some degree of status because of this, most notably with younger pupils where you may be perceived as a parent figure to some extent. If you have a formal post of seniority in the school, such as being the headteacher or the deputy head, then this will also add to your status.

The most important thing about status, however, is not that you simply have such status, but that you act as though you have status. This conveys to pupils a sense of you being in charge and in authority that they simply take for granted. Behaving as though you have status will be conveyed by your appearing relaxed, self-assured and confident, as indicated in particular by your tone of voice, posture, facial expression and use of eye contact. When you issue an instruction, your tone will indicate by its matter-of-factness that you simply expect without question that the instruction will be followed.

Status is also conveyed by various actions that indicate you have status, such as the fact that you are free to wander around the classroom, initiate

Figure 7.1: Conveying your status

conversations and direct activities. You also take the decisions about when pupils are to start and stop particular activities. Again, it is by acting in these ways, in a manner that indicates that you are in charge, that you create a climate in which your authority is taken for granted. This requires that as well as behaving in these ways yourself, you control such behaviour by pupils; that is to say, pupils cannot wander about, decide when to stop activities, or when to initiate conversations with you or with each other unless it is with your permission and appropriate. So, for example, most teachers will make a point of picking up on pupils who have started to pack away their books near the end of a lesson before they have been told to do so.

It is perhaps worth noting that one aspect of conveying status you need to be careful about is the use of touch. It is quite common for those in a position of higher status to touch those of lower status, in a friendly and caring manner, but not vice versa. However, you do need to be aware that in the classroom, touching pupils in this way can be misunderstood and, in part depending on the pupil's personal circumstances, experienced as undesirable or unpleasant. As such, touching pupils should be avoided, unless there are specific circumstances, such as dealing with accidents, emotional distress, matters of health and safety, or teaching musical instruments, when touching is fully appropriate.

Teaching competently

The second major source of your authority comes from teaching competently. If you convey to pupils that you are knowledgeable about the topic or subject, are interested in it, and can set up the learning activities skilfully, then pupils will respect your ability to teach; this will confirm your authority to manage their behaviour. This requires that your lessons are well planned and prepared, that your manner conveys interest and enthusiasm, and that you can set up challenging activities effectively.

One of the reasons that teaching competently is so crucial to establishing your authority is because poor teaching is often experienced as insulting. When pupils are taught in a way they regard as unsatisfactory, then one of two interpretations are commonly drawn by pupils: either the teacher has not made an effort, which implies that the pupils are not worth making an effort for; or the school has allocated them a teacher who lacks adequate teaching skills, which implies that the pupils were not worth being allocated a better teacher. Both interpretations strike at the heart of pupils' self-esteem, and the extent to which they react by misbehaviour is largely related to the underlying insult they experience. In contrast, being taught competently engenders a feeling of pride and self-respect, and affirms their sense of worth and importance.

Exercising managerial control

The third major source of your authority comes from exercising managerial control in the classroom. In order to set up learning activities efficiently, lessons need to get off to a prompt start, pupils must be kept involved in the learning activities, and transitions between activities should be handled smoothly. Anything that frustrates these expectations will require you to exert managerial control. Pupils arriving late for lessons, not paying attention or applying sufficient effort, or interrupting your presentation, can frustrate the prompt start and flow of the lesson. Smith and Laslett (1992) famously identified the four main tasks of classroom management as 'Get them in, get them out, get on with it, and get on with them!'

The most crucial aspects of exercising managerial control involve establishing clear conventions, routines and expectations for pupils' behaviour, and imposing your view on a situation when any conflicts arise. For example, when you are ready to start the lesson and have called the pupils to attention, if a pupil points out that they need a new exercise book, rather than allow the start of the lesson to be delayed, you should indicate that you will deal with that later and proceed promptly with the lesson. Once the lesson has started, virtually any activity can frustrate the progress of the lesson. For example, giving out equipment can take too long or become cumbersome, the pace of work by pupils may be rather slow, or pupils may take a long time to pay attention to you after an activity has been completed. To prevent the progress being frustrated, you need to exercise your control whenever appropriate.

In order to exercise managerial control, pupils' behaviour needs to be rule-governed. Indeed, a study by Kyriacou et al. (2007), which explored the views of beginning teachers concerning strategies they thought were effective in dealing with pupil misbehaviour in the classroom, found that the strategy they viewed as most effective was 'establishing clear and consistent school and classroom rules about the behaviours that are acceptable and that are unacceptable'. In contrast, strategies such as issuing reprimands and punishments were regarded as much less effective. In general, the beginning teachers saw a combination of establishing sound classroom rules and counselling pupils towards re-engaging with their work with the minimum amount of fuss as being the most effective approach to dealing with pupil misbehaviour.

Such classroom rules may be explicitly stated by teachers or simply inferred from the teacher's actions. Wragg (2005), in a study of secondary school teachers, identified eleven classroom rules that were explicitly stated by teachers or could be clearly inferred from their actions. These were (in order of occurrence):

- no talking when the teacher is talking

- no disruptive noises

- rules for entering, leaving and moving in classrooms

- no interference with the work of others

- work must be completed in a specified way

- pupils must raise their hand to answer, not shout out

- pupils must make a positive effort in their work

- pupils must not challenge the authority of the teacher

- respect must be shown for property and equipment

- rules to do with safety

- pupils must ask if they do not understand.

In looking at primary school teachers, Wragg (2005) identified a similar set of rules in operation. However, he noted that the primary school teachers' initial encounters with their new classes were generally characterised by a friendly smile, businesslike manner and benign firmness, whereas the secondary school teachers in the earlier study had been more aggressively assertive.

Unpredictable events, such as the appearance of a window cleaner, can be disruptive, although a quick acknowledgement of the situation with a touch of humour is often effective in such circumstances. Imposing your will simply means ensuring that pupils do what you want them to do to ensure that the lesson progresses.

Dealing with pupil misbehaviour effectively

From time to time, pupil misbehaviour will occur. This may range from a trivial incident, such as a pupil not paying attention, to a serious one, such as a pupil punching another in anger. How you deal with pupil misbehaviour is the fourth major source of your authority. Your authority will be enhanced to the extent that you are able to deal with pupil misbehaviour effectively and fairly. How to do this is the subject of the remainder of this chapter. However, it is important to bear in mind that the type of strategy that will work best not only depends on the teacher's skilful use of these strategies, but also their ability to take account of the context in which they are working and in which the misbehaviour occurs.

Dealing with disruptive behaviour requires the teacher to have a well-thought-out repertoire of techniques that can be brought into play in a skilful manner, so that pupils can be guided towards re-engaging with the work as quickly as possible and be given a clear idea of what is regarded by the teacher to be unacceptable behaviour. This needs to be done in a manner that is sensitive to the pupil and the context, and which guides the pupil towards behaving better in future lessons (Ellis and Tod, 2009; Lewis, 2008; Rogers, 2012).

Pre-empting pupil misbehaviour

In considering pupil misbehaviour 'prevention is better than cure'. Skilful teaching can do much to minimise pupil misbehaviour occurring in the first place, and can usefully redirect incidents that were developing before they need be regarded as misbehaviour. The essence of pre-empting misbehaviour lies in vigilance plus action.

Strategies to pre-empt misbehaviour

Careful monitoring of pupils' behaviour and progress during a lesson can ensure that most misbehaviour is nipped in the bud. Successful monitoring requires a conscious decision to do so periodically, as it is all too easy to get wrapped up in particular activities, such as giving individual help, and thereby not to notice another pupil who is disrupting someone else's work. Experienced teachers are adept at such monitoring, while student teachers can usefully remind themselves to do this until it becomes routine.

The main useful strategies to pre-empt misbehaviour are as follows.

- *Set clear expectations regarding behaviour.* All schools have a policy on good pupil behaviour, and guidance on behaviour that is viewed as acceptable or unacceptable. These expectations need to be conveyed to your pupils on a regular basis.

- *Scan the classroom.* Periodically look around the classroom and consider whether any pupils appear to be having difficulties and, if so, go over and investigate in a supportive and helpful manner to ensure that pupils resume working as quickly as possible. Individual contact will be more effective than shouting across the room. The latter both disrupts other pupils unnecessarily and tends to assume the pupil is misbehaving.

- *Circulate.* Circulate around the room periodically and probe whether pupils are having difficulties. Sometimes asking a pupil about their progress usefully uncovers problems that they would otherwise not have drawn to your attention.

- *Make eye contact.* When addressing the class as a whole, make eye contact with individual pupils periodically, but do not look too long at any one individual. If you suspect a pupil may be misbehaving, making eye contact, and prolonging it, will indicate to that pupil your awareness of their need to reinvolve themselves in the lesson without needing to signal this publicly or interrupt the flow of the lesson.

- *Target your questions.* Directing your questions around the class helps to maintain pupils' involvement; targeting questions at particular individuals is also a signal to them to get reinvolved.

- *Use proximity.* While you normally stand at the front of the classroom, how and where you move to can be an effective signal of your monitoring. By moving towards two pupils talking, you can indicate your awareness to them of this without interrupting the lesson. You may also stand near a pair or group of pupils for some time to sustain their working.

- *Give academic help.* Giving advice and guidance to pupils to enable and encourage them to make progress with the task in hand is the single most powerful means of pre-empting misbehaviour.

- *Change activities or pace.* As a result of monitoring pupils' progress you may feel the lesson is proceeding too slowly or too fast and that pupils are ready to move on to another activity or are running into difficulties. Your decisions about altering the pace of the lesson and when to change the activity are crucial to maintaining pupils' involvement. This applies not only to the class as a whole, but also to individual pupils, some of whom will often need to work at a different pace or on a different activity, even when whole-class teaching is taking place, if they are to sustain their involvement to best effect.

- *Notice misbehaviour.* If a pupil is misbehaving, in the vast majority of cases it is important to indicate to the pupil that you have noticed this. Eye contact may be sufficient, or if you wish to do this more forcefully, a stern facial expression or a pause in your exposition will indicate your concern and displeasure, while not interrupting the flow of the lesson for more than a moment. Student teachers often tend to refrain from doing this, in part because they feel misbehaviour needs to be more formally reprimanded once it is noticed or because they hope it might disappear if ignored. In fact, signalling of this sort is very important and effective in exercising managerial control; failing to do so by ignoring simply allows more frequent or serious misbehaviour to develop, whereas too ready a recourse to reprimands serves to create a conflict unnecessarily.

- *Notice disrespect.* When interacting with pupils you should expect pupils to behave with appropriate respect. So, for example, if a pupil is slouched in their seat when addressed by you, it would be a normal courtesy for the pupil to quickly sit up straight while replying. Not doing so might be dealt with by your looking surprised or stern to indicate you are not happy with this, and if that is not sufficient, you might comment explicitly. Lack of courtesy or respect towards you needs to be picked up as it forms part of pupils' impressions concerning the standard of behaviour you expect and the type of relationship you wish to establish. Not doing so will tacitly undermine your authority in behaving with status and exercising managerial control on your terms.

- *Move pupils.* If the circumstances warrant, do not hesitate to separate two pupils who are not behaving acceptably together, after due warning to this effect. Alternatively, you may require a particular pupil to sit at the front where you can monitor the pupil's behaviour more closely. Seating arrangements are a privilege rather than a right of pupils, and if you feel a better arrangement is desirable, a move can be helpful. However, you need to emphasise that this is done in the pupils' interests to ensure that any resentment is minimised.

Maintaining good behaviour largely rests on skilful teaching and skilful use of such strategies to pre-empt misbehaviour. Even so, misbehaviour will still occur from time to time, and to deal with this the best strategy is to combine the use of investigating and counselling with the use of reprimands.

Investigating and counselling

When pupil misbehaviour has occurred despite your use of pre-emptive strategies, you have a choice to make between investigating the nature and cause of the misbehaviour or reprimanding the misbehaviour on the basis of your reading of its most likely nature and cause. Your decision will very much depend on the context, such as the pupil concerned, the nature of the activities taking place, how certain you are about your reading of the incident, and what you anticipate will be the most likely effect of any action you take.

Investigating and counselling refers to a strategy whereby you approach the incident of misbehaviour with a view to finding out the nature of the problem. Indeed, your comment to the pupil might well be 'What's the problem?' Your tone should indicate your concern with a view to helping the pupil return to the work in hand as soon as possible, rather than convey hostility or aggression on your part. In such circumstances, the pupil may admit to having problems with their work, or may attribute the misbehaviour to being bored, for example, or being provoked by another pupil. If the nature of the problem is not primarily an academic difficulty, you then need to decide whether to counsel the pupil towards behaving appropriately there and then or else seeing the pupil at the end of the lesson, during a break time or after school.

Effective counselling

When counselling a pupil it is important to allow the pupil to do much of the talking, with a view to helping the pupil see that the misbehaviour is not in their interests, and that the pupil should agree to behave as required in future. Such counselling is likely to be more effective if conducted in private, in a context of trust and mutual respect, and where you convey a caring and concerned attitude. It is important to the pupils to evaluate their own behaviour and to consider the consequences, such as poor academic progress or punishment if the behaviour does not improve. The most important aspect of counselling is to end with the pupil agreeing to behave well in future as a positive decision.

Where such counselling does not appear to be successful or serious problems appear to be underlying the misbehaviour, it is important to confer with colleagues who have explicit pastoral care concerns. In secondary schools this will be the form teacher and the head of house or year, although in many secondary schools it is usual for the head of department to be involved in the first instance. In primary schools the class teacher is normally the form teacher as well, and so consultation is likely to involve the headteacher or a deputy head with specific responsibility for pastoral care.

Increasing attention has been paid to mentoring pupils who are a cause for concern regarding disaffection and misbehaviour. Mentoring can provide an effective vehicle through which pupils can be helped to engage more positively in schooling and improve their social behaviour towards others. This work can be undertaken by those working as learning mentors or as part of outside support agencies. A particularly interesting development here has been the increasing use of a pupil-centred approach termed 'social pedagogy', which is widely used in mainland Europe and is being more widely used in schools in the UK (Kyriacou, 2015). This pupil-centred form of mentoring is a skill that many effective teachers already employ in their day-to-day classroom practice.

Another important aspect of counselling pupils is to provide them with techniques they can use that will help them improve their behaviour. Dansie (2016) has highlighted ways in which pupils with challenging behaviour can be supported to develop mental techniques that allow them to view themselves more positively and to avoid behaving in a hostile manner towards others. For many troubled pupils facing adverse circumstances in their lives, the help they really need lies in developing socially acceptable ways of behaving when dealing with a situation that has the potential to generate anxiety, anger and frustration.

When counselling pupils you need to be aware of safeguarding issues. You should be careful not to be alone with the pupil, or if you are, you should keep the door open and ensure that a colleague knows this (and when appropriate, is in the vicinity). You also need to make clear to the pupil that you cannot promise confidentiality, as you are duty-bound to pass certain types of concerns on to the appropriate colleague.

Your pastoral care role

In your role as a class teacher, you must bear in mind that simultaneously you have a pastoral care role. Therefore, as well as being concerned about pupils' academic progress, you must also be concerned about their general behaviour and attitudes, their personal and social development, and any individual needs they may have. Dealing with pupil misbehaviour is not simply a matter of behaviour management, but is also bound up with your pastoral care responsibilities.

In addition, in this respect, you should also be alert to pupils' behaviour giving cause for concern that may not be regarded as misbehaviour. For example, excessive shyness, a tendency to work very slowly, or frequent daydreaming may not be in any way disruptive, but may well need to be picked up in monitoring pupils' progress and investigated further. Indeed, non-disruptive behaviours such as inattentiveness or an unwillingness to participate in activities can sometimes be a sign of personal problems occurring in the pupil's life (such as being bullied, or worries about a parent who is seriously ill) and identifying this can enable the teacher and school to offer the pupil appropriate help and support (Kyriacou, 2003). Such concerns are linked to the need for teachers to be aware of national policies regarding the promotion of pupils' well-being.

Although many of the skills involved in establishing and maintaining good behaviour in the classroom may be summarised as involving managerial control, you must never lose sight of the fact that this must take place in the context of your pastoral care concern for each pupil within a classroom climate that pupils feel to be supportive and caring. Therefore, after exercising managerial control, it can be helpful to go up to a pupil and re-establish your caring relationship by saying 'How are things going?' or 'Any problems?', so that your one-to-one positive personal relationship with that pupil is confirmed.

Resulting actions

As a result of investigating and counselling by you alone or in wider consultation with colleagues, there may well be actions you need to take to assist the pupil to behave well. For example, you may discover that the pupil finds it difficult to settle down to work because they are easily distracted by certain other pupils, or the pupil is finding the work too difficult, or is not getting enough sleep because of late nights at home. Some pupils may have a special educational need that requires a formal assessment to be made and explicit provision, such as the help of a support teacher for a period. Some of the necessary actions can be taken by you in the classroom; others may involve collaboration with colleagues, particularly if parents and other agencies are to be involved.

Using reprimands

A reprimand refers to an explicit verbal warning or comment by you to a pupil that indicates your disapproval of the misbehaviour which has occurred. Because the use of investigating and counselling is time-consuming and logistically too difficult to be used for every misbehaviour which occurs, most misbehaviour that has not been successfully dealt with by the pre-emptive strategies will be dealt with by reprimands; only a minority of problems are dealt with by recourse to investigating and counselling. However, the balance between these two strategies will vary greatly from lesson to lesson and from class to class.

Effective use of reprimands

Reprimands are best used sparingly and should complement skilful teaching in general. Too frequent a use of reprimands will lessen their effect, will undermine a positive classroom climate, and will be experienced by some pupils as 'nagging'.

A number of qualities are involved in the skilful and effective use of reprimands.

- *Correct targeting.* The pupil being reprimanded should be correctly identified as the pupil instigating or engaged in the misbehaviour. A particular danger here is to reprimand a pupil who was reacting to another's provocation.

- *Firmness.* Your reprimand should be clear and firm in tone and content. Avoid pleading or implying damage limitation (e.g. 'Let's at least get some decent work done in the last ten minutes') or softening your reprimand once it has been issued.

- *Express concern.* Your reprimand should convey your concern with the pupil's interests or that of other pupils being harmed by the misbehaviour.

- *Avoid anger.* While a firm expression of disapproval is effective, expressing intense anger, shouting at pupils, and appearing to have lost your temper will tend to undermine a positive classroom climate. Frequent expressions of anger are undesirable, are experienced by pupils as unpleasant, and, with younger pupils in particular, may be very upsetting.

- *Emphasise what is required.* Reprimands should emphasise what pupils should be doing rather than simply complain about the misbehaviour itself. 'Pay attention' is better than 'Stop looking out of the window', and

'You may talk quietly with your neighbour' is better than 'There's too much noise in here.'

- *Maintain psychological impact.* When a reprimand is given, its impact is enhanced by non-verbal cues, such as eye contact. After the reprimand is given, a momentary prolonging of eye contact together with a slight pause before continuing with the lesson can increase the force of the exchange.

- *Avoid confrontations.* Do not force a pupil into a heated exchange. Where such a possibility seems likely because the pupil appears tense, agitated or unresponsive to your pre-emptive strategies, postponing a reprimand and instead using investigating and counselling strategies would be appropriate. If you reprimand a pupil who then reacts emotionally, you can usefully curtail the exchange by telling the pupil to stay behind at the end of the lesson in a matter-of-fact manner and quickly resume the lesson.

- *Criticise the behaviour not the pupil.* It is important to emphasise that you disapprove of the misbehaviour not the pupil. This enables you to convey a sense of caring for the pupil and their interests, and gives pupils an opportunity to dissociate themselves from such misbehaviour in future. 'You need to concentrate more on your work and spend less time chatting to others' is better than 'You're an idle person.'

- *Use private rather than public reprimands.* A private reprimand, such as a quiet word, is useful because it is a more personal contact and lessens the likelihood of embarrassing the pupil and the chance that the pupil might react with hostility. It is also less disruptive to other pupils. A public reprimand to a pupil is better only when there is a specific reason to go public, such as when you actually want the whole class to hear the reprimand as an implicit warning to others. A less disruptive use of a public reprimand is to simply call out the pupil's name in a tone that conveys that you have noticed some misbehaviour that must stop immediately.

- *Be pre-emptive.* Reprimands aimed at pre-empting misbehaviour are more effective than those that follow only after repeated and prolonged misbehaviour.

- *State rules and rationale.* A reprimand can usefully consist of a statement of the rule being transgressed together with an explanation of why the rule is required for the benefit of teaching and learning (e.g. 'Please put up your hand and wait until I ask you to speak so that everyone gets a fair chance to contribute and we can all hear what is said').

- *Avoid making hostile remarks.* Hostile and deprecating remarks should be avoided, as pupils may feel personally disliked, and may become disaffected and alienated. Sarcasm and ridicule in particular are felt by pupils to be unfair, and can undermine mutual respect and rapport to the detriment of a positive classroom climate.

- *Avoid unfair comparisons.* Pupils tend to feel that reprimands that involve stereotyping or comparisons with others are unfair, particularly if they relate to other members of the pupil's family or other classes (e.g. 'Your sister's work is much better than this' or 'Just because this is set three doesn't mean you don't have to pay attention').

- *Be consistent.* Reprimands should relate to clear and consistently applied expectations. Pupils will resent being reprimanded if they feel the behaviour was not the type you would normally reprimand or if the severity of the reprimand was unexpectedly great.

- *Do not make empty threats.* Do not issue reprimands that threaten consequences you would not wish to or could not carry out (e.g. 'The next pupil who talks will go straight to the head' or 'If you make another insolent remark, I shall be contacting your parents'). If you explicitly state consequences that will follow, it is very important to carry these out if you are to maintain credibility when you use this strategy in the future.

- *Avoid reprimanding the whole class.* Reprimanding the whole class is a serious act and should only be used when certain misbehaviour or your cause for concern is so widespread that individual reprimands will not have sufficient effect or be appropriate. In order to avoid casting your criticism equally on all pupils, including the blameless, it is useful to indicate your concern with 'too many pupils' rather than all pupils. A useful alternative is to discuss with the class as a whole why certain misbehaviour has become widespread, so that you can identify any particular problems and reinforce the need for good behaviour.

- *Making an example.* Another useful alternative to reprimanding the whole class is to issue a particularly forceful reprimand to one pupil, and add or imply that you will not tolerate other pupils acting in this way. Reprimanding an individual can have just as much impact on the behaviour of the class as reprimanding the whole class. Making an example can be particularly useful in the first few lessons with a new class to highlight your expectations, such as how you deal with the first pupil who arrives late for your lessons without any excuse. It is also useful if certain pupils appear to be trying to challenge your authority publicly. However, you must be sensitive concerning whether you are simply being drawn into a public confrontation that is best dealt with in some other way.

Ideally the use of reprimands can be thought of as adding a few drops of oil to an engine that is running well but very occasionally needs further lubrication to maintain its smooth operation. Once the use of reprimands becomes frequent, the climate of the lesson can change quite markedly, and the tone becomes one of the teacher trying to coerce and cajole pupils towards working well. In such circumstances you need to think carefully whether the academic demands made upon pupils can be modified and consider the nature of the underlying causes of such continuing conflict.

Indeed, frequent misbehaviour by pupils acts as an ongoing critique by pupils of the demands made upon them, and has acted as a major stimulus for curriculum development. The point being stressed here is that if the skilful use of reprimands does not appear to be successful, you should not assume that the best way ahead is to resort to more frequent and more severe reprimands and the use of punishments or other related strategies without first thinking long and hard about the educational context within which the misbehaviour has arisen.

Using punishments

Despite the skilful use of reprimands and other strategies already discussed, pupil misbehaviour may persist. In such circumstances, the use of punishments may be effective in restoring good behaviour.

The nature and purpose of punishment

A punishment is in essence a formal action that the pupil is intended to experience as unpleasant as a means of helping the pupil to behave appropriately in the future. The dividing line between a reprimand and a punishment is often blurred, because reprimands and other strategies are often also experienced as unpleasant. The difference largely lies in the formal way in which a punishment is set up and the explicit intention for it to be unpleasant.

In setting up a punishment, you thus need to emphasise to the pupil that the use of punishment is intended to help the pupil appreciate the gravity and seriousness with which you are treating the misbehaviour and the urgency of the need for good behaviour to occur in future. Indeed, it is essential that the pupil sees the punishment as being in their own interests, and certainly not as an expression of malice or hostility.

Punishments have three main purposes:

- *retribution:* the idea that justice requires that wrongdoing is followed by a morally deserved punishment

- *deterrence:* the idea that the pupil or other pupils will wish to avoid such misbehaviour in the future for fear of the consequences

- *rehabilitation:* the idea that the pupil will be helped to understand the moral wrongdoing of the misbehaviour and the need to behave well in future.

In schools, punishments often involve all three purposes to some extent, but rehabilitation is clearly the most important one and the one that embodies an educational purpose to enable a pupil to choose to behave well in the future. Deterrence is also important and may contribute to the effectiveness of your expressions of disapproval when using reprimands. Retribution tends to be the most evident when a moral code has been broken that the teacher feels needs to be punished in the interests of justice as an expression of the school community's disapproval, the most notable examples being bullying, stealing, cheating, vandalism, and certain types of verbal abuse.

The shortcomings of punishment

The most important aspect of punishment to bear in mind is that its impact largely depends on it being used as a formal and weighty sanction employed for serious incidents of misbehaviour when other strategies have been unsuccessful. There is, however, an element of illusion involved here, since very few sanctions are in fact of any weight, with most involving only a short period of unpleasantness or having a nuisance value. Their impact owes much more to using them in a way that conveys the seriousness with which the misbehaviour is being viewed. It is also largely the case that the type of pupils most likely to be punished, notably disaffected pupils who have little respect for authority and the values and ethos of the school, are the pupils least likely to respond by better behaviour in future. In contrast, those pupils who would be most worried about punishment are those pupils for whom skilful use of other strategies should be sufficiently effective.

The main drawbacks of using punishments are that they:

- form an inappropriate model for human relationships

- foster anxiety and resentment

- have a short-lived 'initial shock' effect

- encourage pupils to develop strategies to avoid getting caught

- do not promote good behaviour directly but simply serve to suppress misbehaviour

- do not deal with the cause of the misbehaviour

- focus attention on the misbehaviour.

Types of punishment

Despite the shortcomings of punishments, they do have a useful role to play in maintaining good behaviour if used skilfully. Each type of punishment has certain strengths and weaknesses that will have a bearing on their effectiveness. The most commonly used punishments are as follows.

- *Writing tasks.* These may range from writing out lines to a short essay on 'Why I misbehaved and will behave better in future'. The main advantage of this approach is that it is done in the pupil's own time without wasting yours. Its weakness is that it is often felt to have a patronising quality and is probably regarded as insulting by older pupils. It is essential not to require pupils to do work that is missing or overdue as a punishment. Doing schoolwork should not be a punishment. Such work must be explicitly justified on other grounds.

- *Detention.* This could entail keeping a pupil in detention for a break period or after school coupled with a writing task (as above) or simply detaining them in silence for a set period of time. Its main advantage is that it is widely disliked by pupils; its main disadvantage is that it can inconvenience you. It is essential to distinguish a detention from requiring to see a pupil for a period of time as part of an investigating and counselling approach or to issue a reprimand. A detention is a formal punishment and should be administered as such.

- *Loss of privileges.* This can range from requiring a pupil to sit alone and in isolation to preventing the pupil going on a school outing. Its main advantage is that it can be quite upsetting to the pupil; its main disadvantage is that it can easily be seen as vindictive and unfair.

- *Exclusion from the class.* This can range from requiring the pupil to wait outside the classroom for a period of time to being sent to another classroom or place in the school. Its main advantage is that it removes the pupil from the classroom and allows them to think about why they were excluded; its main disadvantages are that it is not particularly unpleasant for some pupils and can pose other problems, such as a pupil who keeps looking in through a window or simply wanders off.

- *Verbal intimidation.* A very severe talking to may be considered as a punishment rather than a reprimand, particularly if done by a senior teacher in the school in a formal role. Its main advantages are that it can be very unpleasant and can be administered quickly; its main disadvantage is that it can provoke a confrontation. A severe talking to in this way should only take place in private.

- *Informing significant others.* Informing the headteacher or the pupil's parents is, for most pupils, very punishing. Its main advantage is that it is usually a quite powerful sanction; its main disadvantage is that the pupil may now feel labelled by the school as a disruptive pupil and may even feel the need to live up to this label as a result.

- *Symbolic punishment.* Some schools have a system of recording bad conduct marks that translate into a detention for a given total and may be included on the school report to parents. Its main advantage is that it can use the formal ritual of punishment at a mild level; its main disadvantage is that it can be clumsy to administer and communicate.

- *Exclusion from school.* This is the ultimate sanction. Exclusion can be temporary (usually one to five days in length) or permanent. It tends to be used as a final resort to help the pupil appreciate the immense gravity of the situation and the misbehaviour, either after a long history of problems or in reaction to a particular misbehaviour of the utmost seriousness (such as using drugs or assaulting a teacher). For some, it provides the shock needed to salvage their school careers or acts as a vehicle for the provision of special support. For others, it marks a point of no return. It may result in transfer to another school, with perhaps a fresh start. With pupils approaching the school leaving age, it may lead to a period of prolonged uncertainty during which efforts to place the pupil elsewhere are finally overtaken by time running out.

Effective use of punishments

While it is evident that punishments generally have a more severe and unpleasant consequence for a pupil than strategies based on investigating and counselling or using reprimands, that does not mean they are actually more powerful or effective in dealing with pupil misbehaviour. Research on the effectiveness of different strategies used to deal with difficult classes or pupils indicates that while almost any strategy can be effective if used skilfully in the right situation, generally strategies based on reasoning with pupils are the most effective. Indeed, recourse to a punishment in a situation may be counterproductive if all that might have been necessary and effective was offering some academic help or simply reasoning with the pupil. A major pitfall, facing beginning teachers in particular, is to assume that a punishment is more powerful and hence more effective; as a result, teachers resort to their use too readily and inappropriately.

The skilful and effective use of punishments involves a number of qualities, and includes those considered earlier in relation to the effective use of reprimands. There are, however, some additional qualities worthy of particular note.

- *Use sparingly.* Punishments should only be used sparingly and judiciously, and in the vast majority of cases only after other strategies have been tried.

- *Timing.* Punishments should be given as soon as possible after the misbehaviour. If there is a long delay, the link should be re-established at the time given.

- *Tone.* A punishment should be conveyed as an expression of your just and severe disapproval of the misbehaviour, and given in the interests of the pupil and of the class as a whole. It should not result from you losing your temper or appear vindictive.

- *Fit the crime.* The type and severity of the punishment should be appropriate to the misbehaviour but should also take account of the context.

- *Due process.* It is important that the pupil accepts that the punishment is fair and just. This will normally mean that the pupil has been warned that such a consequence may follow, and that your expectations and actions regarding such misbehaviour are clear and consistent. The pupil should also be asked to explain the misbehaviour and encouraged to understand and accept why the punishment is just, deserved and appropriate.

- *Relates to school policy.* The punishment should relate to the overall policy of the school towards behaviour management.

- *Aversion.* The punishment must be unpleasant for the pupil. Some pupils may not mind being sent out of the room, or may even gain status in the eyes of peers in doing so. As such, each punishment needs to be of a type that is aversive for the pupil concerned and minimises any factors that are likely to weaken its effectiveness, bearing in mind the need to be fair and consistent.

It is also important to consult with colleagues in the school about any pupil giving cause for concern. If a pupil is being punished frequently, this may indicate an underlying problem that is beyond the concern of the class teacher alone. While you may feel you are expected to cope with any misbehaviour yourself as best you can, this does not mean it is desirable to keep problems to yourself as far as possible; in fact, the opposite is the case. You also have a responsibility towards pastoral care and you need to act as a member of a team in monitoring pupils' behaviour, so that any concerns you have are shared with others and appropriate action can then be considered before decisions are taken.

Dealing with confrontations

From time to time a confrontation may develop in the classroom between you and a pupil. Managing very challenging behaviour successfully can be particularly demanding for teachers, most notably when dealing with a direct confrontation with a pupil (Leaman, 2009). A confrontation may be characterised by a heated and emotional exchange, which is upsetting for all concerned. Such a confrontation can develop so quickly and unpredictably that the first thing you are aware of is that you are in the middle of having one. Usually, however, there are warning signals evident that enable you to pre-empt its development.

Triggers for confrontations

There are four major triggers for confrontation in the classroom:

- a pupil may feel emotional and tense as a result of prolonged learning difficulties that are causing increasing frustration

- a pupil may feel that the disciplinary strategy you are adopting towards them is unfair and constitutes a threat to their self-esteem, particularly if linked to loss of face in front of their peers (the use of sarcasm or ridicule may provoke this, or trying to resolve a conflict by making the pupil submit to your authority in some way, such as moving to a seat at the front of the classroom)

- a pupil may react against explicit physical or verbal intimidation, such as a teacher waving a finger in front of the pupil's face or using a forceful reprimand

- a pupil may be trying to avoid embarrassment when you are cajoling or insisting they answer a question or take part in an activity that they feel very anxious about or in which they feel they may make a fool of themselves in front of others.

Clearly, skilful teaching and, in particular, intelligent use of the disciplinary strategies outlined earlier, will do much to minimise the occurrence of such triggers. However, there are circumstances that can lead to a pupil feeling oversensitive to what otherwise would be unproblematic behaviour on your part. For example, there may be acute personal problems the pupil is having to deal with at home, or some upsetting news may have been received in school (e.g. being dropped from a school team, being told that their school report will be critical of poor progress, or even that a best friend has not invited the pupil to a party).

You can usually sense from a pupil's behaviour that something is amiss, such as the pupil looking tense or arriving in the classroom in an uncharacteristically loud manner. Such signals will alert you to the possibility that you may need to be extra sensitive when interacting with the pupil.

Dealing with a confrontation

If a confrontation does develop, there are some useful strategies that will enable you to deal successfully with the situation.

- *Stay calm.* If you remain calm, or regain your composure quickly, and interact calmly with the pupil, the pupil will quickly calm down.

- *Defuse the situation.* Rather than try to pursue the conflict further, you can tell the pupil that 'There's no need for anyone to get upset, I suggest you just calm down and we can deal with this at the end of the lesson' and then back off. If this is not effective, your best course of action is to send for help so that the pupil can be moved elsewhere for the rest of the lesson. Backing off in this way does not mean that you have backed down or lost authority; indeed, it displays your skill in dealing with this as a special circumstance demanding appropriate action, and pupils will generally understand this. Some teachers can use humour to defuse a confrontation, but doing so successfully requires adept sensitivity.

- *Be aware of the heat of the moment.* A confrontation can develop in a matter of seconds, and in the heat of the moment you or the pupil may say or do something that is profoundly regretted later. Bear this in mind before you act and in how you respond to what the pupil says or does.

- *Use your social skills.* A pupil may be horrified by what they have said or done but may lack the social skills to get out of the situation. You need to use your social skills as an adult and as their teacher to help the pupil, for which they may be immensely grateful later once the incident is defused and dealt with.

- *Design a mutual face saver.* In the heat of the moment, your natural tendency may be to feel you must exert your authority by coming out 'on top' in some way. Such a stereotyped reaction is often unhelpful and counterproductive. You need to consider which strategy best fits the situation, and enables you and the pupil to come away from the incident with sufficient grace.

- *Offer the pupil a choice.* Give the pupil a choice of outcomes – such as the pupil agreeing to behave differently in future, or the matter being taken further in some way; it is sometimes useful to walk away for a few minutes, to leave the pupil alone to consider the options offered, as this allows the pupil some thinking time in which to dwell on the gravity of the situation.

- *Get help if necessary.* Do not hesitate to get assistance from another member of staff if this seems appropriate.

Research on how teachers deal with confrontations indicates that almost all confrontations can be avoided or resolved by the skilful use of conflict management techniques. In particular, this requires teachers to be aware of their own emotions during conflicts and confrontations and how these might influence their behaviour, and to be able to stand outside the situation to think rationally about how best to proceed. The biggest danger facing you in dealing with a confrontation is to lose your temper or see the situation as 'I win – You lose', whereby you need to exert whatever power you have. By remaining calm, standing back from the situation, thinking carefully, and using appropriate strategies skilfully, the vast majority of such incidents can be defused and dealt with efficiently and effectively, and without becoming unnecessarily unpleasant.

A range of problems can be triggered as a result of a teacher using aggressive management techniques such as shouting in anger or using sarcasm and humiliation, particularly in terms of the way it can undermine the relationship with the pupil and can disrupt the smooth running of the lesson. A study by Riley et al. (2012) looked at the use of aggressive management by 192 secondary school teachers in Australia and 75 secondary school teachers in China. While very few teachers reported using such techniques often, about 10 per cent of the teachers reported doing so sometimes. Given that such behaviour is regarded as socially undesirable, they argued that this figure is likely to be an underestimate. As such, it is clear that developing skills to maintain emotional control and to employ non-aggressive strategies is very important for quite a few teachers. Of particular concern is that some teachers take the view that aggressive management is the only thing that certain types of pupils understand. Developing skilful use of other strategies would enable such teachers to appreciate that alternative strategies can be both more effective and less damaging.

Figure 7.2: Monitor your pupils' behaviour

Other strategies

As well as the strategies outlined so far, there are other strategies and approaches that are worthy of particular note.

Formal monitoring of behaviour

Formal procedures for monitoring pupils' behaviour can be effective. A frequently used strategy is to put a pupil 'on report', which means that for a period of a few days or a week, each teacher must make a note of the pupil's behaviour at the end of each teaching session on a report card. At the end of this period, the pupil's behaviour is reviewed.

Contracts

The notion of contracts involves promising the pupil an agreed reward of some type if good behaviour is maintained over a specified period. The reward may typically be a merit certificate for good behaviour, allowing the pupil to spend time on a valued activity (such as an afternoon in the craft workshop), or even a tangible reward (such as a bar of chocolate). It is important to note that the real motivation here does not stem from the desire for the reward, but rather the desire to behave well. The procedure and reward simply serve as a helpful vehicle to support the pupil's own efforts.

Getting help from parents and carers

Enlisting the help of pupils' parents and carers is often very important if the behaviour has become a serious cause for concern. Parents and carers should be informed about a cause for concern, not only as part of the desirability of keeping parents and carers informed in general about their children, but also because parents and carers may offer useful and helpful information themselves and assist in various ways to encourage an improvement in the pupil's behaviour. If it is suspected that the pupil may have a special educational need of some sort, then parents and carers should be involved in any discussions at an early stage.

Teachers should be able to communicate effectively with parents and carers and to recognise and respect the role that parents and carers can have in the development of pupils' well-being and in raising pupils' levels of attainment.

Units for disruptive pupils

Many schools are able to make use of on-site or off-site units to which disruptive pupils can be sent for a period of time. This can operate for quite short periods, such as one lesson or half a day to provide a cooling-off period during which the pupil can come to terms with the gravity of the situation. In addition, it can operate for a longer period, perhaps three weeks, during which a detailed assessment and review of the pupils' behaviour and needs are considered. At its best, this strategy can allow a crisis to be defused successfully, followed by a return to normal schooling. At its worst, particularly for pupils near to the school leaving age, it can result in de facto exclusion.

Alternative educational provision

In recent years there has been a rapid growth in alternative education provision. This refers to a range of activities that can take place in school (e.g. a half-day session each week involving creative design activities), or out of school (e.g. a day a week helping on a farm), or in another educational setting (e.g. a free school for challenging pupils). A key feature of alternative education provision is more personalised attention and support for each child, utilising a range of activities designed to enhance their self-esteem and well-being, and enabling them to re-engage in learning, particularly in the areas of literacy and numeracy. The success of such provision depends on the teachers involved taking a more overt role as a trusted and caring adult, and offering emotional support and mentoring. Such activities can be very successful with pupils who have become disaffected with schooling and hard to control in a normal classroom setting.

Positive teaching

Positive teaching refers to an approach to behaviour management based on ideas stemming from behavioural psychology (Porter, 2014; Swinson and Harrop, 2012). The basic underlying principle here is that pupil behaviour that is rewarded is more likely to occur in the same situation in future, and behaviour that is not rewarded, or is punished, is less likely to occur. Advocates of this approach to classroom teaching argue that it enables teachers to be more consistent, systematic and effective in how they deal with misbehaviour. First, the teacher needs to identify desirable behaviours that need to be promoted and which types of misbehaviour need to be discouraged. Having done this, you then use a programme of regularly praising and otherwise rewarding the desirable behaviours, and reminding pupils of the classroom rules that need to be adhered to. The important point about this approach is its emphasis on the use of praise and other rewards to encourage and sustain improved behaviour. Punishments are rarely used. Research studies based on evaluating this approach indicate that its skilful use can successfully improve the behaviour of the class as a whole and also promote better behaviour with individual pupils causing problems.

Strategies for when discipline is lost

One of the most daunting prospects for new teachers is to find themselves in the situation where they feel that a class has lost respect for them, and that discipline is essentially absent. Classes such as these often comprise lower ability pupils with low academic self-esteem who come into the class with the attitude that school is not for them. Disaffected students can target new teachers, making a game of pushing the discipline as far as they can, and maintaining a low level of disruption that is difficult and tiresome to control. In the worst situations, pupils can play games such as persistent humming, pen clicking, or spitballing (paper balls, covered in spit, which are fired across the room by blowing them through a pen casing). In the context of widespread unruly behaviour in the classroom, it becomes difficult to spot and deal effectively with the particular perpetrator, and yet unfair to issue a whole-class punishment. Unchecked, the lesson may feel (and look) anarchic.

The reality of teaching is that the teacher is put in a difficult situation in terms of deciding which acts of indiscipline to act upon and which to overlook. In the case of the pupil who is struggling at home to cope with a family break up, violence or drug abuse, is it really appropriate to discipline them for asking to borrow a pen at an inconvenient moment? Should you allow that pupil to get up out of their seat to borrow a pen from a classmate without asking your permission? Some teachers argue that for some pupils it becomes more important to maintain a positive learning environment and, as such, small misdemeanours (such as wearing nail varnish) should be overlooked if they are not affecting the work. However, it is always important to maintain fairness and firm boundaries.

In the worst cases, a slippery slope of overlooked misdemeanours can lead to a situation where pupils feel that they can talk over you, get up out of their seats, shout at other pupils, throw things across the room, and do very little work. The teacher feels that they cannot possibly discipline the whole class, and any attempt to discipline one or two pupils results in a battle of wills, with students claiming unfairness, such as 'He was doing it too' or 'I was only talking because she asked me a question.' In some such classes, less confident teachers may panic and decide that they have to just plough on with the lesson to at least get some work done. In addition, many teachers may feel that punishing too many pupils could just reflect badly on them, and so might simply struggle on rather than ask for help.

Strategies to deal with such classes could include:

- *Ask for help from senior management.* A stern word at the beginning of the next lesson from a member of senior management sends a clear message to pupils that the school is on your side and such disruption will not be tolerated for any class with any teacher.

- *Ask for help from other colleagues.* Arrange lesson observations with colleagues, both to watch more experienced teachers teach similar classes, or ideally some of the same students in a different subject to observe which techniques work for them. Invite the colleague to watch you with the class, not to grade the lesson but to offer advice. Many schools have a buddy or 'peer mentor' system where reciprocal lesson observations are arranged as part of the in-school professional development.

- *Effective use of teaching assistants.* Speak to any teaching assistants or other support staff working with you prior to the lesson and agree on a strategy, e.g. assign an assistant to particular pupils with an expected amount of work to get through. You can also use them as a second pair of eyes to help with identifying the cause of any future misbehaviour.

- *Establish clear rules.* Remind the class of the school rules and stick them in the front of their exercise books to refer to.

- *Adopt a seating plan.* Whether boy/girl, mixed ability groups, streamed tables or as far apart as possible, use your seating plan to your advantage by separating troublesome students, e.g. you could seat loud pupils with a tendency to shout out at the front.

- *Make sure you are adopting the school's discipline procedures.* Most schools adopt a staged response for dealing with pupil misbehaviour; make sure you are following this (see below).

School policy and procedures

Most schools will have a clear behaviour management policy that should be followed to the letter. When you are dealing with a class where you feel you are in danger of losing control, make sure you are following the school's procedure in a consistent and systematic manner. Once pupils recognise that misbehaviour is dealt with in a consistent manner and that consequences will follow if it continues, then managerial control of the lesson should improve. It is the pupil's sense that their misbehaviour does not have consequences that often lies at the heart of discipline being lost.

School procedures for dealing with pupil misbehaviour commonly have a phased system of warnings and sanctions. The following set of stages is typical.

- *Issue a verbal warning.* Indicate to the pupil that they have done or are doing something unacceptable, and you are giving them a warning that unacceptable behaviour must not continue. This can be given more force if you write the name of the pupil you are warning on the board, which serves to remind them that this is a serious warning, as well as reminding you whom you have given a verbal warning to.

- *Give a written warning.* This warning should be officially recorded, for example in the pupil's planner, and you should indicate that you are now getting very concerned. This is a good time to check carefully whether you can apply a strategy that will get the pupil re-engaged in the lesson, and check whether there is a problem that is preventing them working.

You should also warn the pupil that continued misbehaviour will mean they will have to move to another seat or be given a detention (you need to specify which).

- *Move the pupil to another seat or issue a detention*. At this point you have a choice. Whichever you do allows the alternative to come into play if necessary before moving on to the next stage (removal from the classroom). If the pupil is moved within the classroom, this is normally to a seat at the front. The new location provides you with an opportunity to monitor and talk to the pupil, and gets the pupil away from the location where the problem was occurring. At this point, you may be able to make use of a teaching assistant or other support staff present in the lesson to encourage the pupil to stay focused on the work that is expected of them. The alternative is to issue a detention. This could be a break-time detention or an after-school detention (you will need to make sure you are in line with the school's behaviour management procedures when you issue a detention). If the misbehaviour continues after moving the pupil to another seat and/or issuing a detention, you need to consider the pupil's removal from the classroom.

- *Remove the pupil from the classroom*. Move the pupil out of the classroom, for example to a pre-decided classroom, often timetabled with a senior teacher or with an older group of pupils. In most schools a system is established in the school whereby the pupil will be collected and escorted by another member of staff to the new location. A milder version of this is sending the pupil outside the classroom to wait in the corridor for a specified length of time (e.g. ten minutes) or an unspecified time. You will need to consider beforehand whether the pupil is likely to wander off or cause further disruption by looking through the door or window. You will also need to think carefully about how you handle talking to the pupil while they are in the corridor and, if appropriate, the pupil's re-entry into the classroom and where the pupil will be told to sit. You also need to check whether this is allowed in the school policy on pupil behaviour, as some schools do not allow teachers to send pupils out of the classroom in an unsupervised manner.

- *Further consequences*. If the pupil is sent to another classroom and continues to misbehave in the new classroom, it is likely that a member of the school's senior management team or behaviour management team will take the pupil to another designated room (such as an isolation room). At this stage the school will start to explore the nature of the problem in more depth and consider the most appropriate way ahead.

This may involve contacting the parents/carers and the involvement of professional agencies outside the school. Such further consequences may also be triggered when a pupil is receiving a frequent number of written warnings, which in themselves convey to the pupil the seriousness of the situation and its possible consequences.

Following the school policy not only reinforces the expected behaviour and system of sanctions, but reminds the pupil that you are following a non-negotiable set of procedures. Actions such as telephoning home should only be done in accordance with school policy and usually through the pastoral team or senior management. The school policy on dealing with misbehaviour is reinforced with a positive behaviour policy, including the use of praise and rewards.

What schools can and cannot do is shaped by government policy and legalisation. You will find it helpful to review the advice and guidance on dealing with pupil misbehaviour outlined in national documents and reports (e.g. DfE, 2014). Doing so not only helps develop your own thinking and practice, but can also help you feed your ideas into the discussion of changes to school policy and procedures.

Further reading

Dansie, T. (2016). *Improving Behaviour Management in Your School. Creating Calm Spaces for Pupils to Learn and Flourish.* Abingdon: Routledge. An excellent book that looks at how pupils who exhibit challenging behaviour can be helped to overcome this tendency by thinking differently about themselves and how to react in certain situations. You will find Chapter 7, on practical classroom strategies, particularly helpful.

Leaman, L. (2009). *Managing Very Challenging Behaviour* (2nd ed.). London: Continuum. A clear and helpful guide to key strategies that can be employed when dealing with challenging behaviour by pupils.

Porter, L. (2014). *Behaviour in Schools: Theory and Practice for Teachers* (3rd ed.). Maidenhead: Open University Press. A useful account of different ways of looking at the nature and causes of pupil misbehaviour and their implications for how to promote good behaviour.

Rogers, B. (2015). *Classroom Behaviour: A Practical Guide to Effective Teaching, Behaviour Management and Colleague Support* (4th ed.). London: Sage. An excellent guide to dealing with pupil misbehaviour.

Key questions

1   Is my practice embedded within a positive classroom climate characterised by mutual respect and rapport and positive expectations, and linked with good lesson presentation and management?

2   Is my authority established and accepted by pupils, and do I try out different ways of reducing the incidence of challenges and consult with colleagues on this?

3   Am I clear and consistent in establishing rules and expectations regarding pupils' behaviour?

4   Do I make good use of general teaching skills and pre-emptive strategies to minimise pupil misbehaviour?

5   Do I make good use of investigating and counselling strategies, reprimands and punishments, to deal with pupil misbehaviour skilfully?

6   Are the strategies I use to deal with pupil misbehaviour employed flexibly and skilfully to take account of which strategy is likely to be most effective and appropriate to the situation?

7   Do my strategies encourage good behaviour without undermining a positive classroom climate?

8   Do I avoid confrontations where possible, and efficiently and effectively diffuse those that do occur?

9   Am I sufficiently sensitive to my pastoral care role and alert to any particular needs of individual pupils that give cause for concern?

10 Do I make adequate use of consultation with colleagues and ensure that my actions are in line with the school's policy and procedures on behaviour management?

Chapter 8

Assessing pupils' progress

The regular assessment of pupils' progress is part and parcel of teaching and learning in the classroom. Such assessment may range from simply looking over pupils' shoulders while they are writing during a period of classwork, to the use of formally administered external examinations. There are many types of activities used to assess pupils' progress, each with their own particular processes and procedures (Dix, 2010; Murchan and Shiel, 2017). Nevertheless, the skilful use of assessment techniques can be identified, and will be highlighted in this chapter.

The phrase 'fitness for purpose' applies more importantly to assessment than to any other aspect of your work. Because assessment is very time-consuming, it is very easy to find yourself spending hours collating records of assessment that you later realise you have no productive use for; or to spend hours making detailed notes on pupils' test papers only to find later that pupils are given no opportunity to read and make use of these comments. Therefore one of the key teaching skills involves the skilful matching of the type of assessment activity chosen and the way you make use of it (Boyle and Charles, 2014; Gardner, 2011).

The purposes of assessment

Essentially, assessment can be any activity used to appraise pupils' performance. The learning outcomes promoted by schools concern helping pupils to develop knowledge, understanding, skills, and attitudes. Assessment therefore refers to techniques you can use to monitor pupils' progress in terms of specific learning outcomes. The first and most important question facing you in assessing pupils' progress is 'why?'. What purpose have you in mind for the assessment activity?

Assessment can serve a number of different purposes. The most frequently used purposes are as follows:

- *To help pupils make progress.* Above all, assessment activities are there to enhance pupil learning. We can subdivide this one central purpose into various underlying tasks, but we must never lose sight of this key central purpose.

- *To provide you with feedback about pupils' progress.* Such feedback enables you to consider how effective your teaching has been in achieving its intended learning outcomes. In particular, it may highlight certain problems or misunderstandings that have arisen, which will require remedial action in your subsequent teaching.

- *To provide you with feedback about your teaching.* Pupils' performance in assessment tasks provides you with useful information on what and how you teach, and on how you need to adjust your teaching in order to facilitate better learning.

- *To provide pupils with educative feedback.* Assessment enables pupils to relate their performance to the standard expected, to use detailed feedback to correct and improve their work, and to appreciate more clearly the requirements of the tasks set (e.g. regarding the layout of the work or procedures used).

- *To motivate pupils.* Assessment activities can act as a spur to pupils to organise their work well and to learn what is required so as to achieve at these activities. The spur may be largely based on intrinsic motivation, extrinsic motivation, or a mix of both. Feedback of success at a challenging task is particularly effective in stimulating future motivation.

- *To provide a record of progress.* Regular assessment activities enable you to keep a record of pupils' progress over a long period. This can then form the basis for your decisions about individual pupils' current and future educational needs, particularly if a cause for concern arises. It can also be used when communicating with others, including parents, and may influence your future planning of teaching similar groups.

- *To provide a statement of current attainment.* A specific assessment activity or group of activities can be used to identify the standard of attainment achieved at a particular point in time. Such attainment may form the basis of certification, or a formal statement issued to others, most notably parents.

- *To assess pupils' readiness for future learning.* Assessment can be used to indicate whether pupils are ready for a particular type of learning (e.g. readiness to learn to read), whether they have any specific learning difficulties, or, more simply, whether they have covered the previous learning required for the new topic to be taught effectively (if not, revision or prior preparation will be needed).

- *To provide evidence of teacher and school effectiveness.* Pupils' performance in assessment tasks provides evidence of their progress and acts as a useful indicator of teacher and school effectiveness.

Your decisions about how and what to assess will therefore depend on the exact purpose or purposes you have in mind for the assessment. Part of the difficulty facing teachers in making skilful and effective use of assessment is the need to meet different purposes and uses of assessment at the same time, and to ensure that any undesirable side-effects are avoided or limited as far as possible.

Dangers of assessment

There are three particular dangers to be guarded against when using assessment activities. First, and most serious, is the danger that pupils may become disheartened and upset if they find that the feedback on their progress indicates they are doing less well than peers, or are below some standard of attainment of value to them. This may lead to them becoming disenchanted and alienated from schooling, and sinking into a vicious cycle of increasing underachievement. Second, the procedures and practices adopted for assessing pupils' progress may be too time-consuming and bureaucratic for teachers and pupils, such that it encroaches undesirably on time and energy that could be better spent on other activities. Third, it may lead teachers and pupils to becoming over-concerned with pupils performing well in assessment. In particular, the lessons and assessment activities (both in terms of content and in terms of the teaching and learning processes involved) may become geared to promoting success in attainment tests at the expense of the quality of educational experiences occurring in the classroom.

Because assessment practices are so interlinked with teaching and learning, the skilful use of assessment practices that complement and facilitate the hallmarks of effective teaching considered in previous chapters is essential. Where assessment practices are used that have undesirable side-effects, these can make it much more difficult to teach effectively. Indeed, many of the reforms in assessment practices over the years have stemmed precisely from the recognition of the important role of assessment in promoting effective teaching.

It is also important to note that, when you assess a task in which the pupil has used IT, you need to make a distinction between the quality of the pupil's use of IT and the pupil's subject-related attainment (Briggs et al., 2003). The pupil may well have used the IT well, but this may not have enhanced their understanding and attainment in the subject.

Types of assessment

As a result of the diversity in the type of assessment practices used in schools, a number of key terms are now frequently referred to. The most important of these are as follows:

- *Formative assessment.* This is assessment aimed at promoting effective future learning by pupils. It may do this by giving pupils helpful feedback, or by giving you feedback or information that will enable you to meet the pupil's future learning needs more effectively. Typically, such assessment tends to identify errors, difficulties or shortcomings in the pupil's work and offer advice, guidance and information to improve future performance. Unlike summative assessment (see below), formative assessment occurs throughout teaching and learning.

- *Summative assessment.* This is assessment that identifies the standard of attainment achieved at a particular moment in time, normally carried out at the end of a period of instruction (e.g. end of term, end of course). The most typical examples of these are the grades used on school reports of attainment, or the results of external examinations.

- *Norm-referenced assessment.* The grading of each pupil's performance is related to the performance of others. For example, if a grade A is defined as the level of performance achieved by the top 10 per cent of the assessment cohort, this would mean that no matter how high or low the general standard of work produced was, the best 10 per cent (no more and no less) would always receive a grade A.

- *Criterion-referenced assessment.* The grading of each pupil's performance is judged in terms of whether a particular description of performance (the criterion) has been met. This means that all pupils who meet this criterion would be assessed as achieving the related grade, regardless of how other pupils performed. A typical example of these are graded tests used in music, modern languages and mathematics, the use of grade-related criteria, and level descriptions in attainment tests.

- *Diagnostic assessment.* This overlaps with formative assessment, but specifically identifies learning difficulties or problems. Certain tests can be used to identify particular needs (e.g. dyslexia) and related to pupils' education, health and care plans.

- *Internal assessment.* These assessment activities are devised, carried out and marked by the class teacher, and often used as part of their own programme of teaching.

- *External assessment.* These assessment activities are devised by examiners outside the school, and usually also marked by external assessors, although in many cases marking can be done by the class teacher but is then checked ('moderated') by external assessors on a sample basis.

- *Informal assessment.* Assessment is based on the observation of performance, which occurs in the classroom as part of normal classroom practice.

- *Formal assessment.* This is assessment that is made following prior warning that an assessment will be carried out. This normally allows the pupil an opportunity to revise and prepare for the assessment.

- *Continuous assessment.* The final assessment of the standard of attainment achieved is based on pieces of assessment made over a long period of time.

- *Terminal assessment.* The final assessment of the standard of attainment achieved is based on an assessment made solely at the end of the course or programme of work.

- *Objective assessment.* This refers to assessment activities and associated marking schemes that have extremely high agreement between assessors on the marks awarded. The best example of this is the use of multiple-choice tests.

- *Subjective assessment.* These are assessment activities that are based on a subjective and impressionistic judgement of a piece of work. An example of this would be judging a painting, a vignette of acting, or a piece of creative writing.

- *Process assessment.* This is assessment of an ongoing activity, such as reading aloud a poem or designing and conducting an experiment, in which the assessment is based on direct observation of the performance while in progress.

- *Product assessment.* This is assessment based on a tangible piece of work, such as an essay, project, model or examination script, submitted for the purpose of assessment.

Discussion about types of assessment typically considers contrasting pairs, most notably:

- formative versus summative

- norm-referenced versus criterion-referenced

- internal versus external

- informal versus formal

- continuous versus terminal

- objective versus subjective

- process versus product.

While this is often helpful, the nature of assessment practices is often such that a mixture of each contrasting pair is in fact involved. So, for example, one may imagine that an end-of-year school report was primarily a summative assessment, but inspection of its content may reveal many comments and pieces of information clearly intended to be formative. Similarly, an assessment scheme for marking a coursework project may claim to be primarily criterion-referenced, but close inspection may reveal aspects that are clearly norm-referenced. In tailoring your assessment practice to the purpose you have in mind, it is most important that the assessment is effective in meeting the needs you have for it. Over-concern with its purity, in terms of pigeonholing its type, is likely to be unproductive.

Assessment for learning

The phrase 'assessment for learning' (AfL) refers to the ways in which teachers can make use of a variety of assessment activities to enable pupils to gain a clearer understanding of their learning and how learning is assessed, so that pupils' future learning and performance in tests of attainment are enhanced. This phrase builds upon and extends the notion of formative assessment, and has also been included as an important strand of personalised learning (Bennett, 2011; Black et al., 2003; Wiliam, 2011). The skilful use of formative assessment in promoting motivation and learning is widely recognised (Boyle and Charles, 2014; O'Donnell et al., 2007). The principles that underpin AfL are:

- it focuses on how pupils learn

- it helps pupils know how to improve

- it is sensitive to the context

- it promotes pupils' understanding of goals and criteria

- it develops pupils' ability to assess their own learning.

A simple example of such teaching would be to ask a pair of pupils to mark each other's work in response to an assessment task using a specified set of criteria, and then to ask the pupils to discuss whether the mark they gave had been fair. The teacher can then have a useful discussion with pupils about how and why assessors use specified criteria to mark work, and how this can inform their own learning.

There may, however, be important differences between how teachers perceive using AfL activities in the classroom and how these are perceived by the pupils, which can influence the effective use of these strategies. Pat-El et al. (2013) have argued that for AfL to be successful there needs to be an integration of assessment with learning that the teacher and pupils both understand in the same way. Pat-El et al. developed a 28-item questionnaire to explore AfL practice in the classroom, which was validated with a sample of 237 teachers and 1,422 pupils in secondary schools in the Netherlands. The analysis of their questionnaire highlights two separate aspects of AfL: first, its use to monitor pupil progress, and second, its use to scaffold pupils' understanding of how they can improve. Their analysis also illustrates that what determines whether an assessment activity is summative or formative in nature depends on how it is used.

One of the most important skills you need to develop concerns how to give feedback to pupils, whether it be during classroom interaction or when marking their written work. When giving feedback, you need to think carefully about how the feedback you give will enhance the pupil's learning. Giving feedback to pupils is at its best and most effective when it is purposeful – in other words, when the feedback you give is tailored to the pupil's learning (Dann, 2018).

A number of templates or formats have been developed in order to provide feedback to pupils that will be as helpful as possible to their learning and to their performance in future attainment tests. For example, there are strategies such as giving What Went Well (WWW) and Even Better If (EBI) comments. Providing a WWW comment and an EBI comment enables the pupil to receive some praise for their work as well as explicit advice on how to improve. You might then ask the pupil to respond to your comments with a My Response Is (MRI) comment. In some cases, you might discuss your comments with the pupil and/or ask the pupil to repeat the work in the light of these comments, in order to display a higher level of performance.

Peer and self-assessment activities are a widely used aspect of the formative assessment approach. These activities can not only help pupils to develop the habit of self-reflection regarding their own work, but can also help them to better understand the quality of their work by both thinking about how their peers evaluate their work, and how they evaluate their peers' work.

Organising such activities, however, is not simply a matter of allowing pupils to engage in them. Rather, the teacher also needs to engage in a dialogue with pupils during and after these activities, in order to enhance what pupils have understood and gained. This can also lead to a fruitful whole-class discussion of what pupils have learned from their peer and self-assessment.

Improving assessment practices

Looking at the types of assessments listed from page 166, and bearing in mind the range of *learning outcomes* that can be assessed (knowledge, understanding, skills and attitudes), the type and nature of the *performance involved* (oral, written, practical, coursework, tests, examinations) and the *educational domains* (academic subjects, study skills, personal and social education), it is perhaps not surprising that a number of complex issues underlie the skilful assessment of pupils' progress. Attempts to improve the nature and quality of assessment practices used in schools are continually evident in many countries.

National tests and examinations are used in many countries to monitor and accredit pupils' progress and attainment. The results of these tests and examinations can provide an indication of each pupil's individual progress as well as the general progress made by pupils in each school compared with other schools. However, a number of problems and issues have emerged concerning the use of national tests and examinations that generate 'league tables' to monitor standards and make judgements about relative school effectiveness. In particular, it has generated a culture that puts teachers under pressure to 'teach for the test' in a way that emphasises performativity (pupils performing well in an attainment test) at the expense of real understanding and enjoyment (Gardner, 2011). For example, a teacher may prepare pupils strategically by emphasising only certain parts of the programme of study. Teaching for the test provides a good example of how teachers with high levels of teaching skills still have to make ethical judgments about aspects of their classroom practice when placed under pressure to meet targets. On the one hand, you want your pupils to do as well as possible in examinations; on the other hand, you also want the learning experience to be positive and engaging, to promote high-quality learning, understanding and interest, and to enhance pupils' attitudes towards themselves as learners. Teaching is not just about grades, but is also about offering high-quality educational experiences.

Value-added and baseline assessments

One major problem that has been highlighted in respect of using league tables based solely on giving the final level of attainment of each pupil is that such tables do not provide a fair indicator of a teacher's or a school's effectiveness; rather, what needs to be considered is each pupil's progress. Value-added refers to the difference between a pupil's initial level of attainment and their final level of attainment. It is argued that by taking account of pupils' prior levels of attainment, we can see whether a teacher or school is performing better or worse than one would have expected. Such an initial assessment is called a 'baseline assessment'.

Many primary and secondary schools carry out baseline assessments for each new intake of pupils, in the areas of language and literacy, mathematics, and personal and social development. These are based on the class teacher's observations of a range of classroom activities during pupils' first few months at the school or by making use of standardised tests developed for this purpose.

The use of data on pupils' initial levels of attainment, whether based on teacher assessments, standardised tests, or the results of national tests and examinations, together with information about the general socio-economic circumstances of the pupils, allows comparisons to be made between teachers and schools based on measures of value-added. Nationally produced tables of pupil progress and attainment at each school now include information about value-added.

It is now common practice for schools to make use of data that compares pupils' progress in their own school with the progress of pupils with similar prior attainment nationally. This can sometimes put teachers under pressure to explain why pupils in their school may be doing less well than similar pupils in comparable schools. While comparative data of this sort can provide a useful guidance, it is certainly not an exact science that enables a fair comparison to be made that takes proper account of all the relevant differences in circumstances. This includes the problem of a school using a baseline measurement carried out by others who may seek advantage in the baseline measure being slightly higher or lower than is valid.

Skills in assessing pupils' progress

Developing skills in the ability to assess pupils is very important; this is recognised by being included in various lists of the skills teachers are expected to have. These typically include elements regarding assessment such as the following:

- knowledge of the assessment requirements for the subjects/curriculum areas and age ranges they teach

- knowledge of a range of approaches to assessment, including the importance of formative assessment

- knowledge of how to use local and national statistical information to evaluate the effectiveness of their own teaching, to monitor their pupils' progress, and to raise their pupils' levels of attainment

- making use of a range of assessment, monitoring and recording strategies

- assessing the learning needs of pupils in order to set challenging learning objectives

- providing timely, accurate and constructive feedback on pupils' attainment, progress and areas for development.

Records of achievement

One of the criticisms made for many years concerning assessment was that pupils were often awarded a single mark or grade to indicate their attainment, and that this provided very little useful information to pupils and others (including parents, employers, and university admissions tutors). This has led to a major development in assessment practice over the years: the introduction of ways in which a much fuller record of pupils' progress in a school can be recorded, including both academic and non-academic aspects. This includes the introduction of documents that provides the pupil with a record of their achievements while at the school. These are typically given to pupils when they reach school-leaving age, and aim to include as full a range of their achievements during their school careers as possible, both academic and non-academic. A number of primary schools also produce such records. Evaluation studies, however, have indicated that teachers need to develop a host of new assessment practices and procedures, and to operate these skilfully, for these documents to be produced efficiently and with validity.

Assessment materials

Another major development in assessment practice has been the provision by awarding bodies of sample assessment materials in order to help teachers understand what type of work by pupils equates to particular levels of grades. One of the most powerful learning experiences for a teacher regarding the assessment of pupil attainment is to become an examiner for an awarding body. This provides you with a clear understanding of what examiners are looking for in awarding marks, which you can then pass on to your pupils.

Assessment activities in the classroom

As discussed earlier, assessment activities are going on in the classroom all the time, ranging from asking pupils questions during classwork to administering a formal written examination. In carrying out assessment activities, you need to be clear about the main purpose or purposes of the assessment and the type of assessment you want to use. After this, you are then ready to think about how best to select, design and carry out the appropriate assessment activities themselves.

It is important to note here that AfL activities, and, in particular, formative assessment strategies, permeate all teaching and learning in the classroom. This could take the form of asking a pupil to use a whiteboard to generate ideas on which you can monitor and give feedback, either individually or to the class, to help improve the next stage of their work. Alternatively, it could take the form of exit cards, on which pupils have to write down three things they've learned from the lesson, which can then feed into your planning for the next lesson.

In addition, summative assessment is also occurring in various forms in order to generate data about pupil progress. This can also provide formative opportunities to pupils in helping them to understand what they need to do to reach or exceed individual progress targets.

Figure 8.1: You should use a wide range of assessment activities

Monitoring classwork activities

Monitoring classwork activities is a central aspect of teaching, and is bound up with your decision-making about the progress of the lesson and the feedback you give to pupils to facilitate their learning. The most important aspect of such assessment is that you ensure that you monitor all pupils' progress regularly (not just those who frequently demand or require more attention). Furthermore, your monitoring should be investigative and active, in the sense that you actively probe pupils' current understanding and difficulties rather than simply rely on this being drawn to your attention in some way. Many forms of assessment in common use now involve teachers monitoring pupil performance during classwork.

Designated assessment tasks integrated within classwork

There is a thin line between monitoring classwork activities and using designated assessment tasks integrated within classwork. Some activities that need to be assessed occur in classwork on a regular basis, whereas others need to be specifically designed and introduced for the purpose of the assessment. The latter is often the case if it is important for the task to be carefully standardised and assessed in terms of specific criteria that require close attention. In either case, however, you need to consider how you should forewarn pupils that a particular assessment activity is to take place and indicate its purpose and use.

As the range of activities that can occur within the classroom increases, so does the range of assessment skills teachers need to develop. For example, the skills needed to give formative assessment for a slideshow presentation and the skills needed to then assess the final product will be quite new for a teacher who has not taught and assessed such work before. A study by Postholm (2006) looked at the skills involved in the ways in which teachers can monitor and support pupils undertaking project work, encourage and help pupils to assess their own work and the work of other pupils, and in discussion with the pupil explain how the final grade for the finished piece of work was arrived at and justified. In particular, Postholm focused on the quality of the dialogue that occurred between the teacher and pupil to illustrate how the teacher was able to help foster pupils' learning during the ongoing assessment of the project work they were undertaking.

Homework

The use of homework tasks is very important in providing feedback on how well a pupil can perform when unaided. Homework is particularly useful in developing pupils' organisational skills and power of commitment to meet the demands made on them. It can also provide stark feedback to the pupil and to you on the nature of any difficulties or problems that arise which are less evident in the class, where you may be readily available to provide help. Unfortunately, in this respect, parent help is both useful in providing further tuition, but also unhelpful if it readily enables the pupil to enlist assistance rather than persevere with their own efforts. Parental help has also posed problems for the assessment of independent project work done partly or largely at home, and much of such work now has to be based solely on classwork activity.

It is common for homework to be used to assess pupils' previous learning in lessons, which often involves consolidation and practice-type tasks, or to prepare for a test by revising. In addition, however, it is important to use homework to good effect by encouraging new learning. This involves not simply the learning of new material, but also creative investigation and application of the topic area to life outside the school (e.g. listing cubes, spheres and cylinders that can be found in your living room, or exploring the earliest recollections of the pupil's parents about when they first went to school).

You need to think carefully about how you will mark homework, as this can be very time-consuming. You might decide to mark just one aspect of the work, or to make use of generic phrases to indicate areas for improvement. Some teachers make use of a checklist or a grid that can quickly highlight areas of strength and areas that require attention.

Short tests

Short tests devised by you can motivate learning in preparation for more formal attainment tests. Regular tests can be particularly useful in conveying the importance of making progress with new learning, but they can also be very threatening. They must therefore be used with sensitivity and in a way that will facilitate rather than discourage learning. Short tests vary immensely in type and form, ranging from a spelling test based on homework, to an end-of-course or topic tests used to assess academic progress.

Standardised tests

Standardised tests are widely used to monitor progress and attainment in key areas of learning. Such tests are standardised by giving the tests to a large number of pupils of a given age (usually a nationwide sample), so that the score of pupils who are well above average, average, and well below average can be identified. Standardised tests are thus *norm-referenced* tests. Thereafter, when a pupil takes this test, it is easy to see how well they have performed on the test relative to an average pupil of the same age. Intelligence tests are standardised tests. The most commonly used standardised test in learning is for reading, where a pupil's score is normally given in terms of a reading age. If a 10-year-old pupil, for example, takes the test and achieves a reading age of 12 years, this indicates that the pupil's reading level is comparable to the reading level of an average 12-year-old.

A range of other standardised tests in learning include language tasks, mathematics, and tests used as part of screening procedures to identify pupils who may have special educational needs. Such tests are useful in enabling the teacher to compare the result with that expected for a pupil of that age. In using standardised tests, however, you must be alert to their appropriateness for the use you are making of them. In particular, a dated test may well include words, formats or tasks that are no longer commonly used. A mathematics test may explore attainment based on different coverage or a different approach to the one your pupils have experienced. In addition, a test result, of course, can only be based on what was tested, which means that other aspects of performance that may be difficult to test are largely excluded. Given the increasing diversity of learning skills and qualities being fostered in schools, written tests in particular are likely to be inadequate as the major or sole assessment activity used to measure attainment.

Administering some standardised tests will involve particular skills and training, so these may need to be administered by specialist colleagues in your school or by external professionals.

Formal examinations

Formal examinations devised by the school are a common feature of school life. The formality varies, from classroom-based examinations designed and administered by the class teacher at an appropriate time, to examinations designed in collaboration and administered as part of an examination timetable. As well as providing a useful measure of attainment to be used in school reports, they also help pupils to develop examination skills and techniques that prepare them for externally set tests and examinations.

Formal examinations and tests that are set and marked externally by government agencies or examination boards are of major importance in most countries. As such, your role in helping pupils to achieve the highest possible mark in such examinations puts pressure on you to consider how best you can do this. One key aspect of improving your work in this area is to be become as familiar as possible with the type of questions that will appear in external examinations and how the marking scheme works. If you can take up the opportunity to act as an external marker, this can provide you with major insights into how what you teach in the classroom, and in your revision lessons prior to an examination, will maximise your pupils' chances of answering questions in a way that aligns with the marking scheme. Most awarding bodies require you to have had at least a year's experience of teaching a subject before you can apply to be an external marker, and may also require you to undertake some training in this role.

Making use of local and national data on pupil attainment for target setting

Data are available to enable teachers and schools to compare pupil attainment in their own class and school with the standards of pupil attainment achieved locally and nationally. They can also do this in a way that enables them to make comparisons with those schools that have a similar intake of pupils (in terms of their range of ability and the type of community catchment they serve). Such comparisons enable teachers and schools to set sensible targets for raising standards. Comparative school data of this sort can also be used to test whether changes in practice and funded interventions are having the expected beneficial effect on the pupils targeted (Sobel, 2018).

Schools are also making much more use of school-generated data to monitor pupil progress, so that the school can intervene when a pupil appears to be falling below the expected progress based on the previous progress they had made. This can provide useful information to the school and teachers concerning which interventions appear to be helpful to pupils in such circumstances.

As well as tracking an individual pupil's progress, school data systems, such as SIMS, can allow a school to compare various groups of pupils, to identify trends in their progress and whether a particular group has benefited from targeted interventions.

Carrying out assessment activities

In carrying out assessment activities, a number of important points need to be borne in mind.

- The assessment activity must be a fair one, in the sense of relating to the work covered, so that pupils can be reasonably expected to perform well on the activity if progress has been made during the appropriate coursework.

- The assessment activity should relate to the learning outcomes planned by the school, which may be documented in terms of the programmes of study being followed.

- The programme of assessment activities used over a long period should be varied in type and form, so that the full range of learning outcomes intended are assessed in different ways.

- Pupils should be informed about the nature and purpose of assessment activities, how they are used, and the criteria employed that characterise successful performance.

- The conduct of assessment activities should facilitate performance by taking place in appropriate circumstances and, in particular, avoiding disruptions and, so far as possible, minimising pupils' anxieties.

- Assessment activities should be carefully designed to ensure that tasks are unambiguous and the type and nature of performance expected is clear to pupils.

- Most importantly of all, you need to ensure that the assessment activity actually provides a valid assessment of what it is intended to assess.

Skills underlying assessment

Two examples will suffice to illustrate the complex skills needed to carry out assessment activities effectively. The first example concerns designing a multiple-choice test in science. Consider the following question:

In very cold weather, pipes sometimes burst because:

(a) water expands when it freezes.

(b) ice is harder than water.

(c) unlagged pipes always burst.

(d) cold water softens pipes.

In designing this item, the teacher needs to check that the question is clear and appropriate, and that the four options will effectively discriminate between pupils who have the understanding being tested from those who do not. You also need to consider whether this test item is a good example of the particular learning outcome being assessed: knowledge, understanding, ability to relate science to real-life applications, or appreciation of the nature of cause and effect.

A second example is asking a class of junior school-age pupils to write a short story about someone who fell into a river. Such a task could be used to assess a whole range of aspects concerning progress in writing, including technical aspects such as handwriting, grammar, punctuation, and use of capital letters, and aspects of its content, such as creativity, use of ideas, and intelligibility to the reader. In designing this assessment activity, it is important to think first of all about what the task is intended to assess, and to discuss with pupils prior to taking the test what criteria will be used in assessing their work, and what they are expected to do in order to gain a higher mark. So, for example, if you want to test imaginative writing, you could tell pupils to try and make the story as imaginative as possible, as this is the aspect you are assessing, and what characteristics of imaginative writing they could employ (as such, a very imaginative story should still get a high mark even if there are technical shortcomings).

It will be evident from consideration of these two examples that carrying out assessment activities involves a whole range of skills regarding selection, design, implementation, match of activity to purpose, marking procedures, feedback, and appropriate and valid use of the results of the assessment.

Each type of assessment task involves its own set of skills. Teachers who are competent in designing a certain type of task may be much less competent in designing another type of task. Therefore take care not to jump into preparing types of assessment tasks that are new to you, as though all you need is common sense. Rather, see what examples of similar assessment tasks colleagues in the school may have used and get their advice.

Marking, recording and reporting

A number of studies and reports concerning assessment practices in primary and secondary schools have highlighted the importance of sound and appropriate practice regarding the marking of pupils' work and the recording and reporting of pupils' progress (McGill, 2017; Tanner and Jones, 2006). The way in which pupils' work is marked, recorded and reported has a major impact on pupils' subsequent motivation and the effort and strategies they use regarding further learning. As such, the skills displayed by a teacher in this area are of crucial importance.

Marking classwork and homework

The marking of pupils' work during and after lessons needs to be thorough and constructive, and returned in good time. Good practice in marking acts as an important model for pupils in setting them an example of the care and attention that needs to be devoted towards academic tasks, and can thereby maintain a high expectation for the standard of work required. The formative aspect of marking is of fundamental importance to effective teaching and learning. Feedback that enables the pupil to make further progress by understanding more clearly what needs to be done can enhance motivation and self-confidence. For example, a pupil who gets a low mark for the imaginative quality of an essay or for a description of an experimental procedure, but who has had no guidance as to how the work could have been improved, will tend to be disheartened. Constructive and helpful guidance on how a better piece of work could have been produced will help stimulate further progress.

The marking of pupils' work completed as part of classwork and homework tasks is simply an extension of the normal process of teaching and learning. The major challenge facing you in marking pupils' work is how to be helpful and encouraging for the whole range of attainment in the class. The main problem is that norm-referenced marking, based on comparing the work of pupils with each other, will tend to discourage the lower attainers. Therefore most teachers try to make greater use of marking related to attainment standards expected of each pupil, taking account of previous progress. In this respect, good use can be made of tasks that are more clearly matched to each pupil's ability or using tasks that are graded in terms of increasing difficulty. In addition, you may decide to keep the written record of marks in your own record books but not report these to pupils. Instead, your feedback to pupils will take the form of comments about the work, and areas of improvement that are required. It is also important to give feedback about effort, if you feel a pupil has done less well or better than expected as a result of their efforts.

It is also useful to make use of a variety of marking methods, including allowing pupils to mark their own work or each other's from time to time. In addition, marks over a period of time should also be based on a variety of assessment activities, to ensure that the run of marks reflects different aspects of attainment. The most important function of marking to bear in mind is that it should provide helpful and encouraging feedback to pupils about their progress. Part of this may mean that pupils will need help in their thinking about their study skills and how they organise their work, so that they can better prepare for such assessment tasks in future.

The importance of developing the skills involved in assessing pupils' work is highlighted in a study by Smith and Gorard (2005). It is increasingly recognised that formative assessment has a much greater emphasis on providing pupils with more detailed formative feedback on their work. One school studied by Smith and Gorard sought to take this one step further by exploring whether giving pupils formative feedback without an overall grade or mark would be more effective in promoting pupil attainment. Smith and Gorard found that the use of the 'formative feedback only' approach showed no evidence of being more effective, and in some areas of the data on pupil attainment, it appeared to be less effective. However, what was perhaps most evident from the study were apparent shortcomings in the quality of the formative feedback given at this school. The study highlights how a school cannot simply take what is advocated to be good practice 'off the shelf' and apply it at their own school; rather, the teachers involved have to develop the necessary understanding and skills underpinning the practice being adopted, In addition, it is important for everyone at the school to be able to apply the school's marking policy consistently.

There is another lesson to draw from this study, which is the importance of taking account of the context and prevailing practice within a school when a new initiative is evaluated. For example, if the school placed a lot of emphasis on the grade awarded, that alone might lead to pupils becoming habitually used to just focusing on the grade, rather than being open to making use of formative feedback designed to help them improve their grade.

Marking formal assessment tasks

As well as marking classwork and homework, you will also be marking a whole range of formal assessment tasks, including tests and examinations. The skills involved in such marking have become increasingly complex with the growth of more detailed marking practices. Performance in a subject or area of the curriculum is now typically divided into a number of components or elements, and the marking scheme is devised so that the mark awarded on a particular aspect of performance is clearly related to the component or element being assessed. This enables attainment to be recorded in terms of a profile of components rather than as an overall single mark or grade, or if the latter is the case, the single mark or grade is based on a specified weighting of the different components involved. For example, assessing a practical project might involve making a separate assessment on each of three stages involved: (i) planning the project, (ii) carrying out the project and analysing the data collected, and (iii) drawing conclusions.

Therefore the marking of formal tasks involves careful consideration, not so much of the correctness of the pupil's performance, but rather a judgement of what the quality of the performance indicates. A programme of study needs to specify the knowledge, understanding and skills that comprise educational attainment. Designing and marking assessment tasks requires a clear appreciation of how performance relates to educational attainment.

So, for example, a programme of study in science might require pupils to be able to measure variations in living organisms. The task used to measure this must carefully take account of what precise type of pupil performance would exemplify this statement. Doing this needs to reflect a clear understanding of what the statement means and requires a mark scheme for performance that is fair, reliable, valid and practical.

Marking personal qualities and attitudes

The assessment of personal qualities and attitudes has always posed problems of reliability and validity. While most teachers form impressionistic judgements about these, some forms of assessment, such as Records of Achievement, have demanded that such judgements be based on performance related to particular tasks where a fair opportunity to display particular qualities or attitudes (such as acting responsibly, showing initiative, working conscientiously when unsupervised) can be given. Again, it is important to prepare pupils for such assessment and to discuss with them what is expected, and how marks or grades are achieved.

Recording and reporting pupils' progress

The need for teachers to keep good records of pupils' progress has been emphasised frequently by Ofsted in their inspections of schools. However, it is also important to recognise that the usefulness of keeping records is dependent on the extent to which the records are in fact used. Keeping records that are much too detailed or in a form that serves little purpose will not be a good use of your time.

Figure 8.2: Keep good records of your pupils' progress

Keeping a good record of pupils' progress should serve three main functions:

- It should provide a useful basis from which reports to others (e.g. the pupils themselves, parents, other teachers, other establishments) can be made.

- It should highlight any cause for concern if a pupil's performance shows a marked drop compared with previous progress.

- It should facilitate the planning of future work with each pupil by building upon previous progress and, in particular, by ensuring that progress is adequate in its breadth and depth of coverage and that areas requiring remedial work receive attention.

In addition, such records can usefully contribute to the school's general decision-making about their own effectiveness and their coverage of the programmes of study. In this respect, notes about the work covered, including samples of pupils' work and test scores, can help to ensure that the curriculum provided each year matches pupils' needs and abilities adequately.

As noted earlier, school data systems, such as SIMS, have transformed the amount of data that a school can use to track the progress of individual pupils or particular groups of pupils. This also means that information on pupils' progress can be shared with pupils and their parents much more frequently than in end of term reports.

Feedback to pupils about their progress is extremely important in contributing to motivation and further progress, as has been noted already. In addition, however, you also need to report on pupils' progress on a regular basis to parents, both in the form of written reports and during meetings with them.

Written reports to parents have been the subject of much debate. On the one hand, parents typically complain that they would like to receive reports more frequently, in more detail, and for reports to be more meaningful. On the other hand, teachers complain that producing such reports is very time-consuming and involves a number of problems that are not easy to resolve. For example, there is a tension between giving honest reports and not being demoralising if the comments are critical or reflect low attainment; in addition, it is difficult to summarise performance in a way that is concise but that still provides useful information for parents.

Writing reports that are fair, valid, meaningful to the reader, and have a positive effect on future progress involves a number of skills. As well as making good use of your knowledge about each pupil and your records of progress, you need to make comments that are helpful and constructive. Where you need to be critical, this should usefully point to what needs to be done in future to improve matters. In addition, school reports also need to adhere to relevant national guidance concerning their content and format.

The time you spend on assessment activities, whether it be formative assessment, recording and reporting pupil progress, or the use of school data systems, is an area of your workload where you have to think carefully about how best to make the most efficient use of your time (DfE, 2018).

Further reading

Boyle, B., & Charles, M. (2014). *Formative Assessment for Teaching and Learning.* London: Sage. A very useful guide to how teachers can use assessment to improve the quality of pupil learning.

Dann, R. (2018). *Developing Feedback for Pupil Learning: Teaching, Learning and Assessment in Schools.* Abingdon: Routledge. An excellent consideration of the role played by the effective use of feedback to enhance pupil learning.

Gardner, J.R. (Ed.). (2011). *Assessment and Learning.* (2nd ed.). London: Sage. An excellent analysis of the issues involved in considering how the 'assessment for learning' approach can contribute to improved classroom practice. You will find Chapter 7, on quality assessment practice, and Chapter 11, on the role of assessment in developing motivation for learning, are especially helpful.

Murchan, D., & Shiel, G. (2017). *Understanding and Applying Assessment in Education.* London: Sage. A very clear and helpful overview of aspects of assessment in schools, with excellent guidance on how to apply these ideas in the classroom. The illustrative examples given in Chapter 5 are very helpful.

Key questions

1   Do I audit my use of a variety of assessment strategies in my teaching, and evaluate which of these are the most useful in helping pupils to make progress?

2   Do I make use of the various purposes for assessment, including both formative and summative purposes and also as a means of monitoring the success of my own teaching and further planning?

3   Do I ensure that each assessment activity is well tailored to the purpose for which it is intended?

4   Is my marking of assessment tasks and feedback to pupils sufficiently speedy, thorough, constructive and helpful, so as to foster and sustain pupils' motivation and self-confidence and facilitate further progress?

5   Do I help pupils to prepare for assessment tasks so as to enable them to achieve success by having a clear understanding of the expectations required and how these can best be achieved?

6   Are the assessment activities I use fair in terms of being well matched to the work covered and to pupils' abilities, and in terms of being valid indicators of the learning outcomes being monitored?

7   Are the assessment activities carried out in a way that will facilitate achievement?

8   Do I help develop pupils' ability to evaluate their own progress through the use of self-assessment activities?

9   Are my records of pupils' progress based on a variety of types of assessment activities and different aspects of performance, and are they well suited to the purposes for which the records are kept, including for my own use, for use by parents and colleagues, and for the assessment of good practice in the school by external assessors?

10 Do I make the most efficient use of the time I spend on assessment activities, whether it be formative assessment, recording and reporting pupil progress, or the use of school data systems?

Chapter 9

Reflection

All teachers spend a great deal of time reflecting about and evaluating how well they are performing their work, both with particular regard to their classroom teaching and to other aspects of their work in general. Reflection and evaluation are inherent in the job and are an essential part of developing your teaching skills (McGregor and Cartwright, 2011). All teachers need to be able to:

- evaluate the impact of their teaching on the progress of all pupils, and modify their planning and classroom practice where necessary

- reflect on and improve their practice and take responsibility for identifying and meeting their developing professional needs

- identify priorities for their professional development.

It is impossible to meet the various demands of teaching without planning, organising and evaluating the activities you carry out. What differs between teachers, however, is how skilfully and systematically they carry this out. It is easy as a teacher to operate within the bubble of your classroom and school, and in a trial-and-error manner gradually develop your own style of teaching, which becomes a set of well-used habitual practices. However, an important part of your professionalism is that your practice must be continually informed and updated by considering other approaches. An essential aspect of doing this is to make use of meetings, conferences, courses, and Internet-based literature dealing with the improvement of teaching and learning in schools. There is a wide variety of government agencies, teacher unions, subject associations, educational research associations, and other national and local organisations, which provide activities and materials to enhance your reflection on your current practice.

Reflective teaching

Over the years, this quality of critically thinking about your own performance in the classroom, often referred to as 'reflective teaching' (Pollard et al., 2014), has been widely advocated as needing to be fostered and encouraged as part of teachers' normal practice and professional development.

All teachers do this intuitively most of the time. The quality of a teacher's reflection about their own practice is seen by many to underpin the teacher's ability to develop and improve their teaching. Many writers have made an important distinction here between reflecting on one's teaching while the teaching is in progress, in order to be able to make effective adjustments to a lesson in the light of how well the intended learning by pupils is progressing, and reflecting on one's teaching after the lesson, in order to inform one's teaching in the future (Zeichner and Liston, 2014).

In addition, some teachers have also been involved in more systematic self-appraisal processes, either as part of a specific scheme of self-evaluation within the school or as part of a network of teachers who have been involved in researching aspects of their own practice within the teacher action research movement (Baumfield et al., 2013).

Working with other teachers as part of a learning community has been increasingly recognised as a powerful and effective way of enabling teachers to reflect upon and develop their classroom practice. Teachers need to be able to:

- have a creative and constructive critical approach towards innovation, being prepared to adapt their practice where benefits and improvements are identified

- act upon advice and feedback and be open to coaching and mentoring

- work as a team member and identify opportunities for working with colleagues, sharing the development of effective practice with them

- ensure that colleagues working with them are appropriately involved in supporting learning, and understand the roles they are expected to fulfil.

Teachers have increasing been encouraged to undertake research looking at their own practice as part of a collaborative activity with other teachers in the same school, or as part of a network with teachers in other schools. This has increasingly been seen as an important aspect of a teacher's professional development and as an activity that can have a positive impact on school improvement. A study by Colucci-Gray et al. (2013) explored the experiences of thirteen primary and secondary school teachers in Scotland involved in small action research projects. Of particular interest here, is their finding that many of these teachers felt conducting action research had increased their confidence in innovating with a more pupil-centred approach to their teaching, and that they had become more skilled in reflecting on and evaluating the consequences of their practice for pupils.

The establishment of formal schemes of teacher appraisal and performance management (Jones et al., 2006; Middlewood and Abbott, 2017) and the publication of guidance for schools on how school inspectors evaluate the quality of classroom teaching have also contributed to the extent to which teachers are engaged in regularly and systematically reflecting on their own classroom practice.

Teachers also need to continuously update and develop their understanding of their subject matter, and how this can be taught in the classroom, as well as their knowledge and understanding of how pupils learn and develop, and how pupil learning can be affected by a variety of developmental, social, religious, ethnic, cultural, and linguistic influences. While some initial grounding in these areas will be established during initial teacher training, this needs to be revisited in the light of new research findings, as well as in the light of changes in policies.

Self-evaluation

There are two key aspects of self-evaluation. First, what aspects of your teaching need to be considered in order to improve your future practice? Second, how can you best go about improving your practice in the area that could usefully be developed? The first aspect involves setting yourself, or being set by others, an agenda about classroom teaching to consider, and then collecting some data that will enable you, or others, to judge the area that could usefully be developed. The second aspect deals with the programme for development.

Setting the initial agenda for your classroom teaching can be done in a number of ways. Studies of teacher self-evaluation indicate that most teachers tend to take as their starting point some problem that they are concerned about, rather than attempt to formally review their teaching as a whole. For example, a teacher may feel that they ought to make greater use of group work activities, or that coursework activities need to be more clearly planned, or that too many pupils in the class become restless and inattentive during lessons. Such concerns may lead the teacher to explore carefully their own current practice with a view to considering how best to improve future practice. This process would constitute the first part of a teacher action research strategy, which would then lead on to devising a solution to improve practice, implementing the solution, and then evaluating its success.

Teachers who attempt to review their teaching as a whole are usually involved in a formal scheme of some sort, in which a checklist of questions about current practice or a set of rating scales is used. For example, the following list of statements is fairly typical as a means of stimulating a teacher's reflections on their current classroom practice. The teachers are asked to rate themselves on each statement as either 'I am happy with this aspect of my teaching' or 'I think I could usefully look at this aspect further'. The statements are:

- I plan my lessons well, with clear aims and a suitable lesson content and structure.

- I prepare the materials needed for the lessons, such as worksheets and apparatus, in good time.

- My explanations and instructions are clear and pitched at the right level for pupils to understand.

- I distribute questions around the classroom well and use both open and closed questions.

- I use a variety of learning activities.

- My lessons are suitable for the range of ability of pupils in the class (able, average, less able).

- I maintain a level of control and order that is conducive for learning to occur.

- I monitor pupils' learning closely during the lesson and give help to those having difficulties.

- I mark work, including homework, thoroughly, constructively and in good time.

- I have good relationships with pupils based on mutual respect and rapport.

- My subject expertise is fine for the work I do.

In order to help ensure that teachers are honest in using this list of statements, they are told that it is for their own personal use, simply to help them think about which areas of their classroom teaching they might like to focus on as part of the self-evaluation or teacher appraisal process. It is useful to note that the description of the second rating category is carefully worded so that it does not imply that, by wanting to look at this aspect further, your current practice is unsatisfactory. This is essential, since the need for change in your teaching often has nothing to do with your current practice being weak nor mean your previous practice was wrong. Not appreciating this point has caused many teachers faced with the need to change much unnecessary anguish.

Rating scales

As well as such checklists, many teachers have made use of more sophisticated rating scales in the role of appraiser when observing the teaching of a colleague. Such classroom observation instruments vary greatly in format and content, and in particular whether the rating scale is norm-referenced (e.g. above average, average, below average) or criterion-referenced (i.e. describes the behaviour indicative of each category on the rating scale), or a judgmental and ambiguous mixture of both (e.g. outstanding, good, average, poor).

There is no definitive description of what constitutes effective teaching, as was noted in Chapter 1; a whole variety of different classroom observation instruments have been used to explore classroom practice, including those devised by governmental agencies, researchers, teacher trainers, and schools. In addition, the ways in which such observation schedules have been used have also varied. At one extreme are observers who maintain a detached stance by sitting at the back of the classroom for the whole lesson, while at the other extreme are those who frequently circulate around the room at appropriate times, talk to pupils, look at pupils' work, and even assist with the lesson when possible. What is of crucial importance in the use of such rating scales is that they lead to an informative and constructive dialogue between the observer and the observed that helps to stimulate the quality of the latter's thinking about their own classroom practice.

Using an agreed list of teaching skills

Over the years, many attempts have been made by governmental agencies to clearly define the teaching skills that should be developed during the course of initial teacher training, and which should then develop further during a teacher's career supported by appropriate in-service education and other professional development activities. Unfortunately, the main problem with doing this is that it tends to emphasise the summative assessment aspects of teaching skills, rather than the formative aspect. This then implies that the main aim of teacher appraisal and school inspection is to identify weaknesses that need development. As was noted earlier, however, most teachers need to develop their classroom practice to meet new demands stemming from changes in the curriculum and patterns of teaching, learning and assessment, rather than to correct weaknesses. Teacher appraisal and school inspection schemes need to emphasise the formative aspects of appraisal and provide a supportive ethos that will foster and encourage teachers' own reflection and evaluation about their classroom teaching, if such schemes are to facilitate teachers' efforts to monitor and develop their own classroom practice.

Monitoring a teachers' performance

As noted in Chapter 8, the increasing use of school data systems to collate data on pupil progress now enables the senior management team in schools to identify a teacher who is doing less well than others in keeping individual pupils at or above their target level of progress. This can be viewed as beneficial to the teacher and pupils, in that it may alert the school to the need to offer the teacher and the pupils support to rectify the situation, but at its worst it can simply put the teacher under greater pressure to deliver the level of pupil progress expected.

Portfolios and profiles

One of the means by which teacher training courses aim to encourage student teachers to reflect regularly on their classroom practice is to require them to build up a portfolio of their teaching based on their lesson plans, their notes on how the lessons went, and feedback from observation of their lessons by course tutors and school mentors. In addition, some teacher training courses make use of a variety of profiling documents to comment on individual lessons and to record their progress during the training course, both in respect of the general classroom teaching and with respect to more specific aspects of the development, such as the use of a profiling document to record students' development of skills in the use of information technology.

Mentoring

Mentoring can be very influential in developing your teaching skills, both as a beginning teacher (Boreen et al., 2009: Hounslow-Eyre, 2017) and as an experienced teacher (Burley and Pomphrey, 2011). Discussing and exchanging ideas on teaching and learning can benefit not only the teacher being mentored, but also the teacher doing the mentoring. Sharing ideas about practice not only enables you to think about what you do, but also to think about the reasons behind your practice. Beginning teachers in most countries can now expect that a teacher in the school will act as their mentor during their initial phrase of training as a student teacher and during the first year or two as a newly appointed teacher.

In the past, mentoring largely took the form of giving advice and coaching beginning teachers, where an experienced teacher was drawing on their expertise to guide novices in the art of good practice. More recently, mentoring has been taken a stage further by encouraging all teachers at all stages of their career development to mentor each other through collaborative activities. This development recognises that mentoring has the power to be transformative in how you view yourself and your practice, and can help you to develop new skills and incorporate new practices throughout your career. Indeed, the Department for Education (2016) views teachers' collaboration with colleagues as an essential part of their professional development.

Research on mentoring in schools indicates that high-quality mentoring is not only important in helping you to improve your teaching skills, but is also effective in enhancing your professional commitment. In some schools mentoring may simply focus on general advice and guidance given by a more experienced teacher in order to help a beginning teacher to settle into their new school. However, genuine mentoring is now widely regarded as involving a close collaboration and ongoing dialogue with the mentor that aims to enhance the teacher's pedagogical understanding and the development of their teaching skills. In a review of research on the mentoring of beginning teachers, Spooner-Lane (2017) reported that the professional growth of beginning teachers was more enhanced in those mentoring schemes where mentors discussed specific teaching practices or teaching beliefs with their mentees.

Mentoring can play an important part in helping you to develop your skills as your career in teaching progresses, from newly qualified teacher to expert teacher, and in helping you to respond to new pedagogies. As a mentor yourself, you are also able to help those colleagues that you mentor to benefit from your advice and guidance.

Induction as a newly qualified teacher

One of the benefits of building up a portfolio and having a profile of one's skills at the end of initial teacher training is that such documents can form a very useful basis from which to consider your professional development needs during the first few years as a qualified teacher. Indeed, many schools have a well-established programme to support newly qualified teachers during their first year of appointment (the induction year), in which opportunities to review their progress and their development needs are provided. This is coupled with having another teacher in the school formally appointed to be your mentor, and to whom you can go for advice and guidance. The career entry and development profile completed at the end of the initial teacher training programme is designed to help make the induction year programme more effective.

Research on the experience of beginning teachers during the induction year has highlighted the importance of the quality of mentoring that new teachers receive to enable their confidence and teaching skills to develop. A study by Kyriacou and Kunc (2007) tracked a group of beginning teachers over a three-year period, covering their PGCE year and their first two years in post. The quality of mentoring they received in schools had a major impact on the progress they felt they made in the development of their teaching skills.

Becoming an expert teacher

The growth of expertise in classroom teaching is clearly crucial for your professional growth and for the effectiveness of the whole school system. As such, much attention has been paid to how teachers can be helped to develop and extend their teaching skills and to meet the demands for changes in the classroom practice that must inevitably occur from time to time (Kerry and Wilding, 2004; Marzano, 2010). Unfortunately, as teachers develop greater expertise, they are also likely to gain promotion to posts that involve more administrative work and less classroom teaching, with the result that some of the best classroom teachers gradually do less teaching as their careers develop. One way of mitigating this is to establish a grade of expert teacher, which enables a teacher to gain a promoted post (with additional pay) while retaining a full classroom teaching load.

The development of teacher expertise in the classroom covers a number of key areas:

- knowledge and understanding of relevant subject matter in the context of pupil learning

- knowledge and understanding of how best to promote pupil learning

- knowledge and understanding of assessing pupils

- knowledge and understanding of how to maintain pupil engagement in learning

- knowledge and understanding of how to constructively critique one's own teaching and that of colleagues, to enable continuing improvement in classroom practice.

While beginning teachers also need to display competence in these areas, what marks out expert teachers from beginning teachers is the depth and breadth of their knowledge and understanding, and the skilfulness they display in carrying out the tasks of teaching. Expert teachers are able to deal with a variety of situations with consistent high-quality teaching and make critical and well-informed adjustments in the light of how a lesson is progressing.

Defining the skills of an expert teacher has been particularly problematic (Berliner, 1995; Eaude, 2014). It is easy to assume that expert teachers are simply teachers who display the same range of skills as 'competent' teachers but only more so. However, research on the differences between expert teachers and other teachers reveals that expert teachers seem to have additional qualities that go beyond those displayed by other teachers. These additional qualities seem to be:

- the highest level of commitment to their work

- some degree of charisma that flows from the quality of their interest in the work they do and for the pupils they teach

- an insightful grasp of the essence of what needs to be learned and how best to get pupils from where they are now to where they need to be

- an attunement to pupils' prior experience and current emotional state

- an awareness of how the cognitive and affective aspects of teaching and learning interact

- an insightful ability to anticipate problems and to intervene effectively when problems do occur so that pupils' learning can progress smoothly.

Responding to new pedagogies

All teachers need to develop new skills in response to changes in pedagogy. This highlights the importance of your ability to reflect upon your professional development needs and to take the action needed to develop new teaching skills in response to new pedagogies. Inspections and evaluations of the quality of school management typically consider the role played by school and teacher self-evaluation in contributing to the development of new teaching skills.

A particularly effective way in which teachers can be helped to develop their teaching skills and classroom practice is to become part of a professional learning community within the school or across schools, where teachers can explore, discuss and share ideas about how to develop their teaching. This can usefully complement and enhance the role played by mentoring. Schools that are proactive in setting up and supporting professional learning communities are sending an important signal to the teaching staff about the need for constant development and innovation in order for high-quality teaching to be sustained. A particularly interesting development regarding professional learning communities is the role played by e-learning networks. It is quite common for teachers making use of a new approach to teaching to be able to network with other teachers via Twitter, using resource-sharing websites, and sharing best practice on exam-board-specific Facebook pages. Such activities alleviate the problem of the time and financial cost involved in travelling to face-to-face meetings, and are immediately accessible whenever needed.

Interestingly, a study by McConnell et al. (2013) in the USA explored teachers' experiences of taking part in a project to improve their teaching of inquiry-based science lessons in primary and secondary schools that involved a monthly videoconference with other teachers. A challenge for the project was to set up the videoconference in ways that would enable the typical benefits of traditional face-to-face meetings (such as being mutually supportive, having shared leadership, and collective learning) to occur. The findings indicated that videoconferencing can act as an effective vehicle through which teachers can develop their teaching skills, but there are pluses and minuses. For example, while it is extremely convenient to take part in videoconferencing from the comfort of your own home, you are also vulnerable to home-based distractions such as your pet dog barking at the other participants.

The mentoring relationship

For mentoring to play a successful part in helping you to develop your classroom teaching skills and those of your colleagues, the nature of the mentor–mentee relationship is crucial. The relationship needs to be equal and collegial: it is not a question of the mentor telling the mentee what they could and should be doing differently. The communication should take the form of a constructive dialogue within which ideas are explored, and the advice of the mentor is based on their wider experience but is not treated as a directive. Indeed, given the rapid development in classroom practice, there are now many instances where a less experienced mentee is more in tune with newer approaches to teaching than the mentor, and where the mentor has more to learn from the mentee than vice versa. As such, mentoring very much needs to be seen as collaborative: the mentor and the mentee have the joint responsibility for taking things forward.

Perhaps the biggest challenge facing a mentor is the notion of what Stephens (1996) termed 'principled mentoring'. This refers to the importance of looking at the wider picture of what education is all about, the values one believes in, and the moral purpose of education to empower and inspire children. It is all too easy for a mentor to simply focus on the practicalities of teaching, and helping the mentee just to do what is expected by others. However, for the relationship to be honest and authentic, there are times when what really matters is reminding each other, and thinking about, what it means to be part of a caring profession.

Collecting data about your current practice

Whatever the circumstances by which you come to appraise your classroom teaching, whether self-initiated or as part of a formal scheme of appraisal, whether based on a list of teaching skills or some type of observation schedule, you will need to consider detailed information about aspects of your teaching in order to base your plans for further development on a systematic analysis of your current practice. Collecting and receiving such feedback is the area we turn to next.

During a period when there are major changes in the curriculum relating to patterns of teaching, learning and assessment, it will be relatively clear from the new demands made on you what areas of your current practice will need to be developed. It may be that, as a primary school teacher, you need to develop your teaching of science or history topics, or, as a secondary school teacher, you need to develop your teaching of investigational work in mathematics or assessment of coursework tasks in English.

However, it is just as important during periods when major changes are not taking place in the curriculum for you to be able to undertake self-initiated reflection on your current practice, with a view to thinking about aspects of your teaching that you are broadly happy with but that nevertheless might usefully merit attention. It is in exploring your current practice during such periods, when there is no obvious problem or demand for you to change your practice, that collecting data in some way can be particularly helpful.

Figure 9.1: Collect as much information as you can about your classroom practice

Methods of data collection

There are a variety of ways in which you can collect data about your current practice (Baumfield et al., 2013; McAteer, 2013). One or more of the following methods are likely to be the most useful.

- *Writing a diary.* This may be done after each lesson with a particular class or classes, or alternatively at the end of each school day. It can be especially useful in helping you to clarify the nature of your concerns and in noting particular incidents that are examples of the concern.

- *Making a recording of your lessons.* This may be done using audio or video recording equipment. The main advantage of such recordings is that their detail enables you to highlight aspects of your teaching which, during the busyness of the actual lessons, you are unaware of as being worthy of attention and development.

- *Getting feedback from a colleague observing your lessons.* This is an essential feature of formal schemes of teacher appraisal, but has also featured widely in many informal cooperative activities among teachers exploring their own practice. Feedback from an observer appears to work best when you brief your observer about the aspect of your teaching you want feedback on, and when such feedback is descriptive (i.e. describes what happened) rather than judgemental. Judgemental feedback is also valuable, but great care needs to be taken to ensure that the judgements come from a trusted observer, occur in a supportive and non-threatening context, and are fair. Interestingly, observers often claim to learn as much, if not more, about their own teaching from observing colleagues, as from being observed themselves. As such, schemes that involve teachers observing each other have been particularly successful in stimulating teachers' thinking about their own teaching.

- *Getting feedback from pupils.* You can get useful feedback from pupils in a number of ways. You could ask pupils to write a diary about your lessons. In some cases this has been used to encourage pupils to reflect upon their learning experiences linked to a personal and social education programme or records of achievement. You could ask pupils to complete a questionnaire about your lessons that explores aspects of your teaching and their experience of learning. You could interview pupils individually, or in groups, or hold a class discussion. Studies that have looked at teachers' use of feedback from pupils to evaluate their teaching have invariably found that such feedback is very valuable and of high quality, and that the main reluctance by many teachers to solicit such feedback seems to be more to do with a fear that it may undermine the authority inherent in their role rather than concerns about its quality.

- *Getting to grips with the school data systems.* Useful data on individual pupil progress or on the progress made by a particular group of pupils may now be easily available to you. You need to make use of such data to provide you with information that is of interest to you concerning your practice and the progress your pupils are making.

Many teachers have made use of a mixture of methods for data collection, and once you have focused more clearly on the particular aspect of your classroom teaching you wish to explore, the data collection can be made sharper and more specific. For example, a class teacher in a junior school used a diary, observations and an audiotape to explore how well pupils set about various tasks. As a result, he noticed that because he organised the learning activities so that pupils had to complete an English or a mathematics task before they could move on to 'more exciting' tasks, such as art or project work, some pupils simply rushed the first task. Furthermore, pupils with difficulties tended to become frustrated because they could not finish the first task in good time. He then introduced a rotating timetable in which the first task lasted for a specified length of time. This relieved the pressure on pupils, and on him, and the new organisation of the activities led to an improvement in the quality of the work produced and in the pupils' attitudes and motivation towards the work.

Ideas for reflection

A number of writers have produced texts aimed at helping teachers to reflect upon some aspect of their classroom practice by carrying out practical activities that will provide some useful data with which to analyse their teaching (Neil and Morgan, 2003; Pollard et al., 2014). Examples of areas that might be addressed in this way are:

- obtaining a 'measure' of the classroom climate
- exploring your use of classroom rules
- exploring how pupils feel about particular topics
- monitoring a particular pupil's curricular experiences for one week
- examining tasks in terms of their learning demands
- investigating question and answer sessions
- evaluating the techniques you use to assess pupils' progress

- reviewing the motivational qualities of different activities

- looking at the quality of your relationships with pupils

- examining the time pupils spend on different types of activities

- reviewing the work you set for the more able pupils

- reviewing your use of information technology activities.

Many of these activities can be carried out by the teacher acting alone and making use of appropriate materials, while others may require the assistance of colleagues. Indeed, one interesting development in schools has been an increase in the sharing of ideas and data about one's own teaching with colleagues, as part of a collaborative scheme in which teachers try to explore aspects of their own practice. Such schemes may involve a small group of teachers at a particular school or a small group of teachers from different schools. In addition, many in-service workshops for teachers are now based around the collecting and sharing of data about the development of their practice during a specified period, lasting, say, one academic year, during which each teacher focuses on and develops one particular aspect of the classroom teaching. Unlike traditional in-service workshops, which tend to be one-off sessions involving input from 'experts', this approach means that the development is initiated, developed and sustained over a long enough period to have a significant impact on each teacher's practice. Furthermore, the approach makes positive use of the support and insight of colleagues on a regular basis (who are engaged in the same enterprise).

Making use of evidence-based classroom practice

There has been a huge increase in the number of sources of information drawing upon the research evidence for the effectiveness of different aspects of classroom practice (Hattie, 2011; Petty, 2009). These include copies of DfE research reports, which are freely available at the DfE website, and a number of systematic reviews of research, research briefings and research digests, which are freely available at a variety of websites. These include the Evidence for Policy and Practice Information and Coordinating Centre (EPPI-Centre, 2018), the Institute for Effective Education (IEE, 2018), and the Education Endowment Foundation (EEF, 2018). There are also numerous magazines aimed at teachers in which a very accessible style of writing and presentation is used to present the implications of research studies for classroom practice.

In addition, a number of initiatives have been funded that involve teachers doing research on their own practice as part of collaboration with other teachers working in the same topic area (e.g. academic acceleration for gifted pupils;

the use of numeracy recovery programmes for pupils; the use of slideshows in drama lessons; the use of extended coursework projects). A number of studies have indicated that research collaboration between teachers can have a very positive impact on the development of new skills and understanding about aspects of their classroom practice. A study by Erickson et al. (2005) found that collaborative research projects involving teachers and teacher educators were particularly effective in enhancing the professional development of the teachers involved, and helped to improve the learning environment in these teachers' classrooms. They found that such collaborative research was effective because the research was embedded in the teachers' actual classroom practice; the teachers were able to share ideas in an atmosphere of trust; and the teachers also shared a precise mutual understanding of the issues involved in the aspects of the classroom practice they were considering.

There is now a wealth of information available to teachers, and attempts are being made to produce channels for this flow of information in which the information available can be vetted for quality and accuracy and highlighted in terms of its potential importance for classroom practice.

Teacher appraisal

Teacher appraisal (also referred to as teacher performance review) should take place in a context where the aims of the scheme are explicitly stated in written guidelines issued to all staff, together with details of the procedures to be followed concerning how lesson observations are to occur and be recorded and reported. Such guidelines vary markedly from school to school, and certain details of the procedures may even operate differently to some extent within the same school, although they will need to be in line with the national framework for teacher appraisal in schools (Darling-Hammond and Bransford, 2016; Jones et al., 2006; Middlewood and Abbott, 2017).

The stages of teacher appraisal

Teacher appraisal in schools involves four main stages:

- *A pre-appraisal stage.* In this stage, the 'appraisee' (the teacher being appraised) is asked to reflect upon all aspects of their work as a teacher, including, in particular, their current classroom practice and areas of practice they may like to consider in detail or develop in some way. This stage is likely to involve the appraisee completing a questionnaire, which will include open-ended questions designed to encourage them to review and reflect on their current practice and identify any concerns they have.

- *Classroom observation.* This normally involves observation of two lessons. The selection of the lessons to be observed will be based on prior discussion about which lessons might be most appropriate for this, and about whether the appraiser could usefully focus on any particular aspects of the teaching.

- *An appraisal interview.* As part of this interview, the teacher's classroom practice is discussed, and any development needs in this respect are agreed and may form the basis of targets to be met during the subsequent development cycle.

- *Follow-up action.* If problems have been identified during the interview, this may require action to be taken by the school to help resolve them. In addition, support of some kind may be required to help the appraisee to meet agreed development targets.

The role of the appraiser

One of the key tasks of the appraiser is to help a colleague reflect upon and develop their classroom teaching skills. This involves a number of important issues. First, the relationship between the appraiser and appraisee must be based on mutual trust and respect. The appraiser must have credibility with the appraisee and be seen as someone whose observations and comments will be valued. The appraisal process must also be collaborative (i.e. the appraiser and appraisee are jointly helping each other to make the process as valuable and as worthwhile as possible).

Second, the appraiser needs to be extremely careful and sensitive in how they communicate feedback to the appraisee. What is said must be scrupulously fair, and only judgemental insofar as the appraiser is raising an issue for discussion. The tone of the discussion should be one of equals comparing notes and views, and not one of the appraiser telling the appraisee how to teach better.

Third, it is essential that teachers being appraised feel they have ownership over the process. This means that the appraiser needs to help the appraisee reflect on their own practice and offer useful feedback to help them do so. Carrying out this role will require the appraiser to come to an understanding of the teacher's thoughts about their own teaching, their aims and intentions for a lesson, and their concerns about areas that might usefully be looked at in detail. The extent to which the appraiser is able to convey this may be limited by the nature of the scheme itself and how far its emphasis is clearly formative or summative. For example, some schemes have the tone of being a professional review, while others seem to have the tone of being more judgemental and inspectorial.

Recording the results of the appraisal

Part of the appraisal process requires that an agreed record of the appraisal be drawn up. At the very least this will be a written statement of what was agreed at the appraisal interview in terms of the teacher's current performance and development targets. At the other extreme, however, some documents have included a copy of the appraisee's initial self-review, appraiser's comments on the lessons observed, and a summary of the areas and issues covered in the appraisal interview. In some schemes the observations of classroom teaching were recorded in the form of a profile. A typical profile comprises three elements together with a prompt list for each, as follows:

- *Preparation.* The activity was part of a properly planned programme; the aim of the activity was clear; a suitable approach was chosen from the options available; adequate and suitable resources were available; the learning environment had been considered.

- *Teaching skills.* The material was well presented; the pupils were actively involved; the teacher adapted the approach when necessary, was aware of individual needs within the group, and displayed mastery of the subject matter.

- *Follow-up.* Homework is set regularly (if appropriate); pupils' work is marked and recorded regularly; pupils receive appropriate feedback about their work; parents are informed of pupils' work and progress in accordance with school policy; the teacher evaluates the success of their teaching.

This teacher appraisal profile contains a space next to each of these three elements to record a summary of discussion between the appraiser and appraisee. While a detailed listing of the major areas to be covered in an appraisal, together with their specific constituent elements, is helpful in indicating the aspects of teaching that may usefully receive attention, it becomes all too easy for the recording format to dictate what is looked at. As far as classroom teaching is concerned, the elements listed can take on a prescriptive quality and emphasise the summative aspect of appraisal. This will undermine the sense of ownership needed for the formative purpose to be encouraged. Fortunately, the experience of many teacher appraisal schemes indicates that a formative approach designed to encourage self-reflection and development has been widely employed (Jones et al., 2006; Middlewood and Cardno, 2001).

Helping teachers to develop their classroom teaching skills

In helping colleagues to develop their classroom teaching skills, it is often essential to go beyond simply giving advice and guidance. Teachers may need a variety of experiences and support in order to develop in a particular way. Most significantly, they may benefit from observing colleagues in their own school or teachers in other schools, or by taking part in workshops and courses for experienced teachers aimed at developing specific skills and expertise.

Changes in teaching, learning and assessment practices in schools have major implications for in-service training and the provision of new resources. To expect teachers, for example, to be able to use the latest information technology packages, to prepare new coursework assessment activities, and to adopt new investigational tasks, clearly requires major training support for those teachers who are not confident or do not have sufficient current expertise in such approaches. Appraisal must not simply identify such needs, but should also plan for how such needs can best be met.

Further reading

Baumfield, V., Wall, K., & Hall, E. (2013). *Action Research in Education* (2nd ed.). London: Sage. An excellent guide to how research data collected by teachers can inform and develop their classroom practice.

Burley, S., & Pomphrey, C. (2011). *Mentoring and Coaching in Schools: Professional Learning Through Collaborative Enquiry.* London: David Fulton. An excellent treatment of how reflection can be enhanced through working with others. You will find Chapter 5, on professional learning through collaboration, particularly helpful in the way it sets out this important and effective aspect of mentoring.

McGregor, D., & Cartwright, L. (Eds). (2011). *Developing Reflective Practice: A Guide for Beginning Teachers.* Maidenhead: Open University Press. A useful guide to reflective practice that focuses on a range of questions and issues facing teachers in trying to improve their teaching skills.

Ofsted. (2018). Look out for the latest annual report by Ofsted on education in schools. The terminology, phrasing and comments made in this report will help you understand what key issues you need to consider in reflecting on your own practice. The report will also convey Ofsted's agenda regarding areas of practice that it views as good, and other areas where it thinks practice is unsatisfactory.

Key questions

1　Do I regularly consider my current practice with a view to identifying aspects that can be usefully developed?

2　Do I make adequate use of evaluating my lessons to inform my future lesson planning and classroom practice?

3　Do I make use of systematic methods of collecting data about my current practice that may be helpful?

4　Do I try to keep well informed about developments in teaching, learning and assessment in schools that have implications for my teaching?

5　Do I make use of a variety of different ways of developing particular teaching skills, such as attending workshops, using training manuals, and collaborating with colleagues?

6　Do I make the best use of my involvement in a scheme of teacher appraisal to consider my development needs?

7　What opportunities exist in my school to share with colleagues examples of effective teaching and learning strategies, and how do I plan to contribute to this?

8　Do I make use of being mentored to develop my classroom practice, and do I make use of mentoring others to develop their classroom practice?

9　Do I take a leading role in offering skills-development training activities within the school or outside the school?

10　Do I make use of Internet-based training resources?

Chapter 10
Self-management

As a teacher, you need to develop a diverse set of skills: you need to be able to manage teaching and learning, to manage pupils' behaviour, and to manage their dealings with others. It is all too easy, however, to take for granted, and to some extent to neglect, another important area of management: self-management (Day and Gu, 2014; Turnbull, 2013). Two major challenges facing you in terms of self-management are to organise how you use your time to best effect, and to be able to minimise and deal effectively with stress.

Managing your time

There are few jobs that can compare with teaching for the variety of demands you have to deal with. These include lesson planning, classroom teaching, marking, administration, dealing with pupils' personal problems, school-based decision-making, setting examinations, meeting parents, collaborating with colleagues, carrying out managerial responsibilities, helping new members of staff and student teachers, and the purchase of resources and equipment, such as textbooks, machinery and materials. Being able to cope with such demands efficiently and effectively will have a bearing, directly or indirectly, on the quality of teaching and learning that takes place in your lessons.

The DfE (2018) has highlighted three areas where action is needed to reduce teacher workload: marking, planning, and data management. At the teacher level, the DfE has outlined strategies to help teachers make more efficient use of their time. The DfE has also emphasised the importance for policymakers at both the school level and the government level to check that their policy decisions do not make unnecessary demands on teachers' time.

Effective time management

As such, you will need to develop skills that enable you to manage your time and effort to best effect. In addition, because of the changing nature of your work as a teacher, as a result of your own career development and changes in teaching generally, you will need to review and reflect regularly upon how well you are doing this.

Time-management skills are essential to you managing your work and effort to best effect (Capel, 2016; Kyriacou, 2009; Neil and Morgan, 2003). Successful time management involves a number of important elements.

- *Be aware of your time.* You need to think about how much time you spend on particular demands, and decide whether this needs to be altered. For example, you may be spending too much time planning and preparing lessons to the point where you are 'gilding the lily'. Analysis may reveal that you could reduce planning time without any noticeable loss of quality. You may also be able to improve on the efficiency of your planning by, for example, making greater use of lesson plans given previously or by planning a course of lessons at the same time rather than individually.

- *Prioritise.* You have to decide in which order to undertake various tasks, taking account of their importance and urgency. The more important a task is, the more you should budget time to carry it out well in advance of the deadline, so that you do not have to do a rushed job under pressure at the last minute. If the task is urgent, you need to be flexible in postponing another task that can wait. In general, you should loosely try to meet demands in the order they confront you, but be able to prioritise urgent and important tasks as and when necessary.

- *Plan your time.* You need to think about planning your time in the short term (the school day), the medium term (the school week), and the long term (the academic term and year). Your planning for each time frame ought to reflect your prioritising, so that by the end of each period, the tasks with highest priority have been completed effectively, and those with lowest priority have been slotted in as and when appropriate. Advance planning is helpful in enabling you to prepare in good time and make necessary arrangements or take on other commitments in the light of such planning.

- *Match time to tasks.* Everyone has preferences about when and how they work most efficiently for given tasks. For example, some teachers may find marking work late during a weekday evening is particularly productive, while others may find using some time immediately after the end of a school day works better. Organising your time so that you can undertake particular tasks at your most efficient time for each can help you develop regular routines that work well.

- *Deal with small tasks quickly.* There are a number of tasks that can be dealt with in a short period of time, either immediately or at an early opportunity. Getting such tasks done and out of the way as soon as possible helps to keep your desk clear. Leaving them for later often results in finding that you have several rather small tasks needing to be done that begin to clutter up your planning, and their delay in completion may start to cause inconvenience to yourself and others. However, be alert to the fact that some such tasks, although small, may require more considered and careful attention, and you may need to think them through or consult others before acting.

- *Do not procrastinate.* Once you have recognised that there is a task to be done, try to plan when you are going to carry it out, and then do so at that time. Much time can be wasted by thinking about starting a task on several occasions and each time deciding to leave it for no good reason, or because it involves some unpleasantness that you are inclined to put off.

- *Be realistic.* You need to set yourself realistic demands, which means deciding what quality of work you can achieve in the time available. You may be trying to achieve a much higher quality than is really required, or carrying out a task much sooner than is sensible. Try not to accept unrealistic deadlines from others, as often such deadlines can easily be made more realistic.

- *Be able to say 'No'.* Some teachers always say 'yes' when asked to undertake various tasks, and this can easily result in them becoming overloaded and being the first to be approached when a new task needs to be allocated. Saying 'no' occasionally provides others with feedback concerning how busy you may be and whether you feel the task is something you could usefully take on at the moment (this will help others in the school decide how best to manage the allocation of tasks to staff as a whole).

- *Delegate.* There are many tasks you can appropriately ask a colleague or a pupil to undertake and, from time to time, you should review whether some of the tasks you carry out should be delegated. You could easily find yourself, for example, spending a whole day, off and on, trying to find out something about a pupil's circumstances that a colleague was better placed to have found out in just a few minutes. You may also be spending too much time on routine tasks, such as handing out books, equipment, worksheets, collecting marks and checking progress, in ways that can be better done by asking pupils to carry out some of these tasks.

As well as developing time-management skills yourself, you should also be helping others to do so. For example, you should help pupils become aware of how to organise and pace their efforts in meeting deadlines within a lesson or over a longer period. In your dealings with colleagues, you can also help them to plan how tasks that affect you and others need to be organised so that appropriate deadlines and task allocations are set; for example, planning that pupils do not have too many coursework deadlines falling on the same date, or that time to mark examination work does not coincide unnecessarily with other busy periods in the school.

Time-management skills are not a panacea that will alleviate all time pressures on you. Nevertheless, they do have a major impact on keeping avoidable pressures to a minimum and helping you to maintain a high quality of performance in how you undertake the variety of tasks facing you. Indeed, they are one of the important sets of skills a new teacher needs to develop in the early years of teaching, and then needs to develop further as their role and commitments in school alter.

Dealing with stress

When teachers feel angry, depressed, anxious, nervous, frustrated, or tense as a result of some aspect of their work as teachers, this is referred to as 'teacher stress'. Teacher stress has been widely discussed and researched for many years, and it appears that most teachers experience some stress from time to time, and that a sizeable number of teachers, about one in four, experience a great deal of stress fairly often (Kyriacou, 2000, 2011; Rogers, 2011). Being able to deal with the demands of teaching so that sources of stress are minimised or dealt with effectively is another important set of skills needed by teachers. Day and Gu (2014) have set out an analysis of the importance of teacher resilience as underpinning effective teaching and the ability of the teacher to sustain their motivation and enthusiasm for their work.

Sources of teacher stress

The main sources of stress facing teachers fall into ten areas:

- teaching pupils who lack motivation
- maintaining discipline
- time pressures and workload
- coping with change
- being evaluated by others

- dealing with colleagues

- self-esteem and status

- administration and management

- role conflict and ambiguity

- poor working conditions.

How stress is triggered

The particular sources of stress experienced by individual teachers vary greatly from teacher to teacher. However, what appears to be central to the experience of stress is that it is triggered by the teacher's perception that the demands made on them threaten their self-esteem or well-being in some way.

As a teacher, there are a whole host of demands that have to be dealt with, including the need to discipline pupils, get marking done in time, explaining a pupil's poor progress to their parents, and finding that equipment needed for a lesson is out of order. Any one of these situations has the potential to lead to the experience of stress. What seems to be crucial, however, is that two conditions are evident:

- The teacher feels that meeting the demands made is important (i.e. failure to meet the demands successfully may have undesirable consequences).

- The teacher feels that meeting these demands successfully will be difficult or impossible to achieve in the particular circumstances.

If these two conditions are met, the teacher views the situation facing them as threatening, and that immediately triggers the experience of stress. If, however, the teacher does not view the demands as important or feels that they can easily meet the demands, then no threat is perceived, and hence no stress is triggered. For example, if in the middle of a lesson a pupil is rude to you, in a split second you may judge that you are not sure how to deal with the situation, and begin to feel nervous and anxious, particularly if you feel the situation may escalate. Furthermore, if you feel that by failing to deal with the situation, you may be seen by pupils, colleagues, or yourself as having inadequate skills in class control, this will threaten your self-esteem. Your feelings may be particularly strong if you regard the remark as an intolerable insult that embarrasses you in front of the whole class. In such circumstances, you will experience stress. In contrast, if you judge the situation as one you can deal with quite easily, and perhaps even as a rather trivial incident of little consequence, you will experience no stress.

Demands that cause a great deal of stress to one teacher may therefore cause little stress to another teacher, simply because the two teachers perceive the situation differently in terms of its importance and their ability to deal with it.

The impact of stress on your teaching

Teacher stress may undermine the quality of your teaching in two main ways. First, if you find teaching stressful over a long period, it may start to undermine your satisfaction with the work, and may lead to you becoming disaffected with teaching. This is likely to have some impact on the time and effort you are prepared to give to the quality of your teaching. Second, when you experience stress it can undermine the quality of your interaction with pupils in the classroom. Effective teaching very much depends on a positive classroom climate, and, in particular, on a good rapport with pupils, coupled with supporting and encouraging pupils' efforts. When you experience stress, that generosity of spirit towards pupils, which contributes to a positive classroom climate, can disappear, and you may react to problems and difficulties in a less well-tempered or, even worse, in an openly hostile manner. This means that being able to deal effectively with stress will help you to maintain a high quality of teaching.

Coping strategies

Dealing with stress successfully involves using two types of coping strategies: direct action techniques and palliative techniques.

In *direct action techniques,* you need to identify what is causing you stress and why, and then decide on a course of action that will deal successfully with that source of stress. For example, if a particular pupil is disruptive almost every lesson, you may try a new strategy to deal with this. If you feel friction has developed between you and a colleague, you may try to re-establish a good relationship by being overtly more sociable and friendly towards your colleague. If you find that you are not able to mark pupils' work in good time, you may use some time-management strategies to budget your time differently. As well as taking action on your own initiative, you can also usefully consult with colleagues to see if certain problems are common to them, or whether action involving colleagues can help deal with the source of stress. The use of direct action techniques to deal with sources of stress may lead to immediate success, or may involve long term action, particularly if successful action depends on you improving certain skills.

However, there are some sources of stress that you will not be able to deal with successfully by direct action techniques, and here you will need to be able to use *palliative techniques.* Palliative techniques refer to things you can do to relieve the experience of stress, even when the source of stress persists. Particularly useful are mental techniques, such as getting things in perspective, trying to see the humour in a situation, trying to detach yourself from personal and emotional involvement in a situation, and sharing your worries and concerns with others. In addition, physical techniques, such as trying to relax whenever possible, or having a coffee or a bar of chocolate during break time, are useful. Some teachers have developed useful physical techniques based on relaxation exercises that can help them to keep calm and relaxed in a stressful situation. Being able to relax and unwind after work is also very important.

Figure 10.1: Take time to relax and unwind after work

Developing your own approach to coping with stress

In general, direct action techniques should always be tried to deal with a particular source of stress before palliative techniques are used, since if the former are successful, the source of stress is dealt with rather than simply accommodated. Your approach to stress, however, needs to be tailored to your circumstances and personality. For example, while for one teacher more preparation time at home would be helpful, for another more time spent at home relaxing would be better. Nevertheless, the following advice is generally useful.

- Identify and deal with problems as soon as possible.

- Develop skills and procedures to help you deal with the demands on you, particularly organisational and time-management skills.

- See whether some sources of stress are partly of your own making, such as avoidable confrontations with pupils or colleagues, or accepting tasks that are too taxing.

- Keep things in perspective, and try to form realistic expectations about your own performance and that of others.

- Share your worries and concerns with others.

- Maintain a balance between your work as a teacher and your life outside school (a healthy and enjoyable life outside school will enhance your self-esteem and the inner strength you have to deal with problems at school).

It is also important to note that, collectively, teachers can do much to mitigate stress by establishing a supportive climate in the school to help each other overcome difficulties. This could be by ensuring that demands on teachers are organised and allocated in a way that does not create stress that could have been avoided, such as allocating too many important tasks to the same member of staff, or fixing important deadlines too near to each other.

A study by Hobson and Maxwell (2017), which looked at the well-being of early career teachers, noted that teachers' work is subjected to a high degree of external regulation. In this context, they reported that teachers' perceptions that they are a competent teacher, that they relate well to colleagues, and that they are given opportunities to exercise autonomy, can have a positive effect on their sense of well-being. As such, things that you can do for yourself, and things that colleagues can do to support you, in developing positive perceptions in these three areas, are very important for your general sense of well-being.

Further reading

Day, C., & Gu, Q. (2014). *Resilient Teachers, Resilient Schools: Building and Sustaining Quality in Testing Times.* Abingdon: Routledge. An excellent analysis of the challenges facing teachers and how to deal with them.

Kyriacou, C. (2000). *Stress-Busting for Teachers.* Cheltenham: Nelson Thornes. An overview of the nature of teacher stress and what teachers can do to deal with it. You will find Chapter 3, on pre-empting stress, is particularly helpful in outlining the key skills that will enable you to minimise the occurrence of stress, and how these relate to self-management techniques.

Rogers, B. (2011). *The Essential Guide to Managing Teacher Stress* (2nd ed.). Harlow: Pearson. This book covers a variety of practical skills and strategies that teachers can use to minimise and cope with stress.

Turnbull, J. (2013). *9 Habits of Highly Effective Teachers: A Practical Guide to Personal Development.* London: Bloomsbury. A very readable overview of how qualities of self-management underpin the practice of effective teachers.

? Key questions

1. Do I regularly review how I can organise my time and effort to better effect?

2. Do I prioritise when and how much time I spend on tasks over the short term, medium term and long term?

3. How much time do I spend at home on different teaching tasks, and do I discuss my working practice with colleagues?

4. How do I arrive at a sense of 'good enough' in carrying out different tasks?

5. Do I use a range of effective strategies and techniques to deal with sources of stress?

6. Do I take advice from others on how best to deal with challenging situations?

7. Do I develop skills to deal with particular types of demands better so that less stress is generated?

8. Do I have a healthy life outside school?

9. Do I make effective use of teamwork with colleagues, including support staff?

10. Do I help create a supportive climate in my school to help colleagues discuss and overcome problems?

Bibliography

Alexander, R.J. (2008). *Towards Dialogic Teaching: Rethinking Classroom Talk* (4th ed.). York: Dialogos.

Asterhan, C.S.C., Schwarz, B.B., & Gil, J. (2012). Small-group, computer-mediated argumentation in middle-school classrooms: The effects of gender and different types of online teacher guidance. *British Journal of Educational Psychology*, 82(3), 375–397.

Baumfield, V., Wall, K., & Hall, E. (2013). *Action Research in Education* (2nd ed.). London: Sage.

Beere, J. (2016). *The Perfect Lesson* (3rd ed.). Carmarthen: Independent Thinking Press.

Beere, J., & Broughton, T. (2013). *The Perfect Teacher Coach.* Carmarthen: Independent Thinking Press.

Beetham, H., & Sharpe, R. (Eds). (2013). *Rethinking Pedagogy for a Digital Age* (2nd ed.). Abingdon: Routledge.

Bennett, R.E. (2011). Formative assessment: A critical review. *Assessment in Education*, 18(1), 5–25.

Bentley-Davies, C. (2010). *How to be an Amazing Teacher.* Bancyfelin: Crown House.

Berliner, D. (1995). Teacher expertise. In L.W. Anderson (Ed.), *International Encyclopaedia of Teaching and Teacher Education* (2nd ed.), (pp. 46–51). Oxford: Pergamon.

Black, P., Harrison, C., Lee, C., Marshall, B., & Wiliam, D. (2003). *Assessment for Learning: Putting it into Practice.* Maidenhead: Open University Press.

Blatchford. R. (2017). *The Teachers' Standards in the Classroom* (2nd ed.). London: Learning Matters.

Boreen, J., Johnson, M.K., Niday, D., & Potts, J. (2009). *Mentoring Beginning Teachers: Guiding, Reflecting, Coaching* (2nd ed.). Portland, OR: Stenhouse.

Borich, G.D. (2013). *Effective Teaching Methods: Research-Based Practice* (8th ed.). New York: Pearson.

Boyle, B., & Charles, M. (2014). *Formative Assessment for Teaching and Learning.* London: Sage.

Briggs, M., Woodfield, A., Martin, C., & Swatton, P. (2003). *Assessment for Learning and Teaching in Primary Schools.* Exeter: Learning Matters.

Brooks, V., Abbott, I., & Huddleston, P. (Eds). (2012). *Preparing to Teach in Secondary Schools: A Student Teacher's Guide to Professional Issues in Secondary Education* (3rd ed.). Milton Keynes: Open University Press.

Brunn, P. (2010). *The Lesson Planning Handbook: Essential Strategies that Inspire Student Thinking and Learning.* New York: Scholastic.

Buckler, S., & Castle, P. (2014). *Psychology for Teachers.* London: Sage.

Burley, S., & Pomphrey, C. (2011). *Mentoring and Coaching in Schools: Professional Learning Through Collaborative Enquiry.* London: David Fulton.

Butt, G. (2008). *Lesson Planning* (3rd ed.). London: Bloomsbury.

Campbell, J., Kyriakides, L., Muijs, D., & Robinson, W. (2004). *Assessing Teacher Effectiveness: Developing a Differentiated Model.* London: RoutledgeFalmer.

Capel, S. (2016). Managing your time, workload and stress, and building your resilience. In S. Capel, M. Leask, & S. Younie. (Eds), *Learning to Teach in the Secondary School: A Companion to School Experience* (7th ed.), (pp. 45–59). Abingdon: Routledge.

Capel, S., Leask, M., & Younie, S. (Eds). (2016). *Learning to Teach in the Secondary School: A Companion to School Experience* (7th ed.). Abingdon: Routledge.

Carpenter, C., & Bryan, H. (2016). Teaching styles. In S. Capel, M. Leask, & S. Younie. (Eds), *Learning to Teach in the Secondary School: A Companion to School Experience* (7th ed.), (pp. 368–384). Abingdon: Routledge.

Carroll, J., & Alexander, G.N. (2016). *The Teachers' Standards in Primary Schools.* London: Sage.

Cohen, L., Manion, L., Morrison, K., & Wyse, D. (2010). *A Guide to Teaching Practice* (revised 5th ed.). Abingdon: Routledge.

Colucci-Gray, L., Das, S., Gray, D., Robson, D., & Spratt, J. (2013). Evidence-based practice and teacher action-research: A reflection on the nature and direction of 'change'. *British Educational Research Journal*, 39(1), 126–147.

Cooper, J.M. (Ed.). (2014). *Classroom Teaching Skills* (10th ed.). Belmont, CA: Wadsworth.

Cremin, T., & Arthur, J. (Eds). (2014). *Learning to Teach in the Primary School* (3rd ed.). Abingdon: Routledge.

Cullingford, C. (2003). *The Best Years of Their Lives? Pupils' Experiences of School.* London: RoutledgeFalmer.

Dann, R. (2018). *Developing Feedback for Pupil Learning: Teaching, Learning and Assessment in Schools.* Abingdon: Routledge.

Dansie, T. (2016). *Improving Behaviour Management in Your School: Creating Calm Spaces for Pupils to Learn and Flourish.* Abingdon: Routledge.

Darling-Hammond, L., & Bransford, J. (2016). *Preparing Teachers for a Changing World: What Teachers Should Learn and Be Able to Do.* San Francisco, CA. Jossey-Bass.

Day, C., & Gu, Q. (2010). *The New Lives of Teachers.* Abingdon: Routledge.

Day, C., & Gu, Q. (2014). *Resilient Teachers, Resilient Schools: Building and Sustaining Quality in Testing Times.* Abingdon: Routledge.

Day, C., Sammons, P., Stobart, G., Kington, A., & Gu, Q. (2007). *Teachers Matter: Connecting Lives, Work and Effectiveness.* Maidenhead: Open University Press.

Dean, J. (2008). *Organising Learning in the Primary School Classroom* (4th ed.). Abingdon: Routledge.

Department for Education. (2012). *Teachers' Standards.* London: HMSO.

Department for Education. (2014). *Behaviour and Discipline in Schools: Advice for Headteachers and School Staff.* London: DfE.

Department for Education. (2016). *Standard for Teachers' Professional Development.* London: DfE.

Department for Education. (2018). *Reducing Teacher Workload.* London: DfE.

Dix, P. (2010). *The Essential Guide to Classroom Assessment.* Harlow: Longman.

Dymoke, S. (Ed.). (2012). *Reflective Teaching and Learning in the Secondary School* (2nd ed.). London: Sage.

Eaude, T. (2014). What makes primary class teachers special? Exploring the features of expertise in the primary classroom. *Teachers and Teaching: Theory and Practice,* 20(1), 4–18.

Education Endowment Foundation (EEF). (2018). *Education Endowment Foundation.* Retrieved 13 February 2018 from: https://educationendowmentfoundation.org.uk/

Ellis, S., & Tod, J. (2009). *Behaviour for Learning: Proactive Approaches to Behaviour Management.* London: David Fulton.

Erickson, G., Brandes, G.M., Mitchell, I., & Mitchell, J. (2005). Collaborative teacher learning: Findings from two professional development projects. *Teaching and Teacher Education*, 21(7), 787–798.

Evertson, C.M., & Weinstein, C.S. (Eds). (2006). *Handbook of Classroom Management: Research, Practice, and Contemporary Issues.* Mahwah, NJ: Lawrence Erlbaum.

Evidence for Policy and Practice Information and Coordinating Centre (EPPI-Centre). (2018). *Welcome to the EPPI-Centre.* Retrieved 13 February 2018 from: http://eppi.ioe.ac.uk

Fauth, B., Decristan, J., Rieser, S., Klieme, E., & Büttner, G. (2014). Student ratings of teaching quality in primary school: Dimensions and prediction of student outcomes. *Learning and Instruction*, 29, 1–9.

Florian, L., & Black-Hawkins, K. (2011). Exploring inclusive pedagogy. *British Educational Research Journal*, 37(5), 813–828.

Fraser, B.J. (2002). Learning environments research: Yesterday, today and tomorrow. In S.C. Goh, & M.S. Khine (Eds), *Studies in Educational Learning Environments: An International Perspective* (pp. 1–27). Singapore: World Scientific.

Gamlem, S.V., & Munthe, E. (2014). Mapping the quality of feedback to support students' learning in lower secondary classrooms. *Cambridge Journal of Education*, 44(1), 75–92.

Gardner, J.R. (Ed.). (2011). *Assessment and Learning* (2nd ed.). London: Sage.

Garner, P. (2016). Managing classroom behaviour: Adopting a positive approach. In S. Capel, M. Leask, & S. Younie. (Eds), *Learning to Teach in the Secondary School: A Companion to School Experience* (7th ed.), (pp. 180–199). Abingdon: Routledge.

Gillies, R.M. (2004). The effects of cooperative learning on junior high school students during small group learning. *Learning and Instruction*, 14(2), 197–213.

Hammond, M. (2012). Using ICT to support learning. In V. Brooks, I. Abbott, & P. Huddleston (Eds), *Preparing to Teach in Secondary Schools: A Student Teacher's Guide to Professional Issues in Secondary Education* (3rd ed.), (pp. 161–172). Milton Keynes: Open University Press.

Hargreaves, D.H. (1982). *The Challenge for the Comprehensive School: Culture, Curriculum and Community.* London: Routledge and Kegan Paul.

Hargreaves, E. (2017). *Children's Experiences of Classrooms.* London: Sage.

Hattie, J. (2011). *Visible Learning for Teachers: Maximizing Impact on Learning.* Abingdon: Routledge.

Haydn, T. (2012). *Managing Pupil Behaviour: Improving the Classroom Atmosphere* (2nd ed.). Abingdon: Routledge.

Hayes, D. (2006). *Inspiring Primary Teaching.* Exeter: Learning Matters.

Hayes, D. (2012). *Developing Advanced Primary Teaching Skills.* London: David Fulton.

Haynes, A. (2010). *The Complete Guide to Lesson Planning and Preparation.* London: Continuum.

Hobson, A.J., Malderez, A., Tracey, L., Giannakaki, M.S., Pell, R.G., Kerr, K., Chambers, G.N., Tomlinson, P.D., & Roper, T. (2006). *Becoming a Teacher: Student Teachers' Experiences of Initial Teacher Training in England (Research Report RR744).* London: DfES.

Hobson, A. J., & Maxwell, B. (2017). Supporting and inhibiting the well-being of early career secondary school teachers: Extending self-determination theory. *British Educational Research Journal*, 43(1), 68–191.

Holliman, A.J. (Ed.). (2014). *The Routledge International Companion to Educational Psychology.* Abingdon: Routledge.

Hounslow-Eyre, A. (2017). Guidance for ITT mentors: Coaching and mentoring. In R. Paige, S. Lambert, & R. Geeson (Eds), *Building Skills for Effective Primary Teaching* (pp. 253–270). London: Learning Matters.

Huddleston, P., & Bills, L. (2012). Working with parents and other adults. In V. Brooks, I. Abbott, & P. Huddleston (Eds), *Preparing to Teach in Secondary Schools: A Student Teacher's Guide to Professional Issues in Secondary Education* (3rd ed.), (pp. 88–102). Milton Keynes: Open University Press.

Institute for Effective Education (IEE). (2018). *Institute for Effective Education: Empowering Educators with Evidence.* Retrieved 13 February 2018 from: https://the-iee.org.uk/

Ireson, J., & Hallam, S. (2002). *Ability Grouping in Education.* London: Sage.

Ireson, J., & Hallam, S. (2009). Academic self-concepts in adolescence: Relations with achievement and ability grouping in schools. *Learning and Instruction*, 19(3), 201–213.

Jaques, D. (2000). *Learning in Groups: A Handbook for Improving Group Work* (3rd ed.). London: RoutledgeFalmer.

Jarvis, J., & White, E. (2012). *School-Based Teacher Training: A Handbook for Tutors and Mentors.* London: Sage.

Jenkins, A., & Ueno, A. (2017). Classroom disciplinary climate in secondary schools in England: What is the real picture? *British Educational Research Journal*, 43(1), 124–150.

Jones, J., Jenkin, M., & Lord, S. (2006). *Developing Effective Teacher Performance.* London: Paul Chapman.

Kaplan, A., Gheen, M., & Midgley, C. (2002). Classroom goal structure and student disruptive behaviour. *British Journal of Educational Psychology*, 72(2), 191–211.

Kerry, T. (2002). *Explaining and Questioning.* Cheltenham: Nelson Thornes.

Kerry, T., & Wilding, M. (2004). *Effective Classroom Teacher: Developing the Skills You Need in Today's Classroom.* London: Pearson.

Knowles, G. (Ed.). (2011). *Supporting Inclusive Practice* (2nd ed.). Abingdon: Routledge.

Kounin, J.S. (1970). *Discipline and Group Management in Classrooms.* New York: Holt, Rinehart and Winston.

Koutrouba, K. (2012). A profile of the effective teacher: Greek secondary education teachers' perceptions. *European Journal of Teacher Education*, 35(3), 359–374.

Kutnick, P., & Blatchford, P. (2013). *Effective Group Work in Primary School Classrooms: The SPRinG Approach.* London: Springer.

Kyriacou, C. (2000). *Stress-Busting for Teachers.* Cheltenham: Nelson Thornes.

Kyriacou, C. (2003). *Helping Troubled Pupils.* Cheltenham: Nelson Thornes.

Kyriacou, C. (2005). The impact of daily mathematics lessons in England on pupil confidence and competence in early mathematics: a systematic review. *British Journal of Educational Studies*, 53(2), 168–186.

Kyriacou, C. (2009). *Effective Teaching in Schools: Theory and Practice* (3rd ed.). Oxford: Oxford University Press.

Kyriacou, C. (2011). Teacher stress: From prevalence to resilience. In J. Langan-Fox & C.L. Cooper (Eds), *Handbook of Stress in the Occupations* (pp. 161–173). Cheltenham: Edward Elgar.

Kyriacou, C. (2015). Social pedagogy and pastoral care in schools. *British Journal of Guidance & Counselling*, 43(4), 429–437.

Kyriacou, C., Avramidis, E., Hoie, H., Hultgren, A, & Stephens, P. (2007). The development of student teachers' views on pupil misbehaviour during an initial teacher training programme in England and Norway. *Journal of Education for Teaching*, 33(3), 293–307.

Kyriacou, C., & Cheng, H. (1993). Student teachers' attitudes towards the humanistic approach to teaching and learning in schools. *European Journal of Teacher Education*, 16(2), 163–168.

Kyriacou, C., & Kunc, R. (2007). Beginning teachers' expectations of teaching. *Teaching and Teacher Education*, 23(8), 1246–1257.

Kyriacou, C., & McKelvey, J. (1985). An exploration of individual differences in 'effective' teaching. *Educational Review*, 37(1), 13–17.

Lange, J., & Burroughs-Lange, S. (2017). *Learning to be a Teacher*. London: Sage.

Leaman, L. (2009). *Managing Very Challenging Behaviour* (2nd ed.). London: Continuum.

Leask, M., & Pachler, N. (Eds). (2014). *Learning to Teach Using ICT in the Secondary School: A Companion to School Experience* (3rd ed.). London: Routledge.

Lewis, A., & Norwich, B. (Eds). (2005). *Special Teaching for Special Children? Pedagogies for Inclusion*. Maidenhead: Open University Press.

Lewis, R. (2008). *Understanding Pupil Behaviour: Classroom Management Techniques for Teachers*. London: David Fulton.

Lyle, S. (2008). Dialogic teaching: Discussing theoretical contexts and reviewing evidence from classroom practice. *Language and Education*, 22(3), 222–240.

Marzano, R.J. (2003). *What Works in Schools: Translating Research into Action*. Alexandria, VA: Association for Supervision and Curriculum Development.

Marzano, R.J. (2009). *Designing and Teaching Learning Goals and Objectives*. Cheltenham, Vic.: Hawker Bronlow.

Marzano, R.J. (Ed.). (2010). *On Excellence in Teaching*. Bloomington, IN: Solution Tree Press.

Maslow, A.H. (1987). *Motivation and Personality* (3rd ed.). New York: HarperCollins.

McAteer, M. (2013). *Action Research in Education.* London: Sage.

McConnell, T.J., Parker, J.M., Eberhardt, J., Koehler, M.J., & Lundeberg, M.A. (2013). Virtual professional learning communities: Teachers' perceptions of virtual versus face-to-face professional development. *Journal of Science Education and Technology,* 22(3), 267–277.

McCutcheon, G., & Milner, H.R. (2002). A contemporary study of teacher planning in a high school English class. *Teachers and Teaching: Theory and Practice,* 8(1), 81–94.

McGill, R.M. (2017). *Mark. Plan. Teach.* London: Bloomsbury.

McGregor, D., & Cartwright, L. (Eds). (2011). *Developing Reflective Practice: A Guide for Beginning Teachers.* Maidenhead: Open University Press.

McNeil, F., & Sammons, P. (2006). *Improving Schools* (2nd ed.). London: RoutledgeFalmer.

Mercer, N., & Littleton, K. (2007). *Dialogue and the Development of Children's Thinking: A Sociocultural Approach.* Abingdon: Routledge.

Middlewood, D., & Abbott, I. (2017). *Managing Staff for Improved Performance.* London: Bloomsbury.

Middlewood, D., & Cardno. C.E.M. (Eds). (2001). *Managing Teacher Appraisal and Performance.* London: RoutledgeFalmer.

Moyles, J., Merry, R., Paterson, F., & Esarte-Sarries, V. (2003). *Interactive Teaching in the Primary School: Digging Deeper into Meanings.* Maidenhead: Open University Press.

Muijs, D., & Reynolds, D. (2017). *Effective Teaching: Evidence and Practice* (4th ed.). London: Sage.

Murchan, D., & Shiel, G. (2017). *Understanding and Applying Assessment in Education.* London: Sage.

Myhill, D., Jones, S., & Hopper, R. (2006). *Talking, Listening, Learning: Effective Talk in the Primary Classroom.* Maidenhead: Open University Press.

Neil, P., & Morgan, C. (2003). *Continuing Professional Development for Teachers: From Induction to Senior Management.* London: Kogan Page.

O'Donnell, A.M., Reeve, J., & Smith, J.K. (2007). *Educational Psychology: Reflection for Action.* New York: Wiley.

Office for Standards in Education, Children's Services and Skills (Ofsted). (2014). *School Inspection Handbook.* London: Ofsted.

Office for Standards in Education, Children's Services and Skills (Ofsted). (2018). *Ofsted: Raising Standards, Improving Lives.* Retrieved 13 February 2018 from: https://www.gov.uk/government/organisations/ofsted

Opdenakker, M.-C., & Van Damme, J. (2006). Teacher characteristics and teaching styles as effectiveness enhancing factors of classroom practice. *Teaching and Teacher Education*, 22(1), 1–21.

Pat-El, R.J., Tillema, H., Segers, M., & Vedder, P. (2013). Validation of assessment for learning questionnaires for teachers and students. *British Journal of Educational Psychology*, 83(1), 98–113.

Perrott, E. (1982) *Effective Teaching.* London: Longman.

Petty, G. (2009). *Evidence-Based Teaching: A Practical Approach* (2nd ed.). Oxford: Oxford University Press.

Pollard, A., Black-Hawkins, K., Cliff-Hodges, G., Dudley, P., James, M., Linklater, H., Swaffield, S., Swann, M., Turner, F., & Warwick, P. (2014). *Reflective Teaching in Schools* (4th ed.). London: Bloomsbury.

Pollard, A., & James, M. (Eds). (2004). *Personalised Learning: A Commentary by the Teaching and Learning Research Programme.* Swindon: ESRC.

Poore, M. (2012). *Using Social Media in the Classroom.* London: Sage.

Porter, L. (2014). *Behaviour in Schools: Theory and Practice for Teachers.* (3rd ed.). Maidenhead: Open University Press.

Postholm, M.B. (2006). Assessment during project work. *Teaching and Teacher Education*, 22(2), 150–163.

Prain, V., Cox, P., Deed, C. et al. (2013). Personalised learning: Lessons to be learnt. *British Educational Research Journal*, 39(4), 654–676.

Pritchard, A. (2018). *Ways of Learning: Learning Theories for the Classroom* (4th ed.). Abingdon: Routledge.

Putwain, D.W., Symes, W., & Wilkinson, H.M. (2017). Fear appraisals, engagement, and examination performance: The role of challenge and threat appraisals. *British Journal of Educational Psychology*, 87(1), 16–31.

Pye, J. (1988). *Invisible Children.* Oxford: Oxford University Press.

Reid, G. (2005). *Learning Styles and Inclusion.* London: Paul Chapman.

Riley, P., Lewis, R., & Wang, B. (2012). Investigating teachers' explanations for aggressive classroom discipline strategies in China and Australia. *Educational Psychology*, 32(3), 389–403.

Robins, A. (2006). *Mentoring in the Early Years.* London: Paul Chapman.

Rogers, B. (2011). *The Essential Guide to Managing Teacher Stress* (2nd ed.). Harlow: Pearson.

Rogers, B. (2012). *You Know the Fair Rule: Effective Behaviour Management in Schools* (3rd ed.). Harlow: Pearson.

Rogers, B. (2015). *Classroom Behaviour: A Practical Guide to Effective Teaching, Behaviour Management and Colleague Support* (4th ed.). London: Sage.

Rogers, C.R., & Freiberg, H.J. (1994). *Freedom to Learn* (3rd ed.). New York: Merrill.

Savage, J. (2015). *Lesson Planning.* Abingdon: Routledge.

Seidel, T., Rimmele, R., & Prenzel, M. (2005). Clarity and coherence of lesson goals as a scaffold for student learning. *Learning and Instruction*, 15(6), 539–556.

Sellars, M. (2017). *Reflective Practice for Teachers* (2nd ed.). London: Sage.

Shulman, L.S. (1987). Knowledge and teaching: Foundations of the new reform. *Harvard Educational Review*, 57(1), 1–22.

Skinner, D. (2010). *Effective Teaching and Learning in Practice.* London: Continuum.

Skowron, J. (2006). *Powerful Lesson Planning: Every Teacher's Guide to Effective Instruction* (2nd ed.). London: Sage.

Smith, C.J., & Laslett, R. (1992). *Effective Classroom Management: A Teacher's Guide* (2nd ed.). London: Routledge.

Smith, E., & Gorard, S. (2005). 'They don't give us our marks': The role of formative feedback in student progress. *Assessment in Education*, 12(1), 21–38.

Smith, F., Hardman, F., & Higgins, S. (2006). The impact of interactive whiteboards on teacher-pupil interaction in the National Literacy and Numeracy strategies. *British Educational Research Journal*, 32(3), 443–457.

Smith, F., Hardman, F., Wall, K., & Mroz, M. (2004). Interactive whole-class teaching in the National Literacy and Numeracy Strategies. *British Educational Research Journal*, 30(3), 95–411.

Sobel, D. (2018). *Narrowing the Attainment Gap: A Handbook for Schools.* London: Bloomsbury.

Spooner-Lane, R. (2017). Mentoring beginning teachers in primary schools: Research review. *Professional Development in Education*, 43(2), 253–273.

Stankov, L., Morony, S., & Lee, Y.P. (2014). Confidence: The best non-cognitive predictor of academic achievement. *Educational Psychology*, 34(1), 9–28.

Steer, A. (Chair). (2005). *Learning Behaviour: The Report of the Practitioners' Group on School Behaviour and Discipline* (The Steer Report). London: DfES.

Stephens, P. (1996). *Essential Mentoring Skills*. Cheltenham: Stanley Thornes.

Stronge, J.H. (2006). *Evaluating Teaching* (2nd ed.). London: Sage.

Swinson, J., & Harrop, A. (2012). *Positive Psychology for Teachers: A Practical Guide*. London: David Fulton.

Sylva, K., Melhuish, E., Sammons, P., Siraj-Blatchford, I., & Taggart, B. (2010). *Effective Pre-School, Primary and Secondary Education 3–14 (EPPSE 3–14) Final Report from the Key Stage 3 Phase: Influences on Students' Development from Age 11–14*. London: Department for Education.

Tanner, H., & Jones, S. (2006). *Assessment: A Practical Guide for Secondary Teachers* (2nd ed.). London: Bloomsbury.

Tileston, D.W. (2004). *What Every Teacher Should Know About Instructional Planning*. London: Corwin.

Tolhurst, J. (2010). *Coaching and Mentoring* (2nd ed.). London: Longman.

Tolmie, A.K., Topping, K. J., Christie, D., Donaldson, C., Howe, C., Jessiman, E., Livingston, K., & Thurston, A. (2010). Social effects of collaborative learning in primary schools. *Learning and Instruction*, 20(3), 177–191.

Tough, P. (2012). *How Children Succeed: Grit, Curiosity, and the Hidden Power of Character*. Boston, MA: Houghton Mifflin Harcourt.

Turnbull, J. (2013). *9 Habits of Highly Effective Teachers: A Practical Guide to Personal Development*. London: Bloomsbury.

Van Der Valk, T., & Broekman, H. (1999). The lesson preparation method: A way of investigating pre-service teachers' pedagogical content knowledge. *European Journal of Teacher Education*, 22(1), 11–22.

Voight, A., Austin, G., & Hanson, T. (2013). *A Climate for Academic Success: How School Climate Distinguishes Schools that are Beating the Achievement Odds* (full report). San Francisco, CA: WestEd.

Walsh, J.A., & Settes, B.D. (2005). *Quality Questioning: Research-Based Practice to Engage Every Learner*. London: Sage.

Wassermann, S. (2017). *The Art of Interactive Teaching: Listening, Responding, Questioning.* Abingdon: Routledge.

Watkins, C. (2005). *Classrooms as Learning Communities: What's in it for Schools?* London: RoutledgeFalmer.

Watkins, C., Carnell, E., & Lodge, C. (2007). *Effective Learning in Classrooms.* London: Paul Chapman.

Watson, C. (2014). Effective professional learning communities? The possibilities for teachers as agents of change in schools. *British Educational Research Journal,* 40(1), 18–29.

Waugh, C.K., & Gronlund, N.E. (2012). *Assessment of Student Achievement* (10th ed.). New York: Pearson.

Wearmouth, J. (2017). *Special Educational Needs and Disabilities in Schools: A Critical Introduction.* London: Bloomsbury.

Wertzel, K.R., & Brophy, J.E. (2014). *Motivating Students to Learn* (4th ed.). Abingdon: Routledge.

Wheeler, S. (Ed.). (2005). *Transforming Primary ICT.* Exeter: Learning Matters.

Wiliam, D. (2011). *Embedded Formative Assessment.* Bloomington, IN: Solution Tree Press.

Wragg, E.C., & Brown, G. (2001a). *Explaining in the Primary School* (2nd ed.). London: RoutledgeFalmer.

Wragg, E.C., & Brown, G. (2001b). *Explaining in the Secondary School* (2nd ed.). London: RoutledgeFalmer.

Wragg, E.C., & Brown, G. (2001c). *Questioning in the Primary School* (2nd ed.). London: RoutledgeFalmer.

Wragg, E.C., & Brown, G. (2001d). *Questioning in the Secondary School* (2nd ed.). London: RoutledgeFalmer.

Wragg, T. (2005). *The Art and Science of Teaching and Learning: The Selected Works of Ted Wragg.* London: RoutledgeFalmer.

Younie, S., & Leask, M. (2013). *Teaching with Technologies: The Essential Guide.* Milton Keynes: Open University Press.

Zeichner, K.M., & Liston, D.P. (2014). *Reflective Teaching: An Introduction* (2nd ed.). Abingdon: Routledge.

Author index

Subject index

and mentors 192

overwhelming demands 93

pitfalls 82, 92

using punishment 151

behaviour

acceptable and unacceptable 136, 138

challenging 77, 142, 152

consequences of poor 132

criticising 145

disruptive 105

non-disruptive 143

pupils' attitudes to 131

rewards for good 155–6

unruly 158

'behaviour for learning' 129

behaviour management 23, 25, 129, 133–8, 139–61

policy and procedures 159–60

behaviour, monitoring 93, 155

bibliography 217–28

'blended learning' 81

body language 119, 134 *see also* eye contact, facial expression

boredom of pupils 131

building on previous learning 46

bullying 132, 143, 148

C

caring of pupils by teachers 52–3

'catch-up activities' 51

chain of reasoning 82

challenging tasks 111

changing activities or pace 140

choice, lack of for pupils 133

circulating, classroom 68, 95, 139

clarity of explanation 61

class composition 122–3, 125–6

class exclusion 149, 160

classroom appearance 122–4

classroom climate 23, 24, 65, 87–8, 121, 126, 212

establishing positive 105–10

inclusive 108

sense of order 107

studies of 107–9

classroom dialogue 67–8

classroom discussion 66–7

classroom exit 89

classroom layout 123–4

classroom life logistics 95–8

classroom management 17, 136–8

classroom observation 12, 191, 202

classroom practice 22–3, 188, 200–1

classroom rules 137, 138

classroom, scanning 139

classwork activities, monitoring 173–4

'closed' questions 32

coaching 121–2

cognitive activation 17

collaboration with colleagues 193

collaborative problem-solving 70

collaborative research projects 201

collection of data 197–201

competence of teachers 136

confidence, pupils' 117–18

confrontations, dealing with 152–5 *see also* pupil misbehaviour

constructive and helpful feedback 94–5

continuous assessment, pupil 167

co-operative activities 70, 71

correcting pupils' work 94

counselling 141–2, 143

criterion-referenced assessment 166, 191

critical feedback to pupils 120

criticism, unfair 120